MURDER CHRONICLES

A Collection of Chilling True Crime Tales

R. BARRI FLOWERS

MURDER CHRONICLES
A Collection of Chilling True Crime Tales
Copyright © 2014 by R. Barri Flowers

Cover Image Copyright © Claire McAdams, 2014

ISBN: 1503391027
ISBN-13: 978-1503391024

TRUE CRIME BOOKS BY R. BARRI FLOWERS

The Dynamics of Murder: Kill or Be Killed

Masters of True Crime: Chilling Stories of Murder and the Macabre (editor)

Murders in the United States: Crimes, Killers, and Victims of the 20th Century

Prostitution in the Digital Age: Selling Sex from the Suite to the Street

Serial Killer Couples: Bonded by Sexual Depravity, Abduction, & Murder

The Sex Slave Murders: The True Story of Serial Killers Gerald & Charlene Gallego

TRUE CRIME SHORTS

Dead at the Saddleworth Moor: The Crimes of Ian Brady & Myra Hindley

Killers of the Lonely Hearts: The Tale of Serial Killers Raymond Fernandez & Martha Beck

Mass Murder in the Sky: The Bombing of Flight 629

Murder at the Pencil Factory: The Killing of Mary Phagan 100 Years Later

Murder of a Star Quarterback: The Tragic Tale of Steve McNair & Sahel Kazemi

Murder of the Banker's Daughter: The Killing of Marion Parker

Terror in East Lansing: The Tale of MSU Serial Killer Donald Miller

The "Gold Special" Train Robbery: Deadly Crimes of the D'Autremont Brothers

The Amityville Massacre: The DeFeo Family's Nightmare

The Pickaxe Killers: Karla Faye Tucker & Daniel Garrett

The Sex Slave Murders 2: The Chilling Story of Serial Killers Fred & Rosemary West

The Sex Slave Murders 3: The Horrific Tale of Serial Killers Leonard Lake & Charles Ng

PRAISE FOR TRUE CRIME BOOKS
BY R. BARRI FLOWERS

"Selected as one of Suspense Magazine's Best of 2011 books." — John Raab, CEO/Publisher of Suspense Magazine on THE SEX SLAVE MURDERS

"A gripping account of the murders committed by husband-and-wife serial killers Gerald and Charlene Gallego." — Gary C. King, author of Blood Lust on THE SEX SLAVE MURDERS

"R. Barri Flowers always relates an engrossing story." — Robert Scott, author of The Last Time We Saw Her on THE SEX SLAVE MURDERS

"A model of exposition not to be missed by anyone interested in the annals of American criminal behavior." — Jim Ingraham, Ph.D., professor emeritus of American Studies at Bryant University on THE PICKAXE KILLERS

"Striking, well-written tales sparkle in this ocean of murder." — Diane Fanning, author of Mommy's Little Girl on MASTERS OF TRUE CRIME

"Exhaustively researched, each storyteller brings their own unique prose to these pages, creating what will soon become a true crime classic." — Kevin M. Sullivan, author of The Bundy Murders on MASTERS OF TRUE CRIME

"This book should be a mandatory purchase and read for any true-crime buff." — Steven A. Egger, Ph.D., associate professor on MASTERS OF TRUE CRIME

"Incredible cases, psychopathic killers, unwitting victims, along with the very best writers, make for an exciting, no-holds-barred, soon-to-be true-crime classic." — Dan Zupansky, host of True Murder on MASTERS OF TRUE CRIME

"An indispensable sourcebook for anyone interested in American homicide, from law-enforcement professionals to armchair criminologists." — Harold Schechter, author of The Serial Killer Files on THE DYNAMICS OF MURDER

"Vivid case studies of murder to complement this well researched criminology text." — Scott Bonn, Ph.D., criminology professor on THE DYNAMICS OF MURDER

* * *

To true crime readers:

After more than three decades as an award winning criminologist and bestselling crime writer, I am pleased to present to you with **Murder Chronicles: A Collection of Chilling True Crime Tales**.

The ten riveting stories in this collection span nearly a century of murderous crimes in the United States that touched a nerve when I researching and writing about them.

The sad truth is that when it comes to homicides, killers, and victims, history has a very bad habit of repeating itself. This will prove all too true in the pages of Murder Chronicles, where every historical deadly crime explored could easily have occurred today, and vice versa.

Being in the wrong place at the wrong time can often lead to tragic consequences when caught in the crosshairs of a killer. Bringing perpetrators to justice is not always swift or certain, but is something that motivates those on the right side of the law like few other things in society.

Best,

R. Barri Flowers

CONTENTS

MURDER AT THE PENCIL FACTORY
The Killing Of Mary Phagan: 100 Years Later

On Saturday April 26, 1913, Mary Phagan, age thirteen, became the victim of a violent death at the National Pencil Factory in Atlanta, Georgia where she was employed. Her job at the factory was putting erasers into the metal casing atop pencils. The appalling crime left residents of the city outraged and wanting justice for the victim. Fingered for the crime and convicted was factory superintendent Leo Frank, a Jewish-American, who would be hanged by a lynch mob in spite of controversy surrounding Frank's guilt. The century old case was every bit as captivating and publicized as any high profile crime today—complete with a shaky investigation, anti-Semitism, racism, stereotyping, rush to judgment, injustice, and murder—with the effects and outcome of the case still being felt to this day.[1]

* * *

Mary Phagan was born in Marietta, Georgia on June 1, 1899 to tenant farmers John and Frances Phagan. Following her father's death shortly thereafter from the measles, the family relocated to East Point, Georgia where Frances ran a boarding house while her children went to work in the mills.

Mary dropped out of school when she was ten years old and worked part-time for a textile mill. By 1911, she had gone to work for a paper manufacturing plant. The owner of the plant, Sigmund Montag, was the National Pencil Company treasurer. The following year, Frances Phagan married John William Coleman.

During the spring of 1912, Mary went to work for the National Pencil Company in Atlanta, where she operated a knurling machine that fitted rubber erasers into the metal casing atop pencils, earning $4.05 a week for a fifty-five hour work week. The factory superintendent was a twenty-nine-year-old Jewish-American named Leo Frank.

On the cool, crisp late Saturday morning of April 26, 1913, thirteen-year-old Mary Phagan—who had been temporarily laid off earlier in the week because the factory was short on brass sheet metal—took the trolley to Atlanta from East Point in order to collect wages she was due for a twelve hour work week. Afterward, she had plans to get together with friends to celebrate Confederate Memorial Day—a holiday in some Southern states since 1866 that honored soldiers who fought for the Confederacy during the Civil War.

It was around noon when Mary arrived at the Pencil Factory, a four-story stone building in downtown Atlanta that encompassed the entire block of 37 to 41 South Forsythe Street. She came inside the main entrance on the first floor and made her way toward the stairway en route to the second floor, where she had performed her duties in the "tipping department" section of the metal room prior to being laid off. It was also the floor where factory superintendent Leo Frank's office was. Not far away from the stairs on the first floor was a hole, often covered by a hatch, which led to the basement via a ladder.

Mary Phagan went to Leo Frank's office, where he handed her a paycheck for $1.20. Frank would later acknowledge paying her and say that she left his office afterward.

This would be the last time Mary Phagan was seen alive by anyone who could attest to that.

* * *

Leo Frank was born in Cuero, Texas on April 17, 1884 to parents Rudolph and Rae Frank. A few months later, the family relocated to Brooklyn, New York, where Frank would later attend Pratt Institute for his high school education. He graduated in 1902 and enrolled in Cornell University, majoring in mechanical engineering and participating in sports, the debate team, and photography before receiving his degree in June 1906.

He was hired to work as a draftsman for a six-month stint by the B. T. Sturtevant Company in Hyde Park, Massachusetts before going back to New York to work for the National Meter Company as a testing engineer until October 1907.

In December 1907, Frank did a nine-month apprenticeship in Germany's Eberhard Faber pencil factory, learning the skills for pencil manufacturing. The following year, on August 6th, he moved to Atlanta, Georgia where he had a job waiting for him as the supervisor of the National Pencil Factory that his uncle, Moses Frank, had a stake in.

Shortly upon his arrival in Atlanta, Leo Frank met Lucille Selig, a member of a prominent Jewish family whose ancestors had founded Atlanta's first synagogue. In November 1910, the two married, living at the home of Lucille's parents on East Georgia Avenue.

By 1913, Atlanta's Jewish community was the largest in the South. The year before, Frank had been elected as president of the city's chapter of the Jewish fraternal organization B'nai B'rith. The Franks had settled comfortably into a "cultured and philanthropic milieu whose leisure pursuits included opera and bridge."[2]

Leo Frank, who was five-foot-six, of slender build, and on the frail side, wore thick glasses. He had successfully served as supervisor of the National Pencil Factory for five years with seemingly no problems to speak of until the day Mary Phagan became the victim of foul play.

* * *

It was around 3:15 a.m. on Sunday, April 27th that the factory's night watchman, an African American named Newt Lee, went into the basement to use the toilet meant for Negros and came upon the dead body of a young girl. She was dirty, disheveled, and appeared to have been severely beaten.

Aghast at the horrifying image, Lee quickly reported what he had found to the police by phone. When the authorities arrived, Lee met them at the Pencil Factory's front entrance and led them to the basement, which was about 200 feet long with an earthen floor and described as "a filthy catacomb littered with trash, coal dust, sawdust, and ashes, and lighted by a gas jet."[3]

They found the deceased girl's body in the back of the basement close to the incinerator and separated from the elevator shaft by 136 feet. The police noted that the girl, with her face down, was badly bruised, cut, bloodied, and darkened from soot off the floor. She was further described as having "dirt in her eyes, cinders in her mouth and nostrils...a black eye, [tongue that was] swollen and protruding...wounds on her scalp and below the knee and scratches on the elbow, and her clothing ha[d] been torn."[4]

Her dress was lifted up to her waist and there was blood found on her underthings to suggest she had been sexually assaulted. A piece of her undergarment was tied around the girl's neck. There was also a seven-foot piece of wrapping cord looped tightly around the victim's neck.

There were two notes found amidst a mound of garbage near the girl's head. One, written on white lined paper, read: "He said he wood love me land down play like the night witch did it but that long tall black negro did boy his slef."[5] The second note, scrawled on a blank carbon copy of the pencil factory's lined order sheet, read: "mam that negro hire

4

down here did this i went to make water and he push me down that hole a long tall negro black that hoo it wase long sleam tall negro i wright while play with me."[6]

While trying to make sense of the cryptic, unintelligible notes, it was clear to the police that the girl had been cruelly murdered and that a killer was on the loose.

They discovered that someone had messed with a sliding door by a service ramp in the basement that led into an alley, allowing the door to open without the need to unlock it first. Bloody fingerprints were found on the door and a metal pipe that was substituting for a crowbar, as well as on the dead girl's jacket.

In a further investigation of the crime scene, police discovered an intact clump of human excrement in the elevator shaft. Once the elevator car dropped to the basement thereafter and touched the ground, it pressed into the feces and a putrid scent filled the air.

Later in the morning, a worker in the factory who was related to one of the police working the case was brought to the scene. She identified the decedent as her coworker, thirteen-year-old Mary Phagan. Missing was the victim's purse, along with the $1.20 she had purportedly collected from superintendent Leo Frank.

*　*　*

With the media picking up on the murder of young Mary Phagan, the police were under pressure right away to identify and apprehend her murderer.

Given that he had been the one to contact police and allegedly discovered the body with the bizarre notes left near the corpse, suspicion was cast on National Pencil Factory night watchman Newt Lee. On Sunday, April 27th, the dark-skinned, tall, slender man was arrested, suspected of being involved in the crime.

Also arrested the same day was ex-streetcar driver Arthur Mullinax—who had often driven Mary Phagan to work and back—after a witness reported seeing them together on

Saturday, with Phagan giving the appearance of having been in a daze or drugged.

The following day, two more men were under arrest suspected of being a party to Mary Phagan's murder. John Gantt had previously worked for the National Pencil Factory as a bookkeeper and made no secret of his attraction to Phagan. He was taken into custody in Marietta before he could climb aboard a train. The other man arrested in connection with the murder was an unidentified African American.

The *Atlanta Constitution* and *Atlanta Georgian* newspapers offered more than $2,000 in reward money in total to anyone who could provide information that resulted in the capture of Mary Phagan's killer.[7]

At the same time, police had to break up a white mob that wanted to lynch Newt Lee, believing he was Phagan's killer.

* * *

As the suspects in custody were being interrogated, unbeknownst to the public, the police were also routinely questioning National Pencil Factory superintendent Leo Frank about Mary Phagan's murder.

* * *

Suspicion began to fall on Leo Frank nearly from the start. Upon discovering Mary Phagan's body, Newt Lee indicated he had tried phoning Frank for eight minutes, to no avail. The police followed up on this by attempting to call Frank themselves at four a.m. and also got no answer.

They went to his house the morning of April 27th and reported that Frank seemed nervous and was shaking during questioning, and as he was taken to the undertaker in the P. J. Bloomfield's Mortuary to see the dead girl before daybreak and then the factory. According to Frank, he had remained in his office for around twenty or so minutes after Phagan picked up her paycheck. However, another young woman who worked at the factory and came to pick up her own check just after Phagan, claimed she did not see Frank in his office and left a few minutes later empty-handed.

Leo Frank, whom the police remained suspicious of, tried to help his cause by hiring two Pinkerton detectives to assist in the investigation to bring a killer to justice.

* * *

On Tuesday, April 29th, Mary Phagan was laid to rest in Marietta, Georgia even as the investigation into her brutal murder continued. Though Newt Lee was still considered a strong suspect in her death, more and more focus was put on Leo Frank. At eleven-thirty that morning, he was arrested at his office by police and charged with Mary Phagan's murder. The headline for that day's *Atlanta Georgian* in announcing Frank's arrest was: "Police Have the Strangler."[8] For his part, Frank maintained his innocence, as did Lee, with Frank actually interrogating Lee at one point as perhaps the true killer. Earlier, a detective had uncovered a bloodstained shirt from Lee's apartment that was hidden in a burn barrel. Apart from the blood that was mostly around the armpits, the shirt appeared unworn. Newt Lee argued that the blood was his own, caused by an injury. Later, the prosecution in Leo Frank's trial would assert that Frank had planted the shirt in Lee's residence to try to implicate him for the murder of Mary Phagan.

At an inquest into Phagan's death on April 30th, her friend and coworker at the pencil factory, thirteen-year-old George Epps, testified that Phagan was fearful of Leo Frank who had been flirtatious with her and had also made advances toward her. Newt Lee further testified that Frank seemed nervous the day Phagan was murdered and had phoned him to check on things at the factory, something the superintendent had allegedly never done before. Two mechanics, who had been working on the factory's top floor that day, challenged Lee's claim, arguing that Frank's behavior was normal to them.

On May 1st, Arthur Mullinax and John Gantt were set free, no longer considered suspects in Phagan's murder, while Newt Lee and Leo Frank remained in custody.

The press was unaware that another suspect had emerged. That same day at about two in the afternoon, James (Jim) Conley, a twenty-nine-year-old African American janitor at the National Pencil Factory since 1911, was arrested by police. This came after the factory's day watchman, E. F. Holloway, observed him on the second floor scrubbing red stains from a blue shirt. Conley, who was short, brawny, and light brown skinned, initially attempted to hide the shirt. When that failed, he claimed the reddish coloring on it was actually rust that came off a pipe overhead where he had hung the shirt. Detectives gave the shirt a cursory examination and decided the stains were not blood without formal testing, and returned the shirt to the suspect.

The following day, Leo Frank and Newt Lee were adamant in proclaiming their innocence to a reporter for the *Atlanta Constitution*, with Frank expressing confidence that the ongoing investigation would prove he had nothing to do with the crime.[9]

* * *

Detectives were not as easily convinced as they continued to investigate their prime suspects in Mary Phagan's murder. On May 5th, Lemmie Quinn, who was the foreman of the area in which Phagan worked at the factory, testified to seeing Frank on Saturday, the day the murder took place, and found his behavior to be normal. However, detectives accused Quinn of lying after being bribed by Frank, which Quinn flatly rejected.

Over the next two days, Mary Phagan's body was exhumed twice—to search for drugs in her stomach and then fingerprints. As to the former, a number of witnesses had claimed to have seen someone who resembled Phagan attending the Confederate Memorial Day parade, looking as though she had been drugged.

On May 7th, it was established that the blood found on Newt Lee's shirt could not have been present for over a month. According to the wife of a mechanic, who had testified previously, during a visit to see her husband at the factory the day Phagan went missing, she noted a "strange Negro" getting on the elevator at about one p.m.[10] The police believed that false evidence was being planted to throw off their investigation.

On May 8th, Leo Frank and Newt Lee were ordered held by a coroner's jury for Mary Phagan's murder. In the case of Frank, a number of females had testified that they had been the victims of inappropriate advances from him. Other claims were even more troubling for Frank. For instance, on May 9th, according to a fourteen-year-old girl named Monteen Stover, on the day Mary Phagan went missing, she had shown up at the pencil factory at around the same time Phagan was believed to have come. Stover stated that she did not see Frank in his office, contradicting testimony by the superintendent that he had been in the office when Phagan arrived and remained there during the time the girl was believed to have been killed. It was reported by another woman that at about four-thirty in the afternoon, she heard several loud screams coming from the factory's basement while walking by the building.

In a May 12th interview of Leo Frank's mother, Mrs. Rudolph Frank, by a reporter for the *Atlanta Constitution,* she stated emphatically: "My son is entirely innocent, but it is a terrible thing that even a shadow of suspicion should fall upon him. I am sure of his innocence and am confident that he will be proven not guilty of this terrible crime."[11]

* * *

After being in custody for more than two weeks, on May 16th, Jim Conley gave the first of what would be several often-conflicting formal statements. Conley, who had claimed to be illiterate, stated that on the day Mary Phagan was murdered, he didn't leave his house until 10:30 a.m., at which time, he went to a few saloons, did some drinking, shot some dice, bought half a pint of whiskey and other alcohol, and drank at home, never going out again until the following day.

Detectives were skeptical of his story after a witness reported seeing a "negro...dressed in dark blue clothing and hat" hanging around the lobby of the National Pencil Factory the day the crime occurred.[12]

By May 24th, under pressure, Conley admitted that he could read and write, and also now claimed that he, in fact, had written the two notes found near Mary Phagan's body in what would be referred to as "murder notes." However, he placed the onus for the notes squarely on Leo Frank. According to Conley in his sworn statement, on the afternoon of Friday, April 25th—the day before Mary Phagan was murdered—Frank had asked him to come into his office. After asking him if he could write, in which Conley responded in the affirmative, Frank told him what to write and he complied. Upon completing the orders, Conley asserted that Frank said that "he had some wealthy people in Brooklyn," and then asked, "Why should I hang?"[13]

Though detectives came to believe Conley had written the notes, they had misgivings about the part of his shocking story that suggested Frank had included him in what appeared to be a premeditated murder plot.

That same day, Leo Frank was indicted for murder by the Fulton County grand jury in the death of Mary Phagan. They were unaware at the time of Conley's confession to writing the murder notes, which could have led to him being indicted for the crime as well.

The grand jury did not hand down an indictment for murder against Newt Lee, with the prosecution's focus entirely on Leo Frank. However, neither Frank nor Lee's statements or the murder notes found by Mary Phagan's body were presented to the grand jury. Also, Jim Conley was not asked to testify before the grand jury.

According to the undertaker responsible for embalming the body of Phagan, evidence was present of a sexual assault.

However, the county doctor indicated that the evidence was insufficient to reach that conclusion.[14]

In spite of Newt Lee not facing charges, his attorney asked that he remain in custody out of fear that Mary Phagan's killer might try to sway his testimony.

* * *

On May 28th, Jim Conley again changed his tune in a third formal statement—this time saying he had not been truthful about the meeting with Leo Frank and writing the notes the day prior to Mary Phagan's murder. Instead, he now claimed to have met Frank outside on Saturday, the day of the murder, just before one in the afternoon, and went with him inside the pencil factory where Frank told him what he wanted written on the notes. Conley said he was given cigarettes and wrote the notes, and was ordered afterward to get out of the factory. He then indicated he had gone out drinking, to see a movie, and was unaware of Mary Phagan's death until he returned to work on Monday.

The police seemed to believe Conley's latest account, by and large, with the *Atlanta Journal* and *Atlanta Georgian* highlighting the investigation on the front page. Three other National Pencil Factory employees informed the *Atlanta Journal* that Jim Conley had intended to rob another employee that he followed into the building, but turned his attention instead to the more vulnerable young Mary Phagan.[15]

The police dismissed this, though they were troubled by the fact that Conley had not indicated in his confession about writing the notes that he had any knowledge a murder had taken place. In order to gain clarity on this, they sought to bring Conley and Leo Frank together. However, Frank refused to comply without the presence of his attorney, who was currently away from town. In spite of this, the police felt his reluctance to talk face to face with Jim Conley was indicative of Frank being guilty of the crime.

* * *

The following day, Conley was questioned for four hours by authorities. In his fourth sworn statement, he asserted that Frank took him to the second floor and showed him the body of a dead girl and confessed to killing her. According to Conley, Frank said "he had picked up a girl back there and let her fall and that her head hit against something."[16] Conley then helped Frank carry her to the elevator, which they used to bring the girl's corpse to the basement. Afterward, Conley stated he took the elevator to the first floor, while Frank used the ladder through a trapdoor to get to the first floor.

The two men then purportedly rode the elevator to the second floor and went to Frank's office, at which time Frank dictated the murder notes. After writing them, Conley claimed Frank handed him $200, only to take it back and say, "I will make it all right with you Monday if I live and nothing happens."[17]

The affidavit explained at the end the previous inconsistencies, with Conley stating; "The reason I have not told this before is I thought Mr. Frank would get out and help me out and I decided to tell the whole truth about this matter."[18]

William Manning Smith was hired by the *Atlanta Georgian* to represent Jim Conley. Smith had built a reputation for taking on African American clients. He had won a case in which an African American man had been accused of rape by a white woman, and took the civil case of an elderly African American woman all the way to the Georgia Supreme Court.[19] Though Smith reportedly felt that Conley had been truthful in his last written sworn statement, he worried about interviews his client was giving to the press from jail. He was also fearful that reporters working for the William Randolph Hearst owned *Atlanta Georgian* had sided with Leo Frank. Smith was able to have Conley transferred to another jail, while breaking ties himself with the newspaper.

* * *

Leo Frank went on trial on Monday, July 28, 1913 in the Fulton County Superior Court located on Pryor Street in the then City Hall building, which belonged to the Atlanta Chamber of Commerce. Judge Leonard S. Roan sat on the bench. Prosecuting the case were Solicitor General Hugh Manson Dorsey, Frank Arthur Hooper, the Assistant Solicitor General, and E. A. Stevens.

Leo Frank's defense team included eight attorneys, with Luther Z. Rosser and Reuben Arnold the frontrunners. The jury was composed entirely of white males. Two potential African American jurors were eliminated by the defense through peremptory challenges. There were about 250 spectators in the courtroom, who were racially segregated, and many others outside the building who were able to watch the proceedings through the open windows, with scorching temperatures often hovering in the high nineties. The vast majority of those present during the trial were antagonistic toward Frank, while showing unwavering support for the prosecution.

The prosecution's first witness was Mary Phagan's mother, Mrs. J. W. Coleman. In "black mourning clothes and wearing a heavy veil," she did her best to remain composed for much of her testimony.[20] That changed, however, when she tearfully identified the clothing her daughter was wearing on the day of her death.

George Epps, Mary Phagan's friend and coworker at the pencil factory was the second person to take the stand. That fateful morning of April 26th, Epps had accompanied Phagan on the streetcar. The two had made plans to have ice cream and watch the Confederate Memorial Day parade at one p.m. that day. But when Phagan didn't show up, Epps went to see a baseball game.

The last witness of the first day was night watchman Newt Lee, who discovered the corpse of the dead girl and phoned the authorities. In testifying for more than two hours, Lee recounted the story he had initially told police about the gruesome discovery. He spoke as well about Leo

Frank seeming nervous due to John Gantt's appearance, a former employee of the National Pencil Factory; and the fact that Lee received a call from Frank that night, to make sure there were no problems, something that Frank hardly ever did.

* * *

On day two of Leo Frank's trial for the murder of Mary Phagan, Newt Lee finished his nearly five hour testimony under cross-examination by maintaining the story he told the previous day. Sergeant L. S. Dobbs followed Lee on the stand. Dobbs had received Lee's call to the police and hurried to the pencil factory, where he testified to finding Phagan's corpse in the basement. She was lying face down and a cord was wrapped firmly around her neck, while a pair of female underpants was wound looser around the victim's neck. According to Dobbs, the back of Phagan's head was drenched in blood. He spotted the two murder notes, Phagan's shoes, and saw a path from which the girl's body had been dragged to the place where it was left.

Next up was Detective John Starnes, who had phoned Leo Frank and notified him of Mary Phagan's murder. Starnes testified that Frank seemed nervous upon arriving at the National Pencil Factory. Solicitor Hugh Dorsey and defense lawyer Luther Rosser verbally sparred as Rosser sought to discredit Starnes' testimony.

* * *

On July 31st, day four of the trial, National Pencil Factory machinist R. B. Barrett took the stand. He testified that he found some bloodstains by a machine on the second floor of the factory and an empty pay envelope belonging to Mary Phagan. There had previously been no information revealed on the whereabouts of the victim's pay envelope. Monteen Stover, an ex-employee of the pencil factory, testified as well, noting that she had come to the factory at 12:05 p.m. to get her pay and waited in Leo Frank's office for five minutes, but left when he never showed. This was in direct contradiction to Frank's claim of being present in his office during the time Mary Phagan was murdered.

On August 1st, the fifth day of Leo Frank's trial, the secretary of the State Board of Health, Dr. Roy Harris, testified. Having examined the body of Mary Phagan, he estimated that the girl had died within an hour of ingesting her final meal, consisting of bread and cabbage. This indicated that she died somewhere between the time of twelve p.m. and one p.m. According to Harris, Phagan's head wounds were caused by a human fist.

August 4th and 5th, days seven and eight of the proceedings, were the most critical and dramatic days of Leo Frank's trial for the murder of Mary Phagan as Jim Conley, a janitor at the National Pencil Factory and the State's principal witness, took the stand. His testimony was so explicit, grisly, and even sickening at times; it prompted Judge Roan to clear the court of women and children.

Conley stuck to his assertions in his last affidavit, indicating that he had served as the lookout on the main floor factory lobby for Leo Frank on a number of instances on Saturdays while Frank engaged in sexual activity with women in his second floor office. The allegation that Frank was a philanderer in the pencil factory would be substantiated later by witness C. Brutus Dalton, who was a railroad carpenter and had an unsavory reputation, according to other witnesses.

Conley testified that he was ordered to "watch out" for Frank on Saturday, April 26th as Frank "chatted" in his office with Mary Phagan. At some point after, Conley claimed that Frank "whistled" him into the office, where Frank confessed that when Phagan had rejected his advances, he hit her and then left the girl in the machine room.

Having been told by Frank to bring her out of the room, Conley stated that he discovered Mary Phagan dead on the floor with her arms extended. Frank then ordered him to cover up Phagan's body and take her to the basement.

Conley testified that in trying to do as he was told, he found himself unable to lift the girl's body alone. As a result, Frank assisted him in getting the dead girl onto the elevator, whereby they brought her down to the basement. Conley said that he then hauled Phagan's body to a corner.

Afterward, Conley indicated that he and Frank went back to his office. There, Frank told him he would get money as long as he kept quiet about what had happened. Conley reiterated what he had previously stated in a written statement that Frank told him, "Why should I hang?"[21]

It was then that Conley claimed he had written the notes, as dictated by Frank, which were discovered close to Phagan's corpse, in an apparent effort to implicate Newt Lee.

* * *

Under a blistering cross-examination, Jim Conley confessed to lying to the police regarding the crime and changing his story several times, and also acknowledged he had a long history of arrests. He also admitted that he excreted in the elevator shaft the day Mary Phagan was murdered, prior to her death.

In spite of his inconsistencies and the defense being successful tripping him up on a few specifics, overall Conley remained steadfast in his testimony. In all, he would be on the witness stand for sixteen hours.

Though Jim Conley confessed to being an accessory after the fact in the murder of Mary Phagan, his shocking and convoluted story that incriminated Leo Frank was believed by many whites in the courtroom and the general public, who simply felt an African American lacked the intellect to weave such a tale were it not the truth. According to the *Atlanta Georgian*, "Many people are arguing to themselves that the negro, no matter how hard he tried or how generously he was coached, still never could have framed up a story like the one he told unless there was some foundation in fact."[22]

On August 6th, day nine of the trial, Jim Conley's testimony that he had been a lookout for Leo Frank on a number of occasions was ruled admissible by Judge Roan. The same day, Dr. Roy Harris returned to the stand, as his previous testimony had been cut short due to illness. He maintained that Mary Phagan was murdered not long after she ate cabbage and bread, with the cause of death strangulation, as opposed to the blows she took to the head from her assailant's fist.

* * *

On August 7th, day ten of the trial, the prosecution rested its case and it was Leo Frank's defense team's turn to present its case. Over the next two weeks, they called to the stand a number of rebuttal and character witnesses to prove Frank's innocence, and put forth alternative theories on the murder of Mary Phagan—proposing she was really killed by Jim Conley, with Newt Lee assisting Conley in writing the murder notes.

According to defense rebuttal witness Lemmie Quinn, a National Pencil Factory foreman who took the stand on August 13th, on the day that Mary Phagan was murdered, he visited the factory unannounced. He claimed to have seen Leo Frank at about 12:20 p.m. seated at his desk working and alone. This contradicted Jim Conley's timeline of events, which had placed Frank at that time as being with Phagan in the factory's metal room, which was more than 150 feet from his office.

* * *

On Monday, August 18th, day nineteen of the trial, Leo Frank spoke in his own defense with an unsworn statement covering four hours. At the time, Georgia law barred criminal defendants from testifying under oath, but did allow them to offer a statement, and required the defendant's consent to be cross-examined. Frank never underwent cross-examination.

Much of the defendant's long and arduous statement described his activities at the National Pencil Factory and afterward on the day of Mary Phagan's murder. According to Frank, with regard to seeing Phagan that day,

This little girl, whom I afterwards found to be Mary Phagan, entered my office and asked for her pay envelope.... I went to the cash box and took her envelope out and handed it to her, identifying the envelope by the number. She left my office and apparently had gotten as far as the door...when she evidently stopped and asked me if the metal had arrived, and I told her no. She continued on her way out and I heard the sound of her footsteps as she went away.[23]

Frank insisted that he had no knowledge whatsoever of Mary Phagan's death or the circumstances thereof, while denying seeing Jim Conley in the pencil factory or elsewhere on April 26, 1913.

With respect to Jim Conley's damaging testimony, Frank denounced it as untruthful. "The statement of the Negro Conley is a tissue of lies from first to last. I know nothing whatever of the cause of the death of Mary Phagan and Conley's statement as to his coming up and helping me dispose of the body or that I had anything to do with her or to do with him that day is a monstrous lie."[24] He also stated that it was "a base lie" regarding the accusations he had engaged with females at the National Pencil Factory "for immoral purposes."[25]

Frank finished his statement by explaining his anxiety during the initial questioning about the crime, as well describing the shock of viewing Mary Phagan's brutalized corpse. "Gentlemen, I was nervous. I was completely unstrung. Imagine yourself called from sound slumber in the early hours of the morning... To see that little girl on the dawn of womanhood so cruelly murdered—it was a scene that would have melted stone."[26]

* * *

On August 21st, day twenty-two of Leo Frank's trial, closing arguments began. The prosecution painted the defendant as a "a Jekyll and Hyde character who could mask his deviant tendencies from his family and friends;"[27] while the defense argued that Jim Conley was the true killer of Mary Phagan and had invented his tale against Leo Frank in order to save himself.

Over the next few days, the closing arguments continued. Solicitor Hugh Dorsey pulled no punches in attacking the character of Leo Frank, whom he compared to Theodore Durrant, a convicted murderer who had been referred to as the "Demon of the Belfry," for killing two women in a Baptist church in San Francisco, for which Durrant had been sent to the gallows in 1898.[28]

Dorsey depicted the murdered Mary Phagan as "as a symbol of lost innocence and virtue."[29] The prosecutor sought to "deflect charges of anti-Semitism by recalling the great names in Jewish history, arguing that Frank, with his sexually deviant behavior, dishonored them as well as the Southern girl he had so brutally murdered."[30]

In the final arguments, the defense and lead attorney Luther Rosser contended that Leo Frank was but "the latest in a long line of Jews who were persecuted for their religious beliefs;" while maintaining that Jim Conley was the actual killer of Mary Phagan. The defense argued that as a "pillar of the community," Frank was obviously far more trustworthy as an innocent man than Conley.[31]

Rosser described Jim Conley to the jury as "dirty, filthy, black, drunken, [and] lying..."[32] Racism and stereotyping had been part of the defense strategy throughout the trial, as Frank's attorneys portrayed Conley as being "especially disposed to lying and murdering because of his race."[33]

In a statement that received widespread coverage by the press, Frank himself had questioned how the "perjured vaporizings of a black brute" would be given any credibility as truthful in the testimony Conley gave against him.[34]

* * *

The contention that Leo Frank was innocent of this horrific crime fell on deaf ears. At 4:55 p.m. on August 25, 1913, day twenty-five and the last day of the trial, the jury returned a verdict of guilty for the defendant in the murder of Mary Phagan. Leo Frank, along with his attorneys and family, was not in the courtroom when the verdict was read. Fearing for their safety from mob violence in the event of an acquittal, Judge Roan had kept them away for their own protection.

Indeed, upon hearing the verdict they were looking for, the crowd that had gathered outside uttered vindictively, "Kill the Jew!"[35]

According to the *Atlanta Constitution* in describing the feverish setting when Hugh Dorsey moved off the city hall steps, "The solicitor reached no farther than the sidewalk. While mounted men rode like Cossacks through the human swarm, three muscular men slung Mr. Dorsey on their shoulders and passed him over the heads of the crowd across the street."[36]

The following day, August 26th, Leo Frank was sentenced to death by hanging for Mary Phagan's murder. His date of execution was to be October 10, 1913. However, Frank's lawyers quickly filed a motion for a new trial, with the hearing scheduled for October 4th, effectively delaying the pending execution.

On October 31st, the motion for a new trial for Leo Frank was denied by Judge Roan, who set a new date of execution for April 17, 1914.

The Georgia Supreme Court affirmed the conviction of Leo Frank and sentence of death for killing Mary Phagan on February 17, 1914, denying a motion for him to have a new trial.

* * *

A week later, on February 24, 1914, with Solicitor Hugh Dorsey representing the state and William Smith defending Jim Conley, he was found guilty of being an accessory after the fact for his part in the murder of Mary Phagan. Conley received a sentence of one year on a chain gang.

On April 6, 1914, after Leo Frank's lawyers filed a motion with the Fulton County Superior Court to have his guilty verdict set aside—just eleven days before his scheduled execution on April 17th—it was rescheduled to be carried out on January 22, 1915. The motion was denied by the court on June 6, 1914, at which time Frank's attorneys made an appeal for a new trial to the Georgia Supreme Court. On October 14, 1914, this too was denied.

On December 9, 1914, upon serving ten months of his sentence, Jim Conley was released from prison, a free man.

Four months later, Leo Frank's final appeal to the United States Supreme Court was rejected on April 9, 1915. The date of execution, which had previously been delayed three times, was now set for June 22, 1915. An appeal for clemency by Frank's attorneys with the Georgia Prison Commission was denied on May 31, 1915.

* * *

On June 12, 1915, a public hearing was held in Atlanta to debate whether or not Leo Frank's death sentence should be commuted. Presiding over the hearing was Georgia Governor John M. Slaton. Among those in favor of commutation were Frank's lawyers, the presiding judge in his trial Leonard S. Roan, who had handed Frank a death sentence, and William Smith, the defense lawyer for Jim Conley who had now come to believe that it was his client who, in fact, had perpetrated the murder of Mary Phagan.

Those opposing commutation included Solicitor General Hugh Dorsey and a delegation from Cobb County, including former Georgia Governor Joseph M. Brown, who cautioned Slaton that should he wish "to invoke lynch law in Georgia and destroy trial by jury, the way to do it is by retrying this case and reversing all the courts."[37]

Over the next week, Slaton reviewed thousands of pages of documents on the case and visited the National Pencil Factory twice in trying to ensure that justice was being served with the conviction and condemning to death of Leo Frank. Based upon his findings, Slaton began to have serious reservations as to the guilt of Frank.

On June 21, 1915, just one day before Frank was supposed to be put to death by hanging and five days until the end of Governor Slaton's term in office, he commuted Leo Frank's sentence to life in prison. Aware that this move would be very unpopular for the many people who believed Frank should be put to death for Mary Phagan's murder, Slaton arranged to leave Georgia right after the swearing in of his successor. He would stay away for several months.

In defending the commutation, Slaton said, "Feeling as I do about this case, I would be a murderer if I allowed this man to hang. It may mean that I must live in obscurity the rest of my days, but I would rather be plowing in a field for the rest of my life than to feel that I had that blood on my hands."[38]

Fearful that Leo Frank might become the target of a lynch mob with his sentence commuted, Governor Slaton directed that he be transferred in the wee hours of the morning from the Fulton County Jail to the Georgia State Penitentiary, a minimum-security facility located in Milledgeville, which was believed to be more secure under the circumstances.

* * *

The Georgia public was incensed upon learning the news that Leo Frank's death sentence had been given a last day commutation by the governor. Some 5,000 protestors gathered at City Hall in Atlanta that afternoon. "Excited throngs burst into the state capitol building's senate chamber where speaker after speaker excoriate[d] Slaton."[39]

The Georgia National Guard, county police, and deputized friends of the governor managed to break up a mob that threatened to go after Slaton at his residence. As a result of his actions, many in the state would scornfully come to view him as "The King of the Jews and Traitor Governor of Georgia."[40]

* * *

At about eleven p.m. on July 17, 1915, Leo Frank was attacked in his prison bed by another prisoner, William Creen. A convicted killer himself, Creen stabbed Frank's right hand and slashed his throat with a seven-inch butcher knife he had swiped from the penitentiary's kitchen, severing Frank's jugular vein. Creen reportedly said to prison officials that the assault on Leo Frank was to prevent other prisoners from becoming victims of mob violence. Creen further referred to it as disgraceful to have Frank at the prison and somehow believed that by killing Frank, he would receive a pardon as a hero.

Frank barely managed to survive the attempt on his life with the aid of two inmate physicians who were able to stop the bleeding and stitch the wounds. A week later, Georgia's new governor, Nathaniel E. Harris, paid Leo Frank a visit in prison and commented on the knife wound in his neck. He noted that the "gash extended from ear to ear and was so frightful in appearance that I wondered at his being alive."[41]

In speaking briefly with Frank, Harris came to believe he had a "hard, careless heart," which caused the governor to see Frank as "undoubtedly a hardened criminal or a reckless prisoner," and, as such, much more likely to be guilty of the crime for which he was incarcerated than not.[42]

* * *

In July and August 1915, the ire over commuting Leo Frank's sentence to life imprisonment continued to fester in the community, led by former Georgia Populist politician Thomas E. Watson and publisher of the *Jeffersonian* and *Watson's Magazine*. Through his magazines, he let loose with scathing withering editorials against Jews in general and Leo Frank in particular, along with strong disapproval of the commutation. As his readership and personal popularity grew among his supporters, Watson wrote, "This country has nothing to fear from its rural communities. Lynch law is a good sign; it shows that a sense of justice lives among the people."[43]

With accusations of anti-Semitism throughout the case against Leo Frank, Watson's "inflammatory writings are generally credited with pushing the already strong feelings regarding this case past the boiling point. In what is now ominous phraseology, Watson called on the citizens of

Georgia to take justice into their own hands and inflict the death sentence upon Leo Frank."[44]

* * *

It was under an atmosphere of bigotry, hatred, and taking the law into one's own hands that a group of community leaders referring to themselves as the Knights of Mary Phagan enlisted other like-minded men to remove Leo Frank from prison with the intention of killing him.

On August 16, 1915, a convoy of eight vehicles containing twenty-eight armed men left Marietta, Georgia in the afternoon en route to the Milledgeville State Penitentiary. The lynch mob included those with special skills to ensure success in their endeavor, such as car mechanics, an electrician, a locksmith, a medic, a lay minister, and a hangman.

At about ten p.m., the men arrived at the penitentiary where they quickly cut the phone lines, emptied prison vehicle gas tanks, overpowered the guards, and handcuffed the warden. The mob grabbed Leo Frank, clad in an undershirt and nightshirt, from his barracks and drove off in the dark of night. With one vehicle serving as a decoy, the other seven cars headed toward Marietta. "The 175 mile trip took about seven hours at a top speed of 18 miles per hour through small towns on back roads. Lookouts in the towns telephoned ahead to the next town as soon as they saw the line of open cars pass by."[45]

In the early morning of August 17th, the lynch mob arrived on the outskirts of Marietta in Cobb County, where an area had been selected to mete out justice to their prisoner by the corner of Freys Gin and Roswell Road, close to the childhood home of Mary Phagan.

Leo Frank was dragged out of a vehicle by the mob. According to the *New York Times*, a brown piece of canvas had been tied around Frank's waist and he was in handcuffs with his ankles tied. The lynchers put over his head a manila rope, tying it in a hangman's knot—twisted to cause his head to jolt backward, causing Frank's neck to break—and tossed it over a branch of an oak tree. Lifting the condemned man onto a table, Frank's head was turned to face the way of the house where Phagan had resided.[46]

At just after seven a.m., while steadfastly proclaiming his innocence in the death of Mary Phagan, Leo Frank was hanged. According to one description of the tragedy: "Frank die[d] a lingering painful death as he slowly choke[d] to death, his shivering body shaken by violent convulsions, his bare feet jerking spasmodically four feet above the ground. Then the body [was] still and sway[ed] in the wind."[47]

* * *

Once the news of the lynching became known, crowds amassed at the site, including men, women, and children, who came by vehicles, horses, or walked there to witness the macabre scene of a hanging. Some took gruesome photographs of the decedent that would become postcards being sold locally for twenty-five cents; while others ripped off pieces of his clothing or the rope, or snapped branches from the hanging tree to keep as souvenirs. Frank's corpse was assaulted by a few of those gathered before some semblance of order was established. The body was driven away from Marietta to an Atlanta undertaker.

When attempts to keep the location where Leo Frank's body was hidden failed, the decision was made to allow public viewing. With a strong police presence, thousands came to view the corpse. Afterward, the body was hastily embalmed. The following day, Frank's wife Lucille took his body by train to Brooklyn, New York.

On August 20th, Leo Frank was laid to rest at Mount Carmel Cemetery in Glendale, Queens, New York. A day earlier, an unknown person returned Frank's wedding ring to his widow, which was his final request to those who lynched him.

In spite of the gruesome nature of Leo Frank's death, the *New York Times* reported that most people living in Cobb County were unsympathetic, believing the former superintendent of the National Pencil Factory had gotten what he deserved, with the lynch mob merely upholding the law that Governor Slaton had failed to do.[48]

Though a grand jury in Cobb County was convened to indict the lynch party, many of whom were prominent members of the community, no one at the time was identified by name, nor was anyone ever brought to justice for Leo Frank's murder.

It was nearly nine decades later when the masterminds and other participants behind the lynching were finally publicly identified. In June 2000, their names were posted on the Internet by an Atlanta librarian and onetime history professor, derived from data gathered by Mary Phagan Kean, the great niece of Mary Phagan, and supported by other historians.[49]

Those named included:

Joseph Mackey Brown, former Georgia governor

Newton Augustus Morris, a two-time Blue Ridge Circuit superior court judge

E. P. Dobbs, then mayor of Marietta

Eugene Herbert Clay, former Marietta mayor and future Georgia state senator

John Tucker Dorsey, who would later become the Blue Ridge Circuit's district attorney

Bolan Glover Brumby, wealthy businessman and owner of the Marietta Chair Company

Fred Morris, general assemblyman, who would later organize the first Boy Scout troop of Marietta

George Exie Daniell, a jewelry shop owner and Marietta Country Club charter member

Gordon Baxter Gann, attorney and future mayor of Marietta, as well as a state legislator

Newton Mayes Morris, in command of the Cobb County chain gang

George Swanson, then sheriff of Cobb County

William J. Frey, former sheriff of Cobb County

George Hicks, then deputy sheriff of Cobb County

William McKinney, then deputy sheriff of Cobb County

D. R. Benton, uncle of Mary Phagan and a farmer
Emmet Burton, a police officer
Luther Burton, operated a coal yard
Robert A. Hill, a banker who aided in financing the undertaking
Moultrie McKinney Sessions, a banker and attorney
Jim Brumby, garage owner; serviced vehicles used by lynch mob
C. D. Elder, a physician
"Yellow Jacket" Brown, an electrician
Ralph Molden Manning, a contractor
L. B. Robeson, a railroad freight agent
Horace Hamby, a farmer
"Coon" Shaw, a mule trader
Lawrence Haney, a farmer

* * *

With emotions running high after Frank was lynched, an estimated fifty percent of the 3,000 Jews living in Georgia at the time fled from the state. Leo Frank historian Steve Oney declared, "What it did to Southern Jews can't be discounted.... It drove them into a state of denial about their Judaism. They became even more assimilated, anti-Israel, Episcopalian. The Temple did away with chupahs at weddings—anything that would draw attention."[50]

In October 1913, as a direct result of Leo Frank's trial and conviction for the murder of Mary Phagan, the Anti-Defamation League of B'nai B'rith was established. According to its charter:

The immediate object of the League is to stop, by appeals to reason and conscience and, if necessary, by appeals to law, the defamation of the Jewish people. Its ultimate purpose is to secure justice and fair treatment to all citizens alike and to put an end forever to unjust and unfair discrimination against and ridicule of any sect or body of citizens.[51]

* * *

At nightfall on Thanksgiving, November 25, 1915, the Knights of Mary Phagan, who were participants in the lynching of Leo Frank, and several other men convened atop Stone Mountain, just outside of Atlanta, where they burned a large cross and launched a rebirth of the Ku Klux Klan. Leading the gathering was William J. Simmons, with some fifteen "charter members and a few aging survivors of the original Klan."[52]

* * *

In 1916, riding on his popularity as the prosecuting attorney who successfully tried and convicted Leo Frank in the murder of Mary Phagan, Hugh Dorsey was elected the governor of Georgia and reelected in 1918. Dorsey went on to become a superior court judge in the 1930s and 1940s.

According to the *Atlanta Constitution* and the *Atlanta Journal*, on August 1, 1933, William Creen, the convicted murderer who attacked and seriously injured Leo Frank with a knife in prison, was fully pardoned by Georgia Governor Eugene Talmadge.[53]

* * *

On April 23, 1957, Lucille Frank, the widow of Leo Frank, died of heart disease in Atlanta, having never remarried. After requesting in her will that she be cremated, Lucille's ashes were reportedly placed in a shoebox and buried in secret between her parents' headstones in the city's Oakland Cemetery because her family was concerned that a funeral might cause anti-Semitic activity by the Ku Klux Klan locally.

After a previous undertaking to grant Leo Frank a posthumous pardon failed in December 1983, the Georgia Board of Pardons and Paroles reversed its decision and issued Frank a pardon on March 11, 1986. In doing so, while seeming to acknowledge a gross miscarriage of justice, the board did not clear him of the murder of Mary Phagan, per se, saying:

Without attempting to address the question of guilt or innocence, and in recognition of the State's failure to protect the person of Leo M. Frank and thereby preserve his opportunity for continued legal appeal of his conviction, and in recognition of the State's failure to bring his killers to justice, and as an effort to heal old wounds, the State Board of Pardons and Paroles, in compliance with its Constitutional and statutory authority, hereby grants to Leo M. Frank a Pardon.[54]

* * *

While Leo Frank's role in the murder of Mary Phagan was left in limbo by the Georgia Board of Pardons and Paroles, a number of scholars, historians, and criminologists have argued over the last century that the true killer was actually Jim Conley, a career criminal. Conley, a sweeper at the National Pencil Factory, was the chief witness for the prosecution in Leo Frank's trial and conviction. In spite of multiple and inconsistent statements and affidavits, Conley's testimony was key to Frank's conviction.

However, shoddy police work, mishandled or lost evidence, alleged witness intimidation, controversial prosecution witnesses, and an apparent rush to judgment make Conley's testimony, in particular, and the case against Frank, in general, appear less than convincing. The verdict takes on even more significance when considering the frightening turn of events as a result.

A key piece of the puzzle in the murder of Mary Phagan relates to the untouched human excrement discovered by police that day at the bottom of the pencil factory's elevator shaft. Under cross-examination, Jim Conley acknowledged that it came from him before the murder occurred. With this admittance, it would seem to contradict Conley's story about how he and Leo Frank used the elevator to move Phagan's corpse to the basement, as the elevator would have smashed into the feces once it reached the floor of the basement, emitting a foul odor as a result. In fact, the intact excrement only came into contact with the elevator when it was brought down to the basement in the course of the police investigation of the murder.

After he was released from prison as an accessory to the murder of Mary Phagan, Jim Conley seemed to stay out of trouble and the public eye until January 13, 1919. On that day, just after midnight, he was shot while breaking into a drug store by the store's owner. Conley recovered from his injuries and went to trial for burglary, for which he was convicted and given a sentence of twenty years in prison. After serving fourteen years, Conley was released in 1933.[55]

On October 20, 1941, Jim Conley's name once again resurfaced in the press in an *Atlanta Constitution* article, captioned: "Star Witness in Frank Case Arrested Here," that reported he had been arrested for public drunkenness and gambling.[56]

Jim Conley was thought to have died sometime in 1962. It was rumored that he had confessed on his deathbed to Mary Phagan's murder, but this has never been corroborated.[57]

However, nearly five decades earlier on April 24, 1914, in an extraordinary motion filed by Leo Frank's attorneys for a new trial, an affidavit was introduced from Jim Conley's girlfriend, Annie Maude Carter. It alleged that during a jailhouse conversation in which they were both locked up, Conley had confessed to the murder of Mary Phagan and the theft of the payment she received the day of her death.[58] The sworn statement also mentioned lewd letters purportedly written by Conley to Carter that suggested similarities in their grammar and phrasing as the murder notes found near Phagan's corpse that Conley admitted writing. This motion would be denied by the court less than two weeks later, but would seem to bolster the supposed death bed confession by Conley.

* * *

On March 4, 1982 in Tennessee—two decades after Jim Conley's death and almost seven decades since Mary Phagan was murdered—Alonzo Mann, who in 1913 was a fourteen-year-old office boy for the National Pencil Factory, accused Conley of murdering the girl. Now eighty-three and seriously ill, Mann, who had testified for the defense at the trial of Leo Frank, signed an affidavit contending that on April 26, 1913 he witnessed Conley carrying Phagan's lifeless body by himself over his shoulder by the trapdoor that led to the basement.

According to Mann: "I looked to my right and I was confronted by a scene I will remember vividly until I die...." He stated that his eyes locked on Jim Conley holding Mary Phagan. "He wheeled on me and [spoke] in a voice that was low, but threatening and frightening to me."[59]

Mann claimed that Conley had threatened to kill him if he ever spoke a word about what he had witnessed. He admitted to telling his mother about it anyway when he got home, but she too had directed him not to speak out about it, wanting to protect him. Once Frank was convicted, Mann said his parents continued to encourage his silence, believing it would not make a difference at that point, but could hurt their family. Now many years later, he insisted, "Jim Conley, the chief witness against Leo Frank, lied under oath.... I am convinced that he, not Leo Frank, killed Mary Phagan."[60]

Mann, who would pass away in March 1985 at age eighty-five, indicated that he finally decided to come forward to "unburden his soul."[61] In the process of being interviewed by reporters from Nashville's the *Tennessean* newspaper, Mann, while declaring Leo Frank's innocence and Jim Conley's guilt in the murder of Mary Phagan, took lie detector tests and an evaluation for psychological stress. The results indicated that the former office boy at the pencil factory had been truthful in his assertions.[62]

Mann's disturbing revelation was published in the *Tennessean* a few days later on March 7, 1982 and would be validated by the newspaper with its own two month investigation.[63]

In Atlanta on November 10, 1982, Alonzo Mann made a videotaped statement, reiterating his incredible tale that completely contradicted the story told by Jim Conley.[64]

On January 4, 1983, Mann's testimony in exonerating Leo Frank of the murder of Mary Phagan was the driving force behind the Anti-Defamation League's efforts to get the

Georgia Board of Pardons and Paroles to grant Frank a posthumous pardon, which would come a little more than three years later in 1986.

* * *

In spite of Alonzo Mann's sworn statement, persuasive to many in placing the onus for Mary Phagan's murder squarely on the shoulders of Jim Conley, there are some who remain skeptical of his story—wondering, for one, why his white parents "in the White racial separatist Atlanta, Georgia of 1913," would ask Mann to remain silent if he had information for the police that could possibly exonerate the white man who hired him (Frank), while sending instead to the gallows the "Negro janitor" Mann allegedly saw carrying Phagan's body and believed to be guilty of killing her.[65]

Moreover, other points of contention also cast doubts about Jim Conley's guilt and Leo Frank's innocence. According to the point of view of The 1913 Leo Frank Case and Trial Research Library and its "common sense test,"

If we are to believe Alonzo Mann that he saw Jim Conley carrying the unconscious body of Mary Phagan, isn't it rather odd that in a White racial separatist south, given the invitation of an extremely violent lynching, a Southern Negro would assault, rob, and carry the body of a White girl across the highest traffic place in the factory with the front door unlocked?[66]

Apparently, Jim Conley was normally off on Saturdays, as well as a State Holiday, which was the case on the day Mary Phagan was murdered. This has led some historians to question Conley's appearance at all that day at the National Pencil Factory, noting:

In light of the fact Jim Conley had been paid his weekly salary the evening before on Friday, April 25, 1913 at 6:30 PM by Leo M. Frank... Conley coming to work on his day off, on his own, just didn't fit or make sense, unless he was asked to come to work by his boss Leo Frank [as his lookout, according to Conley].[67]

After one hundred years since the violent death of Mary Phagan in Atlanta, and the controversy surrounding key characters involved in the crime and its aftermath, the debate and its impact on society rages on.

* * *

The tragic story of young Mary Phagan, and what followed, has inspired a number of productions about the case over the decades. These include *They Won't Forget*, a 1937 film with Lana Turner cast as the victim in her first role on the screen; *The Murder of Mary Phagan*, a 1988 miniseries, starring Jack Lemmon and Peter Gallagher, with Wendy Cooke as Mary Phagan; a 1999 musical on Broadway, *Parade*, titled to reflect the Confederate Memorial Day celebration that Mary Phagan had plans to attend on the day she was murdered, as well as the lynching of Leo Frank; and a 2009 docudrama, *The People v. Leo Frank*, an episode of *American Experience*, a PBS series starring Will Janowitz, Seth Gilliam, and Katie Adkins.

# # #

THE "GOLD SPECIAL" TRAIN ROBBERY
Deadly Crimes of the D'Autremont Brothers

On Thursday night, October 11, 1923, the Southern Pacific Railroad Express Train Number 13 was headed south across the Klamath range, passing through the Siskiyou Mountains of Southern Oregon from Seattle en route to San Francisco, with crew and passengers going through the motions as they waited to reach their destination. The train was known as the "Gold Special," a reflection of earlier times when it transported large amounts of gold from the mines. As the train reduced its speed, per railway rules, to test the brakes as it reached the Siskiyou Summit's crest, three bandits, armed with sawed-off shotguns, a Colt .45-caliber semiautomatic pistol, and dynamite, climbed aboard. The engineer was ordered to bring the train to a halt upon entering Siskiyou Tunnel 13, which was 3,107 feet long, and did so near the tunnel's west end. An attempt to rob the train—rumored to have as much as half a million dollars in gold on board, along with a cash shipment—went terribly wrong. When the dust had settled, four people were dead and the mail car was in flames as the perpetrators fled from the carnage, with authorities and angry mobs in hot pursuit. In what has been described by many as this country's "Last Great Train Robbery," the tragic tale of greed, poor planning, senseless murders, and three killers who managed to remain at large for years before their capture, is one that still shocks the senses to this day.[1]

* * *

On March 30, 1900, Ray and Roy D'Autremont were born as identical twins in Iowa to parents Paul P. and Isabella Bertha D'Autremont. It was reported that the infant boys looked so much alike that their mother tied ribbons around their wrists in order to tell one from the other. Nearly four years later, on February 21, 1904, their brother Hugh was born in Arkansas. The family settled in Albany, Oregon, where Paul D'Autremont owned a barber shop.

As a teenager, Ray became a member of the Industrial Workers of the World, "a radical, international industrial union," referred to as the Wobblies, which was established in 1905. In 1919, he spent a year in a Monroe, Washington reformatory "for criminal syndicalism during the 1919 Red Scare that followed the Centralia Massacre."[2]

Meanwhile, Roy had become a devout Catholic and also began showing signs of being mentally ill. Both brothers had grown up hearing stories of notorious Old West outlaws, such as Jesse and Frank James and Harry Tracy, and wanted to emulate them.

In 1921, after getting out of jail, Ray, who had grown to resent capitalism, persuaded Roy that they needed to attack what it represented. Ray would later describe his frustrations: "Hatred ate away at my compassion as I saw how the people in power cheated and stole from the masses.... Thousands of women and children were starving and dying, thousands more, honest working men, were receiving less than half of what they should."[3]

Using this pretext to get his brother on the same page, the two first journeyed to Chicago, hoping to latch on with racketeers. Once that failed, they made their way back to Southern Oregon, where the two began committing crimes, including a number of armed robberies that proved disastrous. In one instance, the brothers witnessed the robbery of a Yacolt, Washington bank that they were actually casing, causing them to have second thoughts as would-be bank robbers.

In between their dreams of becoming successful criminals, Ray and Roy found work at a logging camp in Eugene, Oregon that was described as in "the heart of big tree country."[4]

The brothers got renewed motivation to line their pockets with stolen money from U.S. Post Office outlaw Roy Gardiner. During 1922, Gardiner robbed several Southern Pacific mail trains of more than $300,000 as a form of protest for money he had lost through the mail. He was arrested that same year, but the publicity his brazen robberies attracted left an impression on Ray and Roy D'Autremont.[5]

It wouldn't be long before they set their sights on a potential new target to get rich.

* * *

Hugh D'Autremont, nineteen, had always looked up to his older brothers, for better or worse. At high school in Artesia, New Mexico, Hugh was described as popular and a leader among classmates. His teachers viewed the bright young man as "exceptional" and "bound to succeed." He had also mentioned more than once a dream of making fast money and claimed that "all men who worked were fools."[6]

That latter comment didn't prevent Hugh, after graduating from high school in 1923, from following his brothers to work as a logger. He also shared their philosophy of wanting lots of money without having to work hard for it.

It was Ray who led the charge in targeting the Southern Pacific Railroad "Gold Special" Train to rob, driven by a rumor that it would be carrying upwards of $500,000 in gold and a bundle of cash to boot. Moreover, they set their sights on "the 3,107-foot-long Tunnel No. 13 [believing] it would be easy to hop aboard the train as it labored slowly to reach the crest of the summit."[7]

However, the D'Autremont brothers did not just jump into this train robbery without a plan, even if it was a poorly thought out one. For months they camped out in the vicinity, studying the train, the route, and the tunnel before moving forward with their scheme. To increase the odds in their favor, they stole dynamite from a northern Oregon construction site, and would equip themselves with firearms as well.

They decided the end would justify the means in acquiring wealth and leaving the logging work behind them.

The result would put a major dent in their plans, leaving every man to fend for himself.

* * *

On October 11, 1923, Ray D'Autremont and his brothers put their daring plan to plunder the Southern Pacific Express Train Number 13 of its gold and cash into action. As the "Gold Special" Train headed south through the Siskiyou Mountains and approached the Siskiyou station, Roy and Hugh boarded it, with Ray waiting with the explosives at the end of the tunnel. Once the locomotive and several cars had passed, Hugh and Roy hopped onto the baggage car. The brothers then "climbed over the tender and jumped down into the engine cab."[8] The engineer, Sidney Bates, was ordered at gunpoint to stop the train with most of the cars still inside Tunnel 13.

With Roy keeping his eye and a gun on Bates, Ray and Hugh, armed with a .45-caliber semiautomatic pistol and a sawed-off shotgun, headed for the mail car where they believed their fortune in gold and cash awaited them. But the mail clerk, Elvyn E. Dougherty, saw the brothers coming and locked himself inside the car, refusing to let the would-be robbers inside.

Far from willing to let their fortune slip away, Hugh took aim and shot twice at the door to no avail. Undaunted, Ray placed a dynamite charge on the door of the mail car, hoping to blast it open. He and his brothers then took cover while waiting anxiously for the explosion to occur.

It was reported that the "blast ripped open the entire end of the car, killing the clerk and setting fire to the railroad car. The brothers couldn't see into the car because of the smoke and dust. And they couldn't get the train moved out of the tunnel because of the mangled car."

According to the *Slabtown Chronicle*:

The tunnel, rather than muffling the sound of the explosion as the boys had planned, amplified the sound which was heard at the railroad camps at Siskiyou, [Oregon] and at Hilt, [California] several miles away. Rescue crews, thinking that the engine had exploded, left immediately and messages for help were telegraphed to all stations along the line.[9]

With things not going according to plan, panic began to set in for the D'Autremont brothers, who literally saw their fortune in gold go up in smoke and flames.

Coyle O. Johnson, the brakeman, stumbled blindly from a coach through the dense smoke filling the tunnel. He caught the brothers by surprise. Panicking, Ray and Hugh shot him to death.

Having already committed two cold-blooded murders, while coming up empty-handed in their quest for gold and hard cash, the D'Autremont brothers apparently felt they had to eliminate the other witnesses to their ruthless crimes. As such, they rounded up Sidney Bates, the engineer, and Marvin Seng, the railroad fireman, shooting them dead as well.

Later, in a sworn statement, Roy D'Autremont gave his account of the murders:

The [dynamite] blast was so severe that the mail clerk was blown to bits.... The fireman and engineer were then marched to the car. In a few seconds, I saw someone coming with a red lantern from the passenger cars still in the tunnel. I shot at the man, who was a [brakeman], with my shotgun and at the same time Hugh shot him with his .45 Colt. The man staggered and I could see he was dying. Hugh walked over to him and shot him again, in cold blood.... The fireman was standing alongside the engine with his arms in the air. Ray and I had a brief consultation as to what we should do. We decided to kill the fireman. Ray shot him twice with the Colt. Hugh had the engineer covered and I shouted at him to bump him off and then we would clear out. We didn't want any witnesses. Hugh quickly shot the man in the head with his shotgun. We then fled to our cache which was between two and three miles northeast of the south entrance of the tunnel.[10]

As the shots rang through the air, the train passengers awakened to the eerily surreal scene, "half deafened by a rumbling explosion that shook the mountain."[11] According to a newspaper piece on the scary scenario:

Some of the passengers crowded to the car exits, slipped down the steps and moved carefully toward the head of the train. They did not go far before they were driven back by steam, smoke, and gasses from the explosion. The train was afire and the tube was filling with fumes.[12]

With four people dead and the mail car destroyed, along with everything it may have contained, the D'Autremont brothers gave up on their quest and fled the scene of bloodshed and chaos, hiding out in the woods while hoping to somehow escape a terrible predicament of their own making.

* * *

As the gravity of the horrifying crime scene began to settle in for the passengers and remaining crew who were lucky to be alive, a second conductor made his way to an emergency phone close by where he reported what had taken place to the Ashland, Oregon police.

What followed was described in the *New York Times*:

Railroad men and local police soon reached the scene from both directions. The story was plainly written upon the ruins. A bandit or bandits had held up and murdered the engineman and brakeman.... Next he or they had set off a charge of nitro or dynamite against the front end of the mail car.... A steam line had been broken and the hot vapors, mingled with the smoke and the poisonous gas from the charge, had killed the mail clerk and driven the criminals from the tunnel to some refuge in the engirdling mountains.[13]

In what was then billed as "The World's Greatest Manhunt," railroad and police investigators, Oregon National Guard, federal government detectives, and local mobs seeking vigilante justice were in hot pursuit of those responsible.

But Ray, Roy, and Hugh D'Autremont, now mass murderers, against all odds managed to slither out of the area to parts unknown.

The fugitives did, however, leave behind some clues. These included a detonator, a .45-caliber pistol with fingerprints, and a gunnysack that had been "soaked in creosote and dragged along the ground to throw bloodhounds off their trail."[14] Also discovered near Tunnel 13 was a black traveling bag that had a railroad shipping tag containing a pair of grubby green overalls.

However, these items initially led nowhere in the investigation, neither identifying nor resulting in the capture of the bandits who tried to rob the Southern Pacific Train.

As word spread nationally about the Southern Pacific Railroad "Gold Special" Train massacre, frequent sightings of possible perpetrators were made. More than a dozen suspects were taken into custody initially and interrogated by investigators who were under pressure to solve the case, to no avail. Later, when the killers were actually identified, the number ballooned to around five hundred men arrested, but the authorities continued to come up short in apprehending the outlaw brothers.[15]

With the pursuit of the elusive fugitives more or less at a standstill—in spite of rewards from the United States government, the State of Oregon, Southern Pacific

Company, and Railway Express Company totaling nearly $16,000 for information leading to their arrests—police and railroad authorities turned to an American criminologist-chemist to help crack the case.

Edward Oscar Heinrich was a professor of chemistry at the University of California in Berkeley, California. He had often been compared to the fictional British detective Sherlock Holmes. While some of the methods and conclusions reached by the legal chemist were considered dubious at best, investigators were desperate and open to stepping outside the normal investigative techniques of the time in trying to identify the killers.[16]

After his scientific examination of the overalls left behind by the "Gold Special" train bandits, Heinrich concluded that the outlaw who wore them was a lumberjack who had left behind strands of brown hair, was fair complexioned and clean shaven, five feet, eight inches tall, weighed some 165 pounds, and was left-handed, while having personal habits that were fastidious. Based upon finding needles from Douglas firs and "fresh pitch from pine trees," the culprit was thought to have recently worked in camps in western Washington or northwestern Oregon where fir trees were being chopped.[17] Also, dark spots found on the overalls that had looked like car grease to detectives turned out to be gum that came from fir or pine trees.

Heinrich explained that the overalls' size and cut established the probable size and build of the one who owned them. Beneath the left-hand flap were pitch deposits, suggesting that the wearer had used his left hand to remove the clothes, as there was nothing on the right-hand flap. Strands of brown hair had been removed from a button and examined by the chemist, having apparently been ripped away during the course of the bandit getting dressed or removing the clothes. Magnifying the hair strands, Heinrich used standard tables to compare with human hair at different ages in approximating the age of the person wearing the overalls. It was also established that the wearer was standing with the right side of his body closest to the tree that was being chopped by him, indicating that he had to have been using his left hand when working the axe.

Heinrich believed that there were three individuals involved in the train massacre after finding a few grains of rock salt in the gunnysack. He deduced that the outlaws had gathered at a nearby cattleman's cabin that was located around five miles from Tunnel 13. A towel found in the cabin was examined under a microscope, indicating that hairs from shaving belonged to three different faces, based on shade, hair quality, and particles of skin. It also appeared that the bandits had spent around a week in the cabin.[18]

Given that the many lumber camps in the region employed thousands of men—most of who fit the general characteristics attributed to the wearer of the overalls—narrowing this down to discover the identity of the person, much less the other two killers, seemed a daunting task, Heinrich being a forerunner in forensic analyses and deductions aside.

However, in a key piece of evidence, the chemistry professor also found in a pocket of the overalls a registered letter receipt. This was traced by police to a money order of $50 that was sent by an Oregon logger by the name of Roy D'Autremont on September 14, 1923. The recipient was his brother, Hugh D'Autremont, who was in Lakewood, New Mexico.

Authorities quickly interrogated the father of the men, Paul D'Autremont. He acknowledged that his sons were employed as lumberjacks and, of equal importance, one of them, Roy, was a left-hander. Even more damning for Roy was that the Colt .45 left at the scene of the crime was traced to a man named William Elliot. An analysis of his handwriting found it to be a match to Roy D'Autremont's handwriting. Moreover, the railroad shipping tag on the traveling bag discarded by the bandits indicated that it had been mailed from Eugene to Portland by Roy to himself on January 21, 1923.

Given this information, Roy D'Autremont and his brothers, Ray and Hugh, became the chief suspects in the botched robbery and mass murder involving the Southern Pacific Express "Gold Special" Train. Unfortunately, the men had fled the area and showed no interest in turning themselves in.

The federal government would ultimately distribute worldwide, in English and several other languages, more than two million wanted posters for the D'Autremont brothers.

It would take years before any of them were brought to justice.

* * *

In the interim, the authorities worked tirelessly to try to apprehend the killers, as "half a million policemen, sheriffs, constables, customs officers, postal inspectors in all the cities, towns, and villages of the continent, and detectives in ports of the world, were on the lookout" for the fugitive brothers.[19] Dentists, optometrists, and opticians worldwide were made aware of the bandits' dental and eyeglass history and told to be on the lookout for them; while public libraries were put on alert for men who might seek books on radicalism, sociology, and verse, or ask for "the jingles of Robert Service."[20] Furthermore, social bodies and clubs were told to be watchful for young males who may recite "The Spell of the Yukon."[21]

These and other efforts notwithstanding, the D'Autremont brothers remained on the run until 1927. In February of that year, while stationed on Alcatraz Island in San Francisco, California, Army Corporal Thomas Reynolds spotted a familiar face on a wanted poster. It was the face of Hugh D'Autremont, who Reynolds knew as James Price, a fellow soldier in the United States Army with whom he had been acquainted while he was stationed in Los Baños in the province of Laguna, Philippines. Even as he tried to come to grips with this stunning news of D'Autremont as a wanted killer for a Siskiyou Mountains train massacre, Reynolds immediately notified his superiors.[22]

Within hours, Army Private James Price was arrested, relieved of his arms, and sent to "the guard house at points of eight bayonets."[23] Initially, he denied his true identity, but eventually admitted he was the youngest of the D'Autremont brothers, and in March 1927, Hugh D'Autremont was extradited back to the United States to face charges for murder.

While denying he had any information on the whereabouts of his twin brothers, Ray and Roy, the long awaited arrest of Hugh D'Autremont gave authorities reason to believe it was only a matter of time before the other two were also captured and behind bars.

* * *

The hunt for Roy and Ray D'Autremont picked up steam with new wanted posters distributed and a bounty of more than five grand on the heads of both brothers, and law enforcement persistent in their pursuit of the murder suspects. But it would still be months before the fugitives would be apprehended.

In early June 1927, federal authorities received a tip that the D'Autremont brothers were hiding out in eastern Ohio.

Albert Collingsworth, a disabled resident of New Boston, Ohio, recognized the fugitive brothers as factory workers at a steel mill in Steubenville, Ohio. Ray and Roy D'Autremont had been using the aliases Clarence and Elmer Goodwin.[24]

Collingsworth, who was blind in one eye and crippled, asked for assistance from private detective Emma L. Maynard of Portsmouth, Ohio in establishing that the Goodwin brothers were in fact Ray and Roy D'Autremont, wanted for a quadruple murder in Oregon.

On June 8, 1927, Steubenville police officers descended upon the suspects. Roy D'Autremont was taken into custody after leaving work. The authorities located Ray D'Autremont at a rooming house the brothers lived in. He was lured outside by telling him that his brother had sustained a serious injury at the factory. The moment Ray stepped away from the rooming house, well-armed officers placed him under arrest without incident.

While at Police Headquarters, Roy D'Autremont reportedly said: "It looks like some of you guys are in for a reward."[25] The reward money for the twin brothers' arrest had climbed to $20,000.

The twenty-seven-year-old twin murder suspects would later reveal that they had escaped to Detroit, Michigan following the failed Southern Pacific "Gold Special" Train robbery. Ray had gotten married in Detroit before moving to Hanging Rock, Ohio, where Roy would eventually join him. The brothers would keep moving around in an attempt to avoid capture, residing in Portsmouth and Steubenville at one time or another. At one point, Ray had bleached his hair in trying to hide his identity. He had apparently succeeded to some extent as Hazel, his wife of one year and the mother of his infant son, had been stunned to learn about her husband's real name and arrest for multiple murders.

* * *

On June 9th, Ray and Roy D'Autremont waived extradition back to Oregon, where they would stand trial for the Southern Pacific "Gold Special" Train massacre. The two fugitives were returned to the Rogue Valley in southwestern Oregon, and would be tried in Jacksonville. There was great national interest in the case involving American Frontier style bandits, as the press descended on the former county seat for its last noteworthy trial, with Medford becoming the new county seat of Jackson County in 1927.

Ironically, on the same day that Roy and Ray D'Autremont waived proceedings for formal extradition, their younger brother Hugh D'Autremont was put on trial in Jacksonville, Oregon for the second time as a participant in the same murderous crimes. His first trial had ended in a mistrial when a member of the jury died. While awaiting trial, the murder suspect had been held at Alcatraz Federal Penitentiary on Alcatraz Island, off San Francisco's coast.

On June 21, 1927, a strong case by the prosecution against the youngest D'Autremont brother left the verdict all but a formality. Following one hour and twenty minutes of deliberation by the jury, Hugh D'Autremont, now twenty-three years old, was convicted of first degree murder in the death of Coyle O. Johnson, the brakeman on the Southern Pacific Railroad "Gold Special" Express Train Number 13 as it was held up in the Siskiyou Tunnel. D'Autremont was sentenced to life imprisonment at the Oregon State Penitentiary in Salem, Oregon.[26]

The following day, Ray and Roy D'Autremont—who had previously denied being involved in the murders—did an about-face and confessed to the crimes. In contemplating their actions, Ray stated, "Everything we had was invested in the crime. We probably didn't have $3 among us. And we weren't thinking about going back to those logging camps with that hard labor."[27]

With their guilty pleas, the twin brothers were also sentenced to life behind bars at the same Salem, Oregon prison as their younger brother, Hugh.

In an understatement regarding the human cost of the ill-advised attempted train robbery in Southern Oregon's Siskiyou Mountains, and the consequences, the youngest brother of the trio of bandits aptly characterized the crime as, "All for nothing."[28]

Indeed, according to attorney Noreen McGraw, who represented Hugh and Ray D'Autremont at different times, the "get-rich quick scheme" Ray concocted was not supposed to lead to murder and mayhem, with the brothers expressing remorse for their crimes. "They planned to dynamite the mail car," McGraw said. "They didn't think anyone would be riding in it. There was so much smoke and confusion after they blew it up. They thought they'd get all this money and they didn't get anything. That's what's so crazy about it."[29]

"The Last Great Train Robbery," that ended up as no robbery at all, had finally been solved and the perpetrators punished accordingly, allowing the Southern Pacific Company "Gold Special" Express Train Number 13 victims to rest in peace.

* * *

On January 9, 1959, Hugh D'Autremont was released from custody on parole. After moving to San Francisco, California and finding employment as a printer, he received a diagnosis of stomach cancer. Hugh D'Autremont died at age fifty-five on March 30, 1959, the birthday of his older twin brothers. He was buried beside his mother at the Belcrest Memorial Cemetery in Salem, Oregon.

In 1949, after suffering a nervous breakdown, Roy D'Autremont was diagnosed with schizophrenia. He was transferred to Oregon State Hospital in Salem, where he was given a frontal lobotomy. In 1979, he was moved to a nursing home in Salem, and needed to be under twenty-four hour supervision. In March 1983, Roy D'Autremont was paroled. On June 17, 1983, he died at age eighty-three, while still living at the nursing home.

On October 27, 1961, Ray D'Autremont was granted parole. Upon leaving the penitentiary, the convicted killer told reporters, "For the rest of my life I will struggle with the question of whatever possessed us to do such a thing?"[30]

He found janitorial work at the University of Oregon in Eugene and painted in his spare time, as well as studied Spanish and French.

In 1972, after he asked the governor at the time, Tom McCall, to become "a free man before I die," Ray D'Autremont's sentence was commuted.[31] On December 20, 1984, as the last surviving D'Autremont brother, Ray died while living in a nursing home in Eugene. He was eighty-four years old.

Ray and Roy D'Autremont were buried next to their brother, Hugh, and their mother.

On September 28, 1953, Edward Oscar Heinrich, the University of California professor and forensic examiner who was given credit for cracking the Southern Pacific

Express "Gold Special" Train Robbery case, along with thousands of others, died in Berkeley at the age of seventy-two.

In commemoration of the victims of the Siskiyou Tunnel 13 train massacre, a small wreath was placed at the tunnel's south end.

* * *

On Monday, November 17, 2003, vandals started a fire in the Siskiyou Tunnel 13, causing extensive damage, including a collapse of a portion of the tunnel, and closure of the passageway. It reopened seventeen months later in April 2005.[32]

In May 2008, the Siskiyou Summit Rail line closed to steady freight train traffic after big lumber companies balked at a fee increase to use by line owner Central Oregon and Pacific Railroad.[33]

In June 2012, a $7 million grant by the U.S. Department of Transportation was awarded to the Siskiyou Summit Railroad Revitalization project as part of a $9.49 million cost to "repair and revitalize a section of the 296-mile stretch of the short line railroad, including rail, tunnels, ties, and bridges as well as upgrading its freight capacity to handle the 286,000-pound industry standard for rail cars."[34] The work is expected to be completed and the Siskiyou Summit line will reopen to transportation by the end of 2014.

In 2012, a documentary on the infamous train robbery was made, titled, *The Crime of the D'Autremont Brothers.*[35]

* * *

Though the attempted robbery of the Southern Pacific Railroad "Gold Special" Train was one of the most notable train robberies for its failure, terror, and violence, along with the long manhunt for the bandits, it was but one of many trains targeted by outlaws during the latter part of the 19th Century and early 20th Century in search of gold, cash, and other valuables.

Amongst the most infamous were the James–Younger Gang, whose members included outlaw brothers Jesse and

Frank James, whom the D'Autremont brothers idolized. Other gang members included Bob, Cole, Jim, and John Younger, Arthur McCoy, and Bill Chadwell, among others who would come and go over the years.[36]

Jesse Woodson James was born on September 5, 1847 in Kearney, Missouri, and his older brother, Alexander Franklin "Frank" James, was born on January 10, 1843 in Clay County, Missouri.

The James–Younger Gang began as "a group of Confederate bushwhackers who fought in the bitter partisan conflict that wracked the divided state of Missouri during the American Civil War."[37] Their postwar life of crime started in 1866, which included a string of bank robberies and murder.

It was on December 7, 1869 that Jesse and Frank James were suspected of robbing a Gallatin, Missouri Davies County Savings Association, with Jesse gunning down cashier John W. Sheets in a case of mistaken identity. Jesse, in particular, was in the midst of becoming a legend following the crime and successfully escaping a posse, along with writing letters mockingly to newspapers and continuing to commit more crimes that gave him even greater notoriety through the years.

It was on July 21, 1873 that the James–Younger gang committed their first train robbery near Adair, Iowa. After they derailed a Rock Island Railroad locomotive, in which the engineer John Rafferty died, the bandits robbed the express safe of $2,337.

On December 8, 1874, not far from Muncie, Kansas, the outlaw gang came away with a lot more when they robbed a Kansas Pacific Railroad train of $30,000. One gang member, William "Bud" McDaniel, was apprehended after the robbery by a Kansas City policeman. McDaniel would later be shot while trying to escape.

On July 7, 1876, in what would be the last train holdup of the James–Younger Gang, the gang targeted the Missouri Pacific Railroad to rob near Otterville, Missouri at the

"Rocky Cut." New gang member Hobbs Kerry was quickly arrested and pointed the finger at the other robbers.

On September 21st, three of the Younger brothers—Jim, Cole, and Bob—were arrested and faced a variety of charges, including robbery and murder (the other brother, John, had been shot to death by a Pinkerton detective posing as a cattle buyer on March 17, 1874).[38]

On November 20, 1876, the Younger brothers pled guilty and received life sentences at Stillwater Prison in Stillwater, Minnesota. Bob Younger would succumb to tuberculosis while in prison, dying in September 1889. Jim and Cole Younger were released on parole in 1901. The following year, Jim took his own life, while in 1903, Cole was given a pardon. On March 21, 1916, the last surviving Younger brother died in Lee's Summit, Missouri.

With the Younger brothers out of the picture, Jesse and Frank James remained on the loose and continued committing robberies with new gang members. These included on July 15, 1881, robbing of $800 the Rock Island Railroad close to Winston, Missouri, in which the train conductor William Westfall was among the casualties of the bandits.

On September 7th of that year, in what would be his final train robbery, Jesse James and the gang held up the Chicago and Alton Railroad near the Illinois Mississippi River town of Alton. With the express safe all but empty, the gang robbed the train passengers and the bounty grew for the arrest of the James brothers.

As it turned out, Jesse James ended up being shot to death by his gang member, Robert Ford, on April 3, 1882 in St. Joseph, Missouri. Apparently, Ford was hoping to receive the reward money for James's capture, dead or alive. Jesse James was only thirty-four when he died.[39]

His brother, Frank, turned himself in to Missouri governor Thomas T. Crittenden on October 4, 1882. He went to trial for two of the crimes associated with the James brothers, including the Rock Island Railroad train robbery, where two people were killed.

Frank James managed to beat the charges, acquitted in each case.[40] On February 18, 1951, he died a free man at seventy-two in Clay County, Missouri, leaving behind a wife and son.

* * *

Outlaw Harry Tracy also captured the fancy of the D'Autremont brothers as one who made his mark as a desperado with the Old West coming to a close. According to the *Seattle Daily Times*, "In all the criminal lore of the country there is no record equal to that of Harry Tracy for cold-blooded nerve, desperation, and thirst for crime. Jesse James, compared with Tracy, is a Sunday school teacher."[41]

Born October 23, 1875 as Harry Severns, Tracy reportedly spent time with Butch Cassidy as well as the Hole in the Wall Gang. On March 1, 1898, a gunfight involving Tracy and three other bandits took place at Brown's Park, Colorado, leaving Valentine S. Hoy, a posse member, dead. Tracy was apprehended, but managed to escape from the jail in Aspen, Colorado in June 1898. By late 1901, the outlaw had been recaptured and was convicted. He was sent to the Oregon State Penitentiary in Salem, Oregon to serve his sentence.

On June 9, 1902, Harry Tracy escaped from prison, along with a fellow inmate David Merrill, shooting to death correctional officers Frank Ferrell, Thurston Jones Sr., and Bailey Tiffany, along with three civilians.

With the notoriety achieved from the violent escape, a massive manhunt, and widespread coverage by the media about the outlaw, Tracy gained a reputation as "one of the last desperados of the Old West."

On June 28th, Tracy killed fellow escapee Merrill, whose body was found on July 14th. On July 3rd, Tracy ambushed a deputy, John Williams, and a detective, Charles Raymond, killing both in a shootout, before fleeing with hostages. Along the way, he killed two members of a posse.

By the end of July, following a string of crimes in King County, Washington, Tracy cut across the Cascade Mountains and was spotted on a ferry as it crossed the Columbia River.

On August 6, 1902, Harry Tracy's luck finally ran out at a ranch in Creston, Washington, as he was ambushed by a Lincoln County, Oregon posse. Shot twice and seriously injured, "two bullets had ripped through Tracy's leg. One caused a flesh wound in the back of his thigh, but the other had hit mid-calf, shattering both bones. Tracy wrenched himself forward by his hands, and took cover in the waist-high wheat."[42]

When the sheriff arrived and the outlaw was surrounded with no chance of escape, rather than face justice for his violent crimes, Tracy took his own life at the age of twenty-six. He was returned to Salem to be buried.

Harry Tracy's short but action-packed life of crime and evading the law left an impression on Ray, Roy, and Hugh D'Autremont, inspiring them to follow a similar path.

The legend of Harry Tracy inspired books, plays, and a 1982 film titled, *Harry Tracy: Desperado*.[43]

* * *

For better or worse, the D'Autremont brothers' daring and deadly attack of the Southern Pacific Railroad "Gold Special" Express Train Number 13 in search of gold and cash made them part of folklore as notorious outlaws of a forgotten era with the likes of the James–Younger Gang, Harry Tracy, Butch Cassidy, The Dalton Gang, the Jennings Gang, the McCarty brothers, Thomas E. Ketchum, Bill Miner, and "Gentleman" Jack Davis, among others. Their bravado gave them a place in history, while often leading to a life on the run or behind bars, with little to show for their banditry when it was over.

# # #

MURDER OF THE BANKER'S DAUGHTER
The Killing of Marion Parker

On Thursday, December 15, 1927, twelve-year-old Marion Parker, the daughter of a successful banker was boldly abducted from her junior high school in Los Angeles, California. Two days later, the girl's dismembered remains were tossed about the city like garbage by her abductor and murderer.[1] This caused pandemonium, as the vicious killer managed to evade immediate capture, leading to a manhunt by authorities unlike any in recent memory. The horror of the crime was reminiscent of one that occurred fourteen years earlier involving thirteen-year-old Mary Phagan, who was murdered at a pencil factory in Atlanta. It was also similar to the crime five years later when the twenty-month-old son of famed aviator Charles Lindbergh was abducted from the family's New Jersey home and brutally slain. The killer of Marion Parker was identified as former bank employee William Edward Hickman, age nineteen. The career criminal's capture, trial, conviction, and execution captured the public's imagination, while putting attention on the vulnerability of children in this country targeted by child predators and the often tragic consequences.

* * *

Marion Parker, age twelve, was born on October 11, 1915, along with her twin sister named Marjorie, to Los Angeles, California banker Perry Marion Parker and his wife, Geraldine Heisel Parker. The Parkers also had an older son, Perry Willard Parker. The elder Perry Parker was the chief clerk at the First National Trust and Savings Bank in downtown Los Angeles. The family lived comfortably in a residence at 1631 South Wilton Place. The home was less than a mile away from the 17th Street location of Mount Vernon Junior High School in the Lafayette Square area of the city, where Marion and Marjorie attended classes.

On the morning of Thursday, December 15, 1927, Marion was attending a Christmas party in a classroom at her junior high school—likely as a prelude of what she could expect ten days later when the family gathered at home for the holiday—when she was abruptly taken out of the classroom and brought to the school office. It was there that the school registrar, Mary Holt, informed Marion, who was wearing brown Oxford shoes and stockings, that her father had been involved in an automobile accident and was seriously injured. She was supposed to go with the curly brown-haired, slender young man in the office wearing a gray overcoat—who had identified himself as working for Perry Parker as a bank employee—to be with her father.

The fact that her twin sister Marjorie was not present must have seemed odd to Marion, as well as Mary Holt. But the young man had apparently handled this satisfactorily by indicating that Parker requested that he pick up "the smaller one."[2] He had even invited Holt to call the bank for confirmation of his identification and story, a gamble which could have changed the course of history. Instead, the registrar took that as an indication of his truthfulness and released Marion to his custody without making the call. Holt would later say that she would never "have let Marion go but for the apparent sincerity and disarming manner of the man."[3]

For Marion's part, the desire to go to her injured father made her oblivious to the danger the man presented. Unfortunately, her innocence collided with a calculating and ruthless killer, who would see to it that Marion Parker would never live to see her thirteenth birthday and, in the process, put the entire nation on edge.

Sadly enough, one of the last people to see Marion alive was her twin sister Marjorie when she happened to see the stranger walking Marion out to his car. At the time, neither sibling realized that their connection would be broken forever.

* * *

After what turned out to be a daring abduction, a telegraph was sent from a Western Union office in Alhambra, California to Perry Parker at his home that evening, informing him that his daughter had been kidnapped for ransom. The telegraph read: "Marion [is] secure. Use good judgment. Interference with my plans dangerous."[4] It was signed, "George Fox."

The following day, a special delivery letter was sent to Parker, in which the kidnapper demanded $1,500 in order to get his daughter back. The cryptic letter read: "Fox is my name, very sly you know. Get this straight, your daughter's life hangs by a thread and I have a Gillette ready and able to handle the situation.... Fulfilling these terms with the transfer of the currency will secure the return of the girl. Failure to comply with these requests means no one will ever see the girl again—except the angels in heaven. The affair must end one way or another within three days—seventy-two hours. You will receive further notice."[5] This one was signed "Fox Fate."

In a second ransom letter, Parker was ordered to collect $1,500 in $20 gold certificates to be delivered that night. There was also a special delivery letter from Marion, pleading with her parents to do as he asked, so that her life would be spared:

"Dear Daddy and Mother, I wish I could come home. I think I'll die if I have to be like this much longer. Won't someone tell me why all this had to happen to me. Daddy please do what this man tells you or he'll kill me if you don't. Your loving daughter, Marion Parker. P.S. Please Daddy I want to come home tonight."[6]

Though there was a massive police effort underway to try to locate the missing girl while discouraging Parker from succumbing to ransom demands, authorities eventually came to believe that the best hope for getting the girl back alive was to pay the kidnapper the money. Perry Parker agreed to meet with "The Fox" at 10th Street and Gramercy Place on the evening of December 16th, with the ransom in hand while prepared to follow instructions to the letter in making the exchange.

However, the meeting never occurred. Apparently spooked by the presence of police on the scene, the kidnapper aborted the plan, never showing up at the exchange location, leaving Perry Parker without his daughter or even knowing if she was still alive.

Parker breathed a sigh of relief when the kidnapper contacted him again by telegram the following Saturday morning on December 17th, with assurances that the girl was alive and well for now, while placing the blame squarely on Perry for the botched first attempt to exchange the money for the return of his daughter.

The kidnapper warned: "I will be two billion times as cautious and clever, as deadly from now on. You have brought this on yourself and you deserve it and worse."[7]

A renewed ransom demand was made, with the kidnapper threatening to kill Marion should Parker not come alone this time.

At seven-thirty p.m., "The Fox" phoned Perry Parker at home with instructions to bring the $1,500 in $20 gold certificates to the corner of Fifth and Manhattan Place in

Los Angeles. There, the kidnapper would drive alongside Parker's vehicle, demonstrate that Marion was alive and well, grab the money, and release the girl on the next block.

Not wanting to take any chances, Parker followed these orders without informing the police about the exchange. Upon arriving at his destination at 428 Manhattan Place, Parker soon noticed a Chrysler Coupe pull up alongside his car. He could see Marion seated stationary in the passenger seat up front.

The driver of the vehicle, who was wearing a handkerchief to conceal much of his face, aimed a sawed-off shotgun at Marion Parker's father, while saying to him brusquely, "You know what I'm here for. No monkey business."[8]

Parker, noting that his daughter was covered up to the top of her neck and immobile, expressed concern that there was no response from her.

"She's asleep," the kidnapper said simply. "Give me the money and follow instructions."[9]

Eager to get this over with and have his daughter safe from her abductor, Perry Parker did as he was told and gave him seventy-five marked $20 gold certificates. "The Fox" then drove off, and Parker followed the kidnapper to 432 South Manhattan Place. He watched as "The Fox" tossed Marion out of the vehicle like a rag doll and took off.

Parker attempted to get the Chrysler Coupe's license plate number, but Marion's abductor had cleverly turned it inward at the corners, so only part of the numbers could be read.

As "The Fox" fled the scene, Parker hopped out of his car and ran to his unmoving daughter. Holding her in his arms, it became clear to him that she was no longer alive. As he shrieked at the horror before him, others became aware of the tragedy and contacted the authorities.

Marion Parker had been the victim of a brutal murder. Only her head and torso were present, covered in towels. Her arms and legs had been severed right up to the body and the girl had been disemboweled, with rags filling the space where her entrails had been. A wire was fixed firmly around her neck, slicing well into the skin and brought up behind her head and wound securely around her forehead in an effort to prop her head up. Black thread had been used to sew open her eyelids to give the appearance that the girl was still alive, though clearly her assailant went to extremes to ensure otherwise in the viciousness of the attack.

According to an autopsy performed on the victim, Marion Parker had been dead for around twelve hours. There was no indication that she had been sexually assaulted. Unable to establish the exact cause of death, the coroner would attribute it to either loss of blood or asphyxiation. It was later announced by the county chemist that, after analyzing the victim's lungs, there was no evidence of chloroform or ether.[10]

On Sunday, December 18th, five bundles wrapped in newspaper that contained the missing body parts of Marion Parker were found scattered across Elysian Park close by.

What had become abundantly clear to the police and public was that a ruthless kidnapper turned killer was at large and, until he was brought to justice or killed, no one could feel safe. To that end, a reward leading to the capture of the killer quickly swelled to $100,000, even as more than 20,000 law enforcement officers, members of the American Legion, U.S. Secret Service, and firefighters from Los Angeles joined in on the manhunt. Thousands more were on the lookout for the suspect across the Western United States and Mexico.

The brutality of the murder prompted the *Los Angeles Times* to declare it "the most horrible crime of the 1920s."[11] The then Lieutenant Governor of California, Buron Fitts, went even further, calling Marion Parker's murder "the most vicious and atrocious crime in California history."[12]

As such, the race was on to resolve the case as quickly as possible, even as the murderer remained unidentified and on the loose.

* * *

With a violent child killer at large, authorities raced to identify the killer and bring him to justice. In the interim, there was a private funeral service held for young Marion Parker at the Forest Lawn Memorial Park's Little Church of the Flowers in Glendale, California. She was cremated and her remains interred within the Forest Lawn's Great Mausoleum.

On Sunday, the 18th of December, authorities located the 1927 Chrysler Coupe that Marion's kidnapper had driven. It had been abandoned in a Westlake Park district parking garage. It was discovered that the vehicle had been stolen on November 7th in Kansas City, Missouri from Doctor Herbert L. Mantz in the course of a holdup. The license plates found on the Coupe had been stolen as well on December 5th from a vehicle in San Diego.

Also discovered at 620 South Manhattan Place, around one block from where Marion's corpse was discarded, was a suitcase that contained papers soaked in blood and a spool of thread that matched the thread the killer had used to sew Marion's eyes open.

The investigation took a positive turn when a label on one of the towels used to wrap Marion's torso indicated that it belonged to the Bellevue Arms Apartments, located in Angelino Heights, in a district not far from the city center and also within proximity of Elysian Park, where the victim's body parts had been dispersed.

As police descended upon the 88 unit complex on Bellevue Avenue, the manager, John Henry, indicated that the murder suspect's description matched that of a man using the name "Donald Evans," who had rented room 315 on November 23rd.

The tenant in room 315, located in a "quiet area" in the back of Bellevue Arms at his request, was nowhere to be found, but he left behind clues that the police honed in on— including a thumbprint left on a sugar bowl, half of a hazelnut shell tossed in a wastebasket that matched the other half found in one of the towels that enveloped Marion

Parker's body, a piece of thread matching the thread used to tie the bundles that contained the victim's severed body parts, and a notebook on a desk that had the name "Marion" printed on it. There were also razor blades found in the room, which the kidnapper had alluded to in a letter to Perry Parker in threatening his daughter's life, newspapers lying around that talked about Marion Parker's abduction, and leftovers that suggested two people were present. Finally, other tenants linked Evans to the Chrysler Coupe that police believed was the same one driven by Marion's abductor.[13]

It wasn't long before the true identity of the suspect was revealed. Donald Evans turned out to be an alias for William Edward Hickman, a nineteen-year-old with a criminal history and a link to Marion Parker's father.

According to the Chief of Detectives, Herman Cline, the evidence to support Hickman as the kidnapper and murderer of Marion Parker was "overwhelming." In a key piece of evidence, fingerprints taken from the killer's Chrysler Coupe and letters sent to Perry Parker were found by Detective Sergeant Barlow to be a match for Hickman's fingerprints from Juvenile Court records.[14] These records revealed that in June 1927, Hickman had been arrested and charged with check forgery while working as a messenger at the First National Trust and Savings Bank in Los Angeles, where Perry Parker was chief clerk. Hickman, who had been employed by the bank for six months, was fired from the job after he pled guilty to forgeries, which totaled around $400.

Upon his conviction, Hickman was placed on probation and attempted to regain his job as a bank messenger, but the bank and Perry Parker refused to reinstate him. According to Parker, Hickman then tried to get a reference from him for employment elsewhere, which he again declined to do.

William Hickman was also linked to the abduction and murder of Marion Parker by several individuals who gave a positive identification of the suspect. These included Western Union employee Dorothy Snyder from the Alhambra, California office, who recognized Hickman as the person who sent one of the telegrams from there to Perry Parker. John Henry, manager of the Bellevue Arms Apartments, also identified tenant Donald Evans through the Police Rogues Gallery as William Edward Hickman; as did druggist K. D. Jackson and two other druggists from local stores who fingered Hickman as the individual who stole anesthetics from their pharmacies the previous month.[15]

Hickman was further identified as the man who abducted Marion Parker from Mount Vernon Junior High School by school registrar Mary Holt and teacher, Naomi Britton. According to Britton, in her positive identification of Hickman in a photograph, "He is the man. I could tell him anywhere."[16]

On Tuesday, December 20th, William Edward Hickman was formally charged with the kidnapping and murder of the banker's daughter, Marion Parker, and a bench warrant issued for Hickman's arrest.

* * *

William Edward Hickman was born on February 1, 1908, in Sebastian County, Arkansas as one of five children to William Thomas Hickman and Eva Buck Hickman. His father abandoned the family when Hickman was only nine years old. His mother resided in Kansas City, Missouri, and his father took up residence in El Paso, Texas.

Graduating from Central High School in Kansas City, Hickman was only eleven when he committed his first crime, which was stealing candy. Upon relocating to Southern California, his foray into criminality became more violent. In Los Angeles, on December 24, 1926, Hickman and a friend, Welby L. Hunt, held up the Rose Hill Pharmacy on Huntington Drive at gunpoint. The owners, Clarence Ivy Toms and his wife, Ruth, did as they were told. However, during the course of the robbery, police officer J. W. Oliver entered the store and shots were fired. Hickman was armed with a .32 caliber pistol and Hunt carried a .38 caliber revolver. Clarence Toms, twenty-four and a graduate of the

University of Southern California's College of Pharmacy, was fatally shot in the chest; while Oliver was shot in his right hand. In spite of that, he was able to fire shots at the robbers, but missed them as Hickman and Hunt successfully made their getaway.

When Hickman was arrested for forgery in June 1927, he had been living with his mother and sister in a bungalow at 2518 Birch Street in Alhambra. After he received probation, the Hickman family returned to Kansas City, where Hickman got a job as an usher in a theater.

In the first week of November 1927, a gun-brandishing Hickman stole Doctor Herbert Mantz's Chrysler Coupe in Kansas City, driving it to Chicago, before returning to Los Angeles with the stolen vehicle. There, he took the alias "Donald Evans," along with "George Fox," and "The Fox," as his life of crime took another grisly and deadly turn with the kidnapping and murder of Marion Parker.[17]

* * *

With the hunt on for fugitive child killer William Edward Hickman, the authorities spared no expense trying to track down the suspect. Apparently Hickman was last seen and recognized by gas station attendant John Ward on December 20th, at around five a.m., after he put five gallons of gas into Hickman's stolen vehicle at a station near downtown Los Angeles. Without paying for the gas, Hickman took off. Ward went after him, but eventually lost sight of him.

This sighting resulted in an intense effort by the police throughout the city to locate Hickman, to no avail. By evening, with emotions high and people out and about, downtown Los Angeles was the scene of a major fire, as the police station and city jail went up in flames, destroying the upper floors of the timeworn brick building and an adjacent hotel within minutes.[18]

As the search went on, William Edward Hickman's mug shot appeared on the front pages of newspapers nationwide. Men fitting the murder suspect's description were brought in by police for questioning, as reported sightings of Hickman came in from up and down the West Coast and as far away as New York City, along with such cities as Chicago, Des Moines, Iowa, Wichita, Kansas, and Tucson, Arizona, among other places.

In one instance, twenty-seven-year-old Michael O'Neil, a Hickman lookalike who resided just a few miles from where Marion Parker was abducted, was placed under arrest five times before the authorities officially cleared him of any wrongdoing. The Chief of Detectives even sent the innocent man a letter to that effect to keep him from being harassed or arrested again. In another case of mistaken identity, in downtown Los Angeles on Hill and Sixth Streets, a group of vigilantes went after a man who resembled Hickman, threatening him with serious bodily harm before the police finally came to his rescue, questioned him, and determined that he was not the killer. The *Los Angeles Times* noted that the frightening example and "many other occurrences of similar type, demonstrate the fever pitch into which the details of the horrible crime have thrown the citizens of Los Angeles."[19]

In the meantime, authorities picked up other clues into Hickman's mindset in what appeared to be a premeditated murder plot. According to Charles Dowling, a trustee and former cellmate from county jail, Hickman had talked about an interest in poisons and having surgical instruments.[20] Investigators also learned from C. B. Terry, a San Pedro, California Port warden that a young man fitting Hickman's description sought information about employment on a ship bound from Los Angeles to the Orient, indicating he was in a hurry to leave.[21]

* * *

On the day following his fateful encounter with Perry Parker, William Hickman ended up on Hollywood Boulevard where he stole a 1928 green-colored Hudson vehicle from F. R. Peck and made off with $15 from the man, before driving toward San Francisco. There, he spent one night in a hotel and headed for Oregon and Washington.

On Wednesday, December 21st, Hickman used two of the marked $20 gold certificates he had received as ransom from Perry Parker in the state of Washington. In a downtown Seattle haberdashery, Hickman purchased underwear, a pair of black gloves, and a hat with the money, catching the eye of the proprietor, George Willoughby, who phoned the police once the suspect had left the premises. The $20 bill's serial number matched one of those from the ransom money.[22]

And at the Valley Garage in Kent, Washington, a Seattle suburb, Hickman used the other $20 to purchase gasoline. In both instances, Hickman was identified through photographs as the man who passed the marked bills.

On Thursday, December 22nd, in Echo, Oregon, the Pendleton, Oregon Chief of Police Tom Gurdane and State Traffic Officer Clyde Buck Llewellyn had stopped on a curve along the Columbia River Highway on the historic Oregon Trail as they lit their pipes, when a green Hudson sedan flew by. The officers noted that the license plate had been switched, but the vehicle matched the description of one being driven by fugitive William Edward Hickman, wanted in California for the abduction and murder of Marion Parker.

They pursued the vehicle, pulling to the side of it and ordering the driver to stop. When he finally heeded to their demands, Hickman was arrested without incident, in spite of the fact that the child murderer was carrying a revolver, along with the remainder of the ransom money totaling about $1,400. Also in the vehicle was a 45-caliber handgun and a sawed-off shotgun.

A weary Hickman reportedly said as he was taken into custody, "Well, I guess it's all over."[23]

According to Police Chief Gurdane, they had expected Hickman to come their way and were ready for him. "Our information was that he drove to Seattle, intending to go over to Eastern Washington, but finding that the Snoqualmie Pass was blocked by snow, he doubled back on his tracks to the Columbia River Highway."[24] Having been told that the suspect had already driven past Portland, they were certain he would head in the direction of Pendleton.

Hickman was taken to the Pendleton City Jail and interrogated by investigators about the murder case. He initially would not confirm his true identity and denied being responsible for Marion Parker's death. But, under pressure, he acknowledged that he was William Edward Hickman. However, though he confessed to being in on the kidnapping of the girl in order to get the ransom money to pay for college, Hickman named an accomplice, Andrew Cramer, as Marion's killer, throwing investigators in a new and unexpected direction. The suspect claimed that he had no knowledge of the girl's death until Cramer arrived Saturday night with her corpse at his apartment at Bellevue Arms.

It did not take long for the authorities to discredit Hickman's allegations, as Cramer had a concrete alibi that made it impossible for him to have killed Marion Parker. Oliver Andrew Cramer had been in the Los Angeles jail since August—or months prior to the abduction and murder of Marion Parker—serving time for bootlegging.

Cramer, who acknowledged knowing Hickman, scoffed at the notion that he had anything whatsoever to do with the girl's slaying. "It's impossible for me to have been in on that killing, as I was right here all the time," he told police. "It's almost too ridiculous to talk about."[25]

Authorities were inclined to agree with him, all things considered. This placed the onus entirely on Hickman's shoulders, as it became all too clear that the real killer of Marion Parker was now in police custody.

In the meantime, throngs of people had converged on the city jail as news spread that Hickman had been captured in their neck of the woods. Bowing to public interest, Gurdane allowed the press to photograph Hickman in his cell and let locals get a peek at the infamous murder suspect through a window. As reported by the Associated Press:

"Pretty women stopped to peer into the grated room, grim cowmen with their own ideas of justice stalked past with audible comment, and business men made hurried trips to the scene and took their places in the line."[26]

With the real threat of an angry mob taking the law into their own hands and ending Hickman's life for him, the local authorities took no chances. Escorted by Police Chief Gurdane, Officer Llewellyn, Los Angeles Chief of Detectives Henry Cline, and Los Angeles Police Department Inspectors Lucas and Raymond, among others assigned to protect the suspect, William Edward Hickman was transported by train on a special car attached to the Southern Pacific's Cascade Limited back to Los Angeles to face charges in the kidnapping and murder of Marion Parker.

Prior to the journey, Hickman, no doubt depressed and unnerved by the unenviable position he found himself in with such a hostile environment, attempted to commit suicide twice while in his jail cell. The first time was by using a handkerchief to strangle himself. When that failed, he dove head-first from the top bunk to the floor. The guard on duty responded on both occasions, preventing the murder suspect from seriously harming himself.[27]

*　*　*

During his time in custody, Hickman made a number of confessions, some less credible than others. The murder suspect was also flippant when faced with such serious charges and public scorn. For instance, upon a request to pose for a picture, he responded: "What should I look like, a crook?"[28]

In a December 22nd interview with *Pendleton East Oregonian* city editor Parker Branin and court reporter John Beckwith—while still pointing the finger at Andrew Cramer for killing Marion Parker—Hickman indicated that he'd been friendly and gentle with the girl and even took her to see a movie the same day she was kidnapped.

According to Hickman, when the movie was over, Marion said: "I wonder what the school kids will say when I go back. They will want to know what I did and everything."[29]

As to how he went about abducting the girl, Hickman said:

I parked by the house early, so I could see her leave for school and see what school she went to, and it popped in my mind that if I went for her at the school I could get her that way.

There was no plan. But I had been thinking about it.... I went and told the teacher that her father had been in an accident.... They asked me which girl I wanted and I said the younger one and she said, 'Marion?' and I said, 'Yes, that is the one the father was calling for.'[30]

Hickman confessed that the kidnapping was a quick way to make money to go to college. He also claimed that anesthetic was not used when the victim was being dissected, and that the murderer strangled her with wire.

By the time he was en route to Los Angeles on the train, William Hickman confessed to police that the murderer in question was, in fact, him and him alone. In a nineteen-page confession, Hickman admitted to dismembering Marion Parker, feeling he could more easily dispose of her remains that way.

He claimed that after bringing the girl to his apartment, he used a towel to strangle her as he feared she would make sounds. The killer then confessed to putting the banker's daughter in the bathtub, where her limbs were severed, then he "sliced her open at the waist, [before putting] her body on a shelf, with a towel beneath it to soak up the blood."[31]

Hickman would later confess that even after strangling the girl and cutting her throat, he thought that she might still be alive as he was dismembering her.[32]

The child killer indicated that he was not motivated by revenge regarding Perry Parker—who had rebuffed Hickman's attempt to get his messenger job back as well as his request to use the bank as a reference for new employment—in kidnapping his daughter. Instead, Hickman argued that she had been targeted as an opportunity that presented itself, as he had noticed her visiting Parker and wanted the money for college. His desire was to enroll in a Parkville, Missouri religious school called Park College, after which time he planned to turn over a new leaf.

Having already murdered and dissected his victim, Hickman confessed that he knew in order to receive the ransom money; he had to make it appear that Marion Parker was still alive. As such, "he combed her hair, put powder on her face, used a needle and thread to hold her eyelids open, [before carrying] her body out in a suitcase to meet with Parker."[33]

In light of the grisly confession, Kansas City attorney Jerome K. Walsh was hired to represent Hickman, immediately advising him to plead "not guilty by reason of insanity."[34]

* * *

In the wee hours of the morning of December 29th, while in jail in Los Angeles, William Edward Hickman confessed to perpetrating a number of robberies of local drug stores. One of the robberies led to the shooting death of pharmacist Clarence Toms.

According to guard Frank Dewar, when he asked Hickman informally if he had ever murdered anyone else, Hickman answered, "Sure. Remember that druggist at Rose Hill that was shot last December?"[35]

The confessed killer went into detail about the crime with the jailer, implicating sixteen-year-old Welby Hunt in the murder, as well as the other robberies.

After the confession, Clarence Toms' widow, Ruth, was brought in to identify Hickman. Upon looking at him up close, she declared, "That's the man!"[36] Overcome with grief and shock, she fainted.

In the meantime, Hunt was taken into custody, where he admitted his involvement with Hickman in a string of robberies and the shooting death of Toms. However, whereas Hickman indicated that both youths had fired their guns in the drug store owned by the pharmacist, Hunt insisted that Hickman was the only one of them to open fire.

Prison guards would later state that Hickman confessed to being the sole shooter in the murder of Clarence Toms.[37]

* * *

In an effort to avoid what appeared to be a sure trip to the gallows, Hickman became one of the initial murder defendants to make use of a new California law in which offenders could plead not guilty by reason of insanity. His attorney, Jerome Walsh, hoped to offer a dementia praecox or adolescent insanity defense in the case. Clarence Darrow had used the strategy successfully in defending teenagers Richard Loeb and Nathan Leopold, Jr., who on May 21, 1924, kidnapped and brutally murdered fourteen-year-old Bobby Franks in Chicago, Illinois, saving the killers from being executed for the shocking crime.[38]

Walsh relied on a number of mental health professionals and alienists to bolster his argument that Hickman was insane when murdering and dismembering Marion Parker. However, the District Attorney, Asa S. Keyes, countered this by having his own experts on mental disorders, including Doctor Cecil Reynolds and Doctor A. A. Nickels, declare Hickman to be "perfectly sane" after spending several hours examining the accused killer.[39]

On January 11, 1928, with the start of Hickman's trial just two weeks away, the accused child kidnapper and killer's attempt to be made a ward of the juvenile court, thereby circumventing the harsher consequences of adult court, was rejected by Judge Scott. The petition had been filed in August 1927, when Hickman was given probation for the forgery offenses he committed when he was a bank messenger. The dismissal paved the way for Hickman to be tried for murder in Superior Court, where he could face the death penalty.[40]

On January 25, 1928, William Edward Hickman's trial began in Superior Court, with Judge J. J. Trabucco presiding before a packed courthouse. The jury consisted of eight men and four women. Half of the jurors were described as "gray-haired" and the remainder "middle-aged." Dissatisfied with the makeup of the jury, the defense put this in the record, after exhausting its twenty peremptory challenges.[41]

The State chose to rest its case from the start, preferring to prove Hickman was sane and guilty of cold-blooded murder through cross-examination and rebuttal.

Walsh began his case with dozens of depositions and the testimony of alienists and the defendant's father, William T. Hickman, aimed at showing a history of mental illness in Hickman's family, implying a genetic predisposition to insanity. This included portraying his mother, Eva Hickman, as neurotic and suicidal and indicating that his grandfather, Otto Buck, was "subject to fits," and his wife Becky hallucinated that "everyone [was] against her."[42]

Countering the insanity defense, the prosecution produced a letter that Hickman wrote to another inmate, seeking advice on getting a verdict of not guilty due to insanity, in which he said: "I've got to throw a fit in court and I intend to throw a laughing, screaming, diving act before the prosecution finishes their case—maybe in front of old man Parker himself."[43]

There was also testimony from Oregon jail guards that Hickman had sought instruction on "how to act crazy."[44]

The prosecution theorized that Hickman was motivated in the abduction and murder of Marion Parker primarily by revenge against her father, banker Perry Parker, who had testified in Hickman's forgery trial and refused to give him his job back as a bank messenger. Some believe that Hickman may also have been seeking notoriety by committing a shocking crime, after he had allegedly mentioned to a reporter he desired the type of press coverage afforded notorious teenage murderers Leopold and Loeb.

Showing no mercy for the convicted killer, during closing arguments, District Attorney Keyes was quoted as saying:

It is only owing to the fact that we are civilized that a mob did not take this man from the officers of the law, and if it were not that I am an officer of the law I should have wanted to be in the front ranks of such a mob to help put a rope around this man's neck.[45]

In spite of the defense attempts to the contrary through testimony lasting thirteen days, on Friday, February 9, 1928, the jury took just thirty-six minutes to find William Edward Hickman sane during the kidnapping and murder of Marion Parker—and therefore, guilty as charged in the twelve-year-old's abduction and murder.[46]

After the verdict was pronounced, Hickman told the press: "The die is cast and the State wins by a neck. I don't think I have much to live for, and I don't know yet why I killed the Parker girl, but I did it, and I'll take my punishment."[47]

In tipping his hand on what that punishment might entail, Judge Trabucco did not mince words when saying: "I cannot state in advance just what my sentence will be, but you can rest assured that this defendant will be given all the law allows."[48]

The following morning, February 10, 1928, William Edward Hickman was sentenced to die by hanging for the murder of Marion Parker.

* * *

On March 10, 1929, William Hickman's and Welby Hunt's trial for the murder of druggist Clarence Ivy Toms produced a verdict of guilty for the former friends. They were sentenced by Superior Court Judge Elliot Craig to life in prison for the crime.[49]

On March 17th, Hickman and Hunt were accompanied to San Quentin by guards. The two inmates were "shackled together [as they] entered the prison after a night train's ride from Los Angeles."[50]

A *New York Times* article described the grim process the convicted killers, particularly William Hickman, faced as "newcomers": "Their fingerprints were taken, they were photographed and measured. Then they were attired in gray prison clothing. Afterward, Hickman was taken to a row of cells for men awaiting execution. In the cell adjoining his was Edgar Lapierre, condemned to die on the same day as Hickman."[51]

On July 5, 1928, by a unanimous vote, the California Supreme Court upheld the murder conviction of William Hickman. The Court asserted that the defendant's rights had not been violated when he used the new State statute to plead not guilty by reason of insanity.[52]

Hickman also lost his appeal to the U.S. Supreme Court, ending his chances to escape a sentence of death.[53]

* * *

In the days before his execution, Hickman wrote a series of confession letters to police across the country, confessing to the murders he was convicted of, as well as robberies he committed. The death row inmate, who had become religious while incarcerated, claimed that he wished to clear his conscience as the "Christian thing to do."[54]

Hickman spent his last day alive meditating and reading the Bible. He had been transferred the night before from "Condemned Row" to San Quentin's death chamber. Hickman was visited by his father, William T. Hickman, with the elder Hickman holding out hope of convincing the warden of his son's insanity. The condemned killer's mother, Eva Hickman, chose not to visit, as the ordeal was too painful for her.

On October 19, 1928, William Edward Hickman was hanged in San Quentin prison for the kidnapping and murder of Marion Parker, in the process, becoming the one hundred and ninety-fourth person to be executed in the state of California.[55] Unlike the composure that had marked most of his time in custody, Hickman's last moments were decidedly full of anxiety and cowardice, including passing out prior to his execution. This was described in a *New York Times* special report:

On the ninth step [that led to the gallows], Hickman faltered and on the tenth he swayed slightly. The rest of the ascent was accomplished with the help of his guards.... He felt the noose being placed around his neck and looked at the guard with an expression of bewilderment.... Before [the black cap] could be finally secured, his body went limp. Like a flash, the hangman gave the signal.[56]

According to the attending prison physician, Doctor Ralph Blecker, an autopsy would have been needed to determine whether Hickman died of a broken neck or strangulation as a result of his last second loss of consciousness, shortening the killer's drop. But since Hickman's family was against having an autopsy performed, it was not.[57]

Three hours after the execution, William Edward Hickman was buried in an unmarked grave in Holy Cross Cemetery located in Colma, California. Other notables laid to rest at the cemetery include murder victims coffee heiress Abigail Folger and San Francisco Mayor George Moscone, as well as baseball great Joe DiMaggio.

Welby Hunt, convicted with Hickman for the murder of druggist Clarence Toms, would get out of prison on parole. On May 26, 1995, Hunt died at the age of eighty-four and was laid to rest in Cathedral City, California.[58]

Perry Marion Parker, Marion Parker's father, died on December 31, 1944 at sixty-five years of age. He had been employed for forty-four years with the First National Trust and Savings Bank.

Marion's mother, Geraldine Heisel Parker, passed away at seventy-five in San Diego, California in 1963. Marion's brother, Perry Willard Parker, was also seventy-five when he died in 1983 in Torrance, California. As an Air Force veteran, he served during World War II and the Korean War.

Marion Parker's twin sister, Marjorie H. Parker, who managed to escape Marion's fate, got married and relocated to San Diego, dying at seventy-one years of age in 1987, while being deprived of the lifelong bond with her sister.[59]

Undoubtedly, for the entire Parker family, life was never the same with the short life span of Marion Parker and the tragedy of her death.

* * *

Using archive footage, two short documentaries have been made about the murder of Marion Parker: *The March of Crime* in 1936 and *Tragic* in 1998.[60]

A 1990 *Los Angeles Times* article suggested that the house Marion Parker lived in with her family at the time of her death, 1631 South Wilton Place, was haunted with Marion's ghost.[61]

The Los Angeles Police Historical Society Museum has on display pages of William Edward Hickman's confession to abducting and killing Marion Parker; as well as newspaper articles on the horrific crime that still resonates to this day.[62]

# # #

MASS MURDER IN THE SKY
The Bombing of Flight 629

As a literary criminologist for more than thirty years, I have studied and written about many of the most infamous crimes and criminals in U.S. history. One that has always remained with me is a pre-9/11 era bombing of an airliner in flight over Denver, killing all aboard. Though this is stunning and tragic enough, the circumstances and motivation of the mass murderer are even more shocking.

In this true crime short, I revisit this frightening case of mass murder in the sky as part of our dark history and a forerunner to similar acts of terrorism in modern times.

* * *

Jack Gilbert Graham has a unique place in American aviation history. He was not a pilot. Nor was he a passenger on that fateful day in the fall of 1955. Graham's impact was that of a mass murderer. He planted a dynamite bomb in luggage belonging to his mother, who was taking a flight from Denver, Colorado to Portland, Oregon, with her ultimate destination being Alaska to visit her daughter.

Graham's mother never made it to her destination, nor did the other passengers and crew. The plane exploded shortly after takeoff, killing all forty-four aboard instantly. And so began one of our nation's most shocking acts of terrorism.

Jack Graham's motivation was apparently to collect insurance on his mother's death, though some believe it was a difficult relationship between Graham and his mother that led to the tragedy. Either way, the massive explosion not only cost many others their lives, but has also played on the collective psyches of Americans ever since.

Graham's mass murder did not go unpunished. He received the same fate as his mother and the other passengers aboard the ill-fated airliner, when he was executed in Colorado's gas chamber less than two years later.

Now the chilling story of Jack Graham and his date with infamy...

* * *

The evening of November 1, 1955 must have seemed pretty routine for those making their way through Denver, Colorado's Stapleton Airfield, which later became Stapleton Airport. This was likely just as true for the thirty-nine passengers who boarded Flight 629 bound for Portland, Oregon, as well as the five crew members. After all, there was nothing particularly unusual that would have tipped their hand that this was anything but an ordinary flight, much less one for which no one would arrive safely at their destination.

Flight 629 was a United Air Lines four-engine prop Douglas DC-6B airliner. Originating from New York City's LaGuardia Airport, it had made a stop in Chicago before flying to Denver without incident. Piloting the plane was a World War II veteran with extensive experience in the cockpit named Lee Hall.

At 6:52 p.m., Flight 629 took off smoothly for the 1,029 mile trip to Portland, nicknamed the Rose City. It took only minutes before the plane was cruising at 4,000 feet under good visibility. The crew, which included Hall, a copilot, and three stewardesses, went about their respective duties in anticipation of a nice, routine flight that would take them and their passengers over Colorado, Wyoming, and Idaho.

The passengers, taking note of the signs that gave them the green light to unbuckle their seatbelts and smoke if they so desired, likely took advantage of the opportunity. They were ready to relax, receive refreshments, and otherwise enjoy the rest of the journey.

It was a flight that was supposed to take about three hours to complete. With the weather clear and the wind calm, there seemed to be no cause for concern as the aircraft passed over Longmont, a city in northern Colorado, thirty-one miles from Denver and thirty miles from Wyoming.

Then disaster struck. Eleven minutes into the flight, the plane exploded, sending flaming wreckage hurling down onto fields of sugar beets and farmland near Longmont.

Everyone aboard United Air Lines Flight 629 was killed instantly, including an infant traveling with his mother to visit the child's father who was in the military and assigned to a post in the South Pacific; and a passenger named Daisie King, who had hoped to visit her daughter in Alaska, but never made it for reasons that would shock the nation.[1]

* * *

John "Jack" Gilbert Graham was born in Denver, Colorado on January 23, 1932. He was only three years of age when his father, William Graham, passed away without warning. Graham ended up in an orphanage because his mother, Daisie, was not able to adequately care for him. He was in a series of foster homes till age thirteen when it appeared as though his life was changing for the better.

It was then that Daisie, who had married a man named John Earl King in 1941, took Jack out of the orphanage and they moved to a nice sized ranch in northeastern Colorado. However, life was anything but easy for the family as financial difficulties plagued them, forcing King to sell off his land, a little at a time, till the entire ranch was sold by 1950.

The family relocated to Yampa, a tiny town about a hundred miles from Denver. Daisie King proved to be a shrewd businesswoman, finding success in real estate and a drive-in restaurant at 581 South Federal Boulevard in Denver, among other ventures. In the following years, the relationship between Graham and his mother would grow strained, with money or lack of it often at the core. Pent up animosities and greed would later play a role in an unthinkable disaster in the sky.

* * *

According to an article titled, "Sabotage: The Downing of Flight 629," Captain Lee Hall's initial indication that something was very wrong was the sound of a loud noise that appeared to come from underneath the airplane. After the plane shook violently for a few seconds, Hall's seat became unhinged and slammed into the cockpit's metal ceiling. Beneath the pilot, the airliner, moving at "several hundred miles per hour...erupted into one gigantic blast[, ripping] the fuselage apart into a thousand pieces [and] sending debris, luggage and passengers tumbling into space. Both engines separated from the wings and the propellers continued turn[ing] as they began their long, spinning descent to the ground below."[2]

Wreckage stretched far and wide, covering more than two miles of Weld County's flat ground. The whole tail section of the plane had broken apart from the main fuselage, with huge sharp pieces spread across farmland as if to illustrate the magnitude of the deafening explosion.

The locals were horrified and in disbelief. According to farmer Conrad Hopp, who was working his fields just outside of Longmont, "It sounded like a bomb went off.... I turned around and it blew up in the air!"[3]

Twenty-two-year-old Kenneth Hopp, who was the first person on the scene, said he "ran out of the house and saw the burning plane...nosing toward the ground all on fire, with sparks trailing!"[4]

Another witness, Bud Lang, told the *Denver Post*, it "looked like a shooting star;" while farmer Arlo Boda noted that pieces of the plane were "all over these farms." He recalled later digging up "part of the engine manifold."[5]

Under such violent and instantaneous circumstances, survival for any of the forty-four passengers and crew would have been all but impossible. This, it turned out, was the intended purpose of the bombing, though targeting one person, in particular.

* * *

In 1948, Jack Graham joined the U.S. Coast Guard, receiving an honorable discharge the following year, in spite of a less than satisfactory record in the service. He was reported AWOL sixty-three days during his short stint with the Coast Guard. Records show that Graham was stationed last at the Coast Guard's Groton, Connecticut installation, where he held the rank of motorman third class when he was discharged.

Upon returning to Denver, Graham worked a number of jobs. In 1951, while working for a manufacturing plant as a payroll clerk, he stole a number of payroll checks, cashing them for thousands of dollars after forging the company president's name on checks.

He bought a new convertible with his stolen funds and left the state as authorities gathered evidence for theft and forgery charges, issuing an arrest warrant against him.

On September 1, 1951, a policeman sought to arrest Graham outside of Lubbock, Texas for transporting alcohol in his vehicle, but Graham fled. Following a police chase in which Graham managed to evade the law for a while, he was finally captured after crashing into a roadblock set up by police and faced multiple related charges. A .44 caliber pistol was found inside his car on the floor in front.

After being returned to Colorado on the forgery charges, Graham's mother, Daisie King, repaid the funds stolen from the company and he received probation. The relative harmony between mother and son would not last for long.

* * *

After the remains of the passengers of Flight 629 were recovered, they were put in a temporary morgue at the National Guard Amory in Greeley, Colorado. Federal Bureau of Investigation fingerprint experts arrived from Washington, DC to help identify the victims.

Nine of the dead had already been identified by family and friends or personal items recovered. The other thirty-five victims were fingerprinted and twenty-one were positively identified as a result of having fingerprints on file with the FBI's civil section for one reason or another. United Air Lines supplied the FBI with fingerprints of the Flight 629 crew.

The remaining fourteen passengers—twelve women and two men—who were not identified by fingerprints were ultimately identified through their relatives or personal items.

As the victim identification process went on, the Civil Aeronautics Board was investigating the incident in cooperation with FBI agents from the Denver Field Office and United Air Lines personnel. During the initial stages of the investigation, a "minute and detailed examination of all parts of the wreckage was also made by engineers of United Air Lines, the Douglas Aircraft Corporation, and other private manufacturing concerns."[6] However, they were unable to connect the explosion to a breakdown of any area of the aircraft.

On November 7, 1955, the Civil Aeronautics Board's chief of investigations reported that there were signs that United Air Lines Flight 629 had been sabotaged. The FBI was asked to launch an official criminal investigation into this act of terrorism in the air that had taken the lives of forty-four people.

By the following day, the FBI dispatched agents to put the investigation front and center, where their mission was to compare information gathered from those who witnessed the explosion and crash and workers on the plane before it exploded; trace every piece of cargo, baggage, and mail that was on the aircraft; carry out background investigations on the plane's crew and passengers; and oversee and conduct searches of Flight 629's wreckage, recovered luggage, and personal belongings for potential evidence and any possible leads into the investigation.

FBI agents collected information that had been gathered by Civil Aeronautics Board and United Air Lines personnel in the preceding days on approximately two hundred people in a one hundred forty square mile area around the crash scene. Signed statements by thirty-seven of those interviewed were considered most relevant for possible leads in the bombing, which appeared to have caused an initial explosion of "tremendous force" while the aircraft was operating routinely, resulting in "fiery streamers" falling from it. Another explosion was believed to have followed, likely of "one or more fuel tanks...when the engines and forward compartment of the plane struck the ground."[7]

A Stapleton Airfield control tower operator would say later that he had noticed the "flash of light" at precisely 7:03 p.m. on November 1, 1955. Officials from the Civil Aeronautics Board put the explosion's location at "approximately eight miles east of Longmont, Colorado and at a calculated altitude of 10,800 feet above sea level or 5,782 feet above the terrain."[8]

The U.S. Postal Service was given the assignment of retrieving mail from amongst the debris of Flight 629, collecting more than four hundred pounds of post that was "spread out over an area eight and a half miles long and four miles wide."[9] The pattern of the mail—or what was left of it—furthered speculation that there was an onboard explosion that had brought down the aircraft. A postal official was quoted by the *Denver Post* to this effect, stating: "Things appear out of the ordinary.... We are investigating the possibility of sabotage."[10]

* * *

In 1953, Jack Gilbert Graham got married. He and his wife, Gloria, went on to have two children. The family lived with Graham's mother in East Denver in a big house on Mississippi Avenue. Graham was employed as manager of the drive-in restaurant his mother owned.

Things grew sour between Graham and his mother when he was forced to pay back the money she had put up to keep him from going to jail. She also insisted that he pay rent to live in her house. Witnesses noted that the mother and son were arguing constantly over money issues. It was also rumored that Graham was up to his old tricks, this time pilfering from his mother's business.

In the early part of 1955, Graham's Chevy truck was hit by a train outside of Denver. It appeared as though the vehicle had been abandoned inexplicably, though it was never reported as stolen by Graham. While the case went unsolved, Graham filed an insurance claim for the loss of his truck, receiving a few thousand dollars. Some of this was handed over to his mother to repay debt, which was nearly paid in full by October of that year.

Tension continued to remain high between Graham and Daisie King.

* * *

The recovered wreckage from the central section of Flight 629, along with cargo, baggage, and personal items were brought to a vast, guarded warehouse at the airport. The mail was given to postal inspectors, thought it was kept accessible should it be needed for additional scrutiny. The plane sections were wired to a full size "mock-up" of the plane's central portion, constructed of wood and wire netting, as if a "giant jigsaw puzzle." Based on this, it was concluded by the Structure Investigating Committee of the Civil Aeronautics Board chairman and an engineer with the Douglas Aircraft Corporation that there was an explosion "at station 718 in the rear cargo pit, designated as cargo pit number four."[11]

The explosion was thought to have taken place right "across the cargo compartment from the cargo loading door," because the "stringers at this point had failed in outward bending and pieces of heavy fuselage skin recovered and fitted into the area had been shattered into small pieces."[12] Further indication that a powerful explosion had happened was the finding in this area of pieces of material "embedded in shoes contained in luggage and in air freight known to have been carried in cargo pit number four."[13] There were gray soot type deposits on a number of skin fragments next to or inside the station 718 area, as well as the central part of the floor over the cargo pit on the aft side, but none were found on the forward side.

The investigation of freight shipments on the doomed airliner revealed that there were no explosive or flammable items amongst the shipments. Moreover, it was discovered that after arriving in Denver, the cargo and freight from pit four had been transferred to the forward cargo pit. As such, when Flight 629 took off bound for Portland, there was only baggage originating from Denver and loaded from other flights in pit four.

In searching the area of the wreckage, five small pieces of sheet metal were discovered. These were not like any parts of the airplane, nor could they be linked to any identified contents within the cargo. The pieces were burned badly and covered with gray soot residue typically associated with an explosion. One piece was red on one side and contained the letters "HO" in blue. Ultimately, it would be discovered that this piece was part of a six-volt battery's metal side and served as the detonating device for the bomb that brought down Flight 629.

In examining fragments from the wreckage obtained from the scene of the crash, FBI Laboratory technicians found that they contained foreign deposits that were white to dark gray in color. These consisted largely of sodium carbonate, though there were also nitrate and sulfur compounds. The technicians noted that dynamite consisted of "nitroglycerin with varying amounts of sodium nitrate, sulfur, and other materials," and that the "only solid residue to be expected from the explosion of available dynamite is a mixture of sodium carbonate, sodium nitrate, and sulfur-bearing compounds."[14]

The FBI decided that the explosion aboard United Air Lines Flight 629 was caused by dynamite, as indicated in its Laboratory findings sent to the Denver Field Office on November 13, 1955, and that it was likely contained in luggage. Indeed, at one point of the investigation chief investigator James Reyton had suggested to reporters that the luggage in the airliner had a smell "like gunpowder or an exploding firecracker."[15]

Now that dynamite was believed to be the source of the tremendous blast, authorities had to focus their efforts on who may have been responsible for this devastating act of terrorism and mass murder.

* * *

Investigators sought full background information on all forty-four victims of the bombing of Flight 629, along with those who canceled their reservations for the flight or did not show up for the flight or any of its previous stops; as well as anyone who could have had a motive for wanting any of them dead, in hopes of finding the mass killer or killers.

Investigators acquired descriptions of the luggage and likely contents thereof for each passenger so it could be associated with the material recovered from the crash. Then, through an elimination process, they were able to establish which passengers had luggage that was badly damaged or covered with explosive residue.

Recovered from the wreckage were a significant number of personal effects belonging to a victim named Daisie E. King, including such things as personal correspondence, a checkbook, traveler's checks, newspaper articles on her family, keys, and a receipt for safety deposit boxes. The articles were particularly noteworthy in supplying background information about King, as well as her son Jack Gilbert Graham.

One article revealed that the Denver County District Attorney had charged Graham with forgery and put him on the area's "most wanted" list in 1951. Investigators deduced that because these items were located on or close to King's remains, they were being kept in her personal belongings when the plane exploded as opposed to her luggage. In spite of an extensive search for the contents that were in King's luggage, investigators were unable to recover very much. Indeed, only tiny pieces of suitcases thought to belong to Daisie King were ever identified, sending up red flags that her luggage may have been blown to smithereens and therefore the possible location of the dynamite.

The FBI now focused its investigation primarily on Daisie King and who might have wanted her dead badly enough to be the possible perpetrator of mass murder.

* * *

On November 10, 1955, Jack Graham's criminal history was closely examined by authorities through records obtained from the Denver County Probation Department. Though there was nothing to indicate a penchant for violence, let alone mass murder, there were troubling signs. He had spent sixty days in a Texas county jail in 1951 for liquor law violations before being released into the custody of the Denver County District Attorney's Office to answer to forgery charges in relation to a check cashing scheme.

On November 3, 1951 in the State District Court at Denver, Colorado, Graham had been convicted of forgery and sentenced to five years' probation. Cash restitution of $2,500 had been made and, per the terms of his probation, Graham had also been required to make additional restitution totaling $1,805.34, for which he made regular payments till the balance was reduced to just over one hundred dollars. According to his probation report, Graham had apparently not recognized the seriousness of the forgery charges upon his arrest, while his mother was described as "overprotective of her son."

Graham showed up for his monthly appointments with the probation department on a regular basis and also held down a job steadily through 1953 and 1954, where he was employed as a heavy-duty equipment mechanic before going to work in the early part of 1955 at his mother's drive-in restaurant, where he served as manager.

Jack Graham had dropped out of school after finishing the ninth grade, but would later receive a high school diploma after passing Denver University's entrance examinations and being admitted for study. Graham was said to have had a wild streak, spending much of his stolen money on drinking, parties, and females.

* * *

Investigators turned their attention to life insurance on the passengers, particularly Daisie King. They discovered there were three policies on her life. On November 13, 1955, a detailed search of Jack Graham's home uncovered a duplicate travel insurance policy on King for $37,000 that was hidden in a bedroom inside a cedar chest. The original policy named Graham as the beneficiary. The other two policies, amounting to $6,250 each, listed as beneficiaries King's daughter and her only living sister, respectively.

More probing was done on Daisie King's background and family—especially her son, Jack Graham. He had been in and out of public institutions during his childhood and was around sixteen years of age when he left home to be on his own.

Records showed that from April 1948 to January 1949, Graham had been with the U.S. Coast Guard and was honorably discharged, in spite of being AWOL for sixty-three days.

Investigators also learned that King and Graham had repeatedly been at odds with respect to Graham's operation of her Denver drive-in restaurant. One business acquaintance claimed that the two "fought like cats and dogs," and that an explosion had once damaged the restaurant. This person also suggested that Graham may have been stealing money from the drive-in's receipts and, further, that Graham had said he used to do demolition work with the U.S. Navy.

* * *

On November 10, 1955, Jack Graham was first interviewed by the FBI, accompanied by his half sister. He was cooperative and seemed willing to assist in any way he could to solve the bombing that took his mother's life along with many others. Graham shared information about his criminal history and family background. Among other things, he told them his stepfather, John Earl King passed away on October 16, 1954 from heart disease.

After his death, Daisie King and her daughter spent several months in Goodland, Florida on Marco Island, where King owned a home. She returned to Denver in February 1955 to help Graham's wife, who had just had her second child.

Graham noted that in December 1954, his mother had bought the house at 2650 West Mississippi Avenue that they shared, and she had purchased property at 581 South Federal Boulevard in the springtime of 1955 where she built and ran the drive-in restaurant. He suggested the business was not financially successful, per se, but was more successful when he could run it without interference.

He told investigators that vandals had broken windows at the restaurant and that there had been an explosion and fire there in September 1955, caused apparently by someone disconnecting the gas line, enabling gas to fill the room and ignite the water heater's pilot light, which caused the explosion. Graham indicated that there was a small amount of money missing and some vandalism, with damage totaling about $1,200.

Investigators were particularly interested in what Graham knew, or was willing to say, about his mother's actions on November 1, 1955, what she had in her luggage, as well as her intentions in traveling to Alaska. While he did describe the checked luggage and carryon bags she brought on the airplane, Graham indicated he was unaware of what was inside his mother's baggage, which he claimed she always preferred to pack herself. He asserted that he had neither assisted in packing, nor put any items in King's luggage.

According to Graham, his mother had a significant amount of rifle ammunition and shotgun shells with her, which she planned to use in Alaska for hunting caribou.

* * *

On November 11, 1955, FBI agents interviewed Graham's wife, Gloria A. Graham, who had lived with him since they wed in 1953, bearing Graham two children, one nearly two years old and the other nine months of age. She noted that while Daisie King had spent part of her time living at the home on 2650 West Mississippi Avenue since it was purchased in December 1954, King traveled frequently during the summer of 1955, running a business in Steamboat Springs, Colorado.

Gloria Graham, like her husband, was able to describe the luggage King used for her planned trip to Alaska, and concurred that she was picky when it came to packing and insisted on doing so herself without assistance.

Investigators were piqued when Gloria revealed that her husband had presented his mother with a Christmas gift on November 1, 1955. Though unsure exactly what the gift was or when it was purchased, Gloria thought it might have been a tool set with drills and other cutting instruments that could be used to turn sea shells into art forms, something Graham had apparently talked about getting his mother for Christmas. According to his wife, Graham had brought into the house on that very day a gift-wrapped package, around eighteen inches long and fourteen inches wide. He had taken it down to the basement, where Daisie King was busy packing her bags. Gloria assumed the gift was a set of tools.

Authorities interviewed other relatives and acquaintances of Daisie King and Jack Graham over the next couple of days, seeking any additional information that could be helpful to the investigation. At least one neighbor claimed to have heard that Graham was intent on buying a tool kit for his mother's Christmas present and succeeded in this endeavor, and that he had wrapped it and put it in her luggage prior to her boarding the airplane. The same neighbor alleged that just after Flight 629 took off, Graham got really sick and his face turned pale; and that since the fiery explosion that brought down the aircraft, Graham had been unable to eat or sleep, spending much of the time walking around aimlessly.

* * *

With mounting evidence, Jack Graham had become the number one suspect in the bombing of United Air Lines Flight 629. Yet he was allowed to remain free while the case was built to a point where there was no room for error. Or anything short of a conviction.

On November 13, 1955, Graham and his wife came to the Denver field office voluntarily to identify fragments from luggage believed to belong to Daisie King. Afterward, Gloria was allowed to go home and Graham was questioned further.

Specifically, investigators wanted to hear more about the ammunition Graham alleged his mother had taken with her and the Christmas gift set of tools his wife had suggested he had packed in her bags. While Graham stuck to his story on the ammunition, he denied ever buying the tool set, indicating that it had not been the right type for its intended purpose. He seemed at a loss as to why his wife would say otherwise, suggesting she may have mistakenly assumed he had bought the tool set.

The discrepancies with statements provided by Gloria Graham were yet another red flag that pointed the finger at Graham, though he was still an unofficial suspect.

The FBI also wanted details on what Graham did on November 1, 1955 after arriving at the Denver airport with his wife, son, and mother, including why Graham had mailed to himself the trip insurance policy that Daisie King had purchased at the airport for which Graham was the beneficiary. His only explanation on the policy was that he had also mailed similar insurance policies with his sister and aunt named as the beneficiaries.

Graham further indicated that after his mother's plane departed he and his family had dinner at a coffee shop in the airport, where he became ill, speculating that it was due to being excited that his mother had left and bad food at the coffee shop.

It was around this time that Graham was advised he was a suspect in the bombing of Flight 629 and was read his rights, including the right to have an attorney present.

Graham seemed confident at this point that he had nothing to hide. He volunteered to take a polygraph test and agreed to sign statements consenting to a search of his residence, vehicles, and property.

In the process of conducting these searches, FBI agents found a roll of copper wire with yellow insulation in the pocket of Graham's work shirt. The wire was thought to be the kind used to detonate primer caps. More interviews of Graham followed, where he was made aware of the items they found, including the trip insurance policy that had been hidden in a bedroom.

Once again, Graham offered weak or no explanations. He was also told about the FBI Laboratory findings and the examined pieces of the plane's wreckage that were recovered from the scene of the crash.

Faced with the mounting evidence and perhaps feeling the pressure from killing his mother and the others aboard Flight 629, Graham broke down and confessed to committing the mass murder in the air on November 1, 1955.

* * *

Apparently looking to unburden his conscience, Graham first confessed to being responsible for the explosion at the drive-in restaurant he managed for his mother, as well as purposely abandoning the 1955 Chevrolet he owned on a railroad track for an approaching train to hit in order to collect insurance money on the vehicle.

He then confessed to causing Flight 629 to explode, describing in detail to shocked FBI investigators the assembly of a device that was used to carry out the act of terrorism. According to Graham, a time bomb made up of twenty-five sticks of dynamite, a couple of electric primer caps, a timer that was set to go off in sixty minutes, and a six-volt battery were used to commit the offense.

With a signed statement from the suspect, on November 14, 1955, less than two weeks after the incident occurred, Jack Gilbert Graham was charged with sabotage.

Appearing before a U.S. Commissioner, Graham was told of the charges he faced and bond was set at $100,000 by the U.S. Attorney, which he was unable to make and therefore placed in the custody of the U.S. Marshal.

On November 17, 1955, Jack Graham was charged with the murder of his fifty-four-year-old mother Daisie E. King in Denver, Colorado's State Court.

* * *

Further details of the shocking crime began to emerge following the arrest of Graham as a mass murderer. On November 17, 1955, investigators located the supply company in Denver where it was established that Graham had purchased an "on-type" timer on October 26th, exchanging it several days later for an "off-type" timer. Both timers were for sixty minutes.

On November 19th, a Kremmling, Colorado store manager told investigators that he believed it was Graham who purchased twenty to twenty-five dynamite sticks and two blasting caps the previous month. Graham was later picked out of a lineup by the manager, confirming the identification.

Authorities took note of an apparent strained relationship between Jack Graham and his half sister in trying to understand the mass killer's psyche. She admitted feeling uneasy around Graham in recent years, describing him as "sullen" and possessing pent-up aggression. His remarks were equally disturbing. She gave an example in which

Graham had allegedly said to her and his wife after the Flight 629 bombing: "Can't you just see those shotgun shells going off in the plane every which way and the pilots, passengers, and 'Grandma' jumping around."[16]

According to the half sister, Graham had also been physically abusive to her and his wife. She pointed out an instance in the summer of 1955 when Graham had awakened and his wife was not beside him. When he found her playing cards with his mother and half sister, he suddenly grew furious and hit Gloria multiple times. After this incident, Daisie King had allegedly become afraid of her son, believing that she too could become the victim of his domestic violence.

* * *

After Graham's arrest, Gene Amole, the owner of a Denver radio station, and Morey Engle, a photographer for the *Rocky Mountain News*, were able to slip a camera inside the Denver County Jail to interview Jack Graham.

Graham said to Amole, "I loved my mother very much. She meant a lot to me. It's very hard for me to tell exactly how I feel. She left so much of herself behind."[17] After being asked about signing the confession, Graham's latest explanation was that the FBI had noted inconsistencies in his wife's statements during interviews, with the implication that they might go after her as well. For which Graham argued, "I was not about to let them touch her in any way, shape or form."[18]

Denver TV stations refused to show the film, fearful, according to Amole, that it could lead to casting Graham in a sympathetic light, potentially making it more difficult to convict him. "The FBI, United Air Lines and the district attorney wanted Graham tried, found guilty, and executed promptly as a deterrent to others who might plan copycat murders," Amole would later say in a *Rocky Mountain News* column published in 1995.[19] The interview with Jack Graham finally got on the air several decades after the fact in a documentary called "Murder in Midair" that was shown on a Denver PBS station.[20]

* * *

On December 9, 1955, Jack Graham was arraigned in Denver District Court. He had signed over much of his property to his wife upon his arrest. Without the apparent ability to hire counsel, Graham was offered three court appointed attorneys. Charged with murdering his mother Daisie King, Graham pled "innocent" and "innocent by reason of insanity, before, during and after the alleged commission of the crime."[21] The court chose to accept only the pleas that related to the time in which the alleged criminality occurred.

To determine his state of mind, Graham was sent to Colorado Psychopathic Hospital to be examined by two defense psychiatrists and two psychiatrists appointed by the court. While being interviewed by one psychiatrist, Graham recanted his confession, claiming to have confessed to the bombing of United Air Lines Flight 629 only after being given the idea during an earlier interview by FBI agents in an FBI office in which he noticed a photograph on the wall of Nazi saboteurs being taken into custody and agents unearthing a supply of explosives.

He had earlier told reporters during an interview from his jail cell that the confession came as a result of police intimidation, even suggesting there was no recollection in his mind of having ever signed a written confession, stating, "I'm not in the habit of doing anything like that! I respect people's lives as much as my own."[22]

These halfhearted attempts to back pedal from his admitted guilt in the mass murder were summarily dismissed by authorities and psychiatrists. They each found Jack Graham to be legally sane and he was sent back to the Denver County Jail. There, Graham was described as a "model prisoner" who spent much of his time reading and conversing with guards.

On February 10, 1956, Graham attempted to commit suicide in his cell. A deputy sheriff found him around 5:30 p.m. on the floor with socks wrapped tightly around his neck. He had used some rolled cardboard for extra leverage.

Graham was given sedatives and put in a strait jacket for the rest of the night for his own protection, before being sent back to Colorado General Hospital's psychiatric ward the next day. He was strapped to his bed and watched continuously. More examination by psychiatrists followed with Graham maintaining that he was responsible for the dynamite explosion aboard the doomed Flight 629. According to the doctors, Graham claimed he was fully aware that the DC-6B could hold fifty to sixty passengers, but that it "made little difference to me; it could have been a thousand. When their time comes, there is nothing they can do about it."[23]

On February 24th, the insanity plea was abandoned and Graham was brought back to the Denver County Jail.

* * *

Jack Gilbert Graham's trial began April 16, 1956. There was great media and public interest in the case, given the mass murder and, at the time, the unusual act of terrorism in U.S. airspace of bringing down an airliner with dynamite, not to mention the deliberate killing of one's own mother with a bizarre and deadly Christmas gift. In December 1955, the Colorado Supreme Court had enforced a ban on photography in Colorado State courts, but later reversed this decision, giving the judge authority over coverage by the news media. Graham's attorneys sought to have television cameras banned from the courtroom altogether. While the judge in Graham's trial did not allow any live television coverage, some television cameras were permitted in court, along with sound on film, broadcasts for radio, and press photography.

An all-time record was set at the time for the number of persons called in for jury duty in the state of Colorado, with the chosen jury said to represent a "cross section of

American life." The first day of trial and beyond saw throngs of people show up to witness the spectacle. This included the attractive widow of the pilot of United Air Lines Flight 629, who was seated just a few feet from the defendant for the entire course of the trial.

By most accounts, Jack Graham appeared composed and perhaps even confident during the trial, donning a crisp suit daily, and chewing gum or talking with his attorneys. He was thinner than when arrested, but appeared healthy nonetheless.

In opening statements to the jury, the District Attorney promised them the State would prove its case that Jack Gilbert Graham had "coldly, carefully, and deliberately" planned the horrific murder of his mother, Daisie King while callously taking forty-three other lives with her."[24]

Dozens of witnesses were called to the stand by the prosecution, including FBI agents and other law enforcement, Civil Aeronautics Board investigators, crash analysts, technicians, scientists, and various experts, many of whom gave dramatic, detailed, and heart wrenching testimony about the events that led to the devastating explosion aboard the Douglas DC-6B airliner. Evidence of the homemade bomb, exhaustive examination of the wreckage debris and crash site, and incriminating discoveries found at Jack Graham's home were put before the jury; along with the defendant's own twenty-page written confession and solid circumstantial evidence.

On day fifteen of the trial, the prosecution rested its very strong case, having called some eighty witnesses and introducing one hundred seventy-four exhibits during the proceedings.

The defense, facing an insurmountable task, called only eight defense witnesses—none of whom were able to provide testimony or evidence to rebut the prosecution's case that the defendant was, in fact, the person who planted a dynamite bomb in the luggage of his mother, Daisie E. King, causing a massive explosion aboard United Air Lines

Flight 629 on November 1, 1955—before resting its case. Jack Graham was not amongst these witnesses, refusing to testify in his own defense, in spite of insisting to the press that he would take the stand, whereby he would refute prosecution testimony, be truthful, and clear his name.

On May 5, 1956, after deliberating for a mere sixty-nine minutes, the jury found Jack Gilbert Graham guilty of first-degree murder, recommending that he be put to death for the crime.

* * *

A motion for a new trial was filed by two of Graham's attorneys, which was denied by the judge on May 15, 1956. Graham took the stand, requesting that he not be given a new trial and did not wish to have the State Supreme Court review his case, claiming his attorneys had filed such motion without his approval.[25]

Graham was sentenced to be executed the week of August 26, 1956. After the Colorado Supreme Court issued a stay of execution on August 8, 1956, when Graham's attorneys filed an appeal once more without his consent, the Supreme Court confirmed the decision of the lower court and Graham's death sentence was set to be carried out the week that ended January 12, 1957.

On January 11, 1957, John "Jack" Gilbert Graham was executed in the Colorado State Penitentiary gas chamber, pronounced dead at precisely 8:08 p.m. Prior to being put to death, he reportedly said in regard to the bombing and taking innocent lives: "As far as feeling remorse for these people, I don't. I can't help it. Everybody pays their way and takes their chances. That's just the way it goes."[26]

* * *

As with other infamous killers throughout American history, the Jack Graham story was sensationalized in Hollywood in the 1959 Warner Brothers' movie, *The FBI Story*, starring James Stewart, Vera Miles, Murray Hamilton, and Nick Adams as John Gilbert Graham.[27]

However, no film of this tragedy in the sky, no matter how well acted and directed, could possibly measure up to the shock and horror of mass murder that occurred more than half a century ago over the skies of Colorado, when a vengeful killer full of hatred set his sights on his mother with a Christmas gift unlike any other the world has known, assuring Jack Graham a unique place in history few would ever wish to be.

# # #

THE AMITYVILLE MASSACRE
The DeFeo Family's Nightmare

In the wee hours of Wednesday morning on November 13, 1974, shots rang out in the upscale home at 112 Ocean Avenue in Amityville, New York, a village within the town of Babylon. The house belonged to forty-three-year-old Ronald DeFeo, Sr. and his forty-two-year-old wife, Louise, who lived there with their five children, ranging in age from nine to twenty-three. The DeFeos and four of their children—Dawn, eighteen years old; Allison, age thirteen; Marc, age twelve; and John, nine years old—were all shot to death.[1] The surviving member of the family, Ronald "Butch" DeFeo, Jr., twenty-three, was suspected of being the shooter. The police investigated the horrible crime, before it went to court, with solid evidence pointing toward the killer. The case of the Amityville massacre has left many wondering how it happened, and if it could happen again. The chilling scenario, motive, mental state of the accused, the trial, and the shocking supernatural implications of the mass murder of the DeFeo family in Amityville are recounted in this true crime short.

* * *

On September 26, 1951, Ronald "Butch" DeFeo, Jr. was born in Brooklyn, New York at Adelphi Hospital to parents Ronald DeFeo, Sr. and Louise DeFeo. He was the first of four children for the couple. DeFeo, Sr. made a good living for the family as a car salesman for a Buick dealership owned by his father-in-law in Brooklyn. Apart from providing the comforts of a home, where the family had lived since 1965, Ronald DeFeo was described as a "domineering authority figure," who "engaged in hot-tempered fights with his wife and children."[2]

Ronald DeFeo, Jr. was often most victimized by the parental abuse, which was compounded by the overweight, glum youth being frequently taunted by classmates. When he grew older, DeFeo got bigger and stronger and fought back when his father victimized him. According to one authority, "Shouting matches often degenerated into boxing matches, as father and son came to blows with little provocation."[3] Others also became the target of Butch DeFeo's belligerent behavior.

Against his wishes, DeFeo's worried parents forced him to get psychiatric care. Once the therapy ended with no sign of his violent episodes going away, Ronald and Louise DeFeo tried to use money and gifts to calm their troubled son. This included a speedboat that cost $14,000.

Unfortunately, things continued to go downhill for Butch DeFeo, as by the time he reached seventeen years of age, he was using heroin and LSD and engaging in petty theft. He got kicked out of school because of violent conduct.

These issues notwithstanding, the DeFeos sought to pacify their oldest child any way they could. When he was eighteen, Butch was given a job at the family Buick dealership, along with a new car and an allowance weekly with no strings attached. DeFeo took advantage of this generosity by delving further into substance abuse with alcohol and drugs.

He also became interested in firearms during this time, taking it to extremes by once using a 12-gauge shotgun on his father while the elder DeFeo was involved in a domestic altercation with his wife. Though Butch DeFeo attempted to fire the gun at point blank range, it malfunctioned, likely saving his father's life.[4]

In late October 1974, DeFeo's unstable character became even more ominous when he attempted to embezzle over $20,000 belonging to the car dealership that he was supposed to deposit in the bank. He and a friend made plans to divide the money after pretending a robbery had taken place. But a police investigation pointed the finger directly at Butch DeFeo as the culprit for the missing funds, causing him to react with fury.

When Ronald DeFeo, Sr. started to believe his son was responsible for the crime and wondered aloud about his stonewalling the authorities, Butch DeFeo threatened his life.

It was a prelude to the family massacre that was to come.

* * *

At about three a.m. on November 13, 1974, six members of the DeFeo family were shot dead execution style while in bed at their home on 112 Ocean Avenue in Amityville. After entering the bedroom of Ronald and Louise DeFeo, the shooter used a .35 caliber Marlin 336C rifle in shooting each of them twice. According to a Crime Library report, Ronald DeFeo was the initial target, indicating that the "first shot ripped into his back, tearing through his kidney and exiting through his chest. [The shooter] fired another round, again hitting [DeFeo, Sr.] in the back. This shot pierced the base of [his] spine, and lodged in his neck."[5]

Louise DeFeo was then targeted by the assailant, who took aim and "fired two shots into her body. The bullets shattered her rib cage and collapsed her right lung. Both bodies now lay silently in fresh pools of their own blood."[6]

The shooter then methodically stepped inside the bedroom of twelve-year-old Marc and nine-year-old John, shooting both a single time; before moving on to the bedroom of Dawn, eighteen, and Allison, thirteen, and firing a single, fatal shot into each of them.[7]

The shooter was none other than the DeFeo's oldest son, twenty-three-year-old Ronald "Butch" DeFeo, whose bizarre behavior and threats became the family's worst nightmare.

Upon finishing the mass murder, which took around fifteen minutes, DeFeo calmly took a shower and put on fresh clothing to go to work. He stuffed the bloody attire he'd worn during the fratricide and the murder weapon inside a pillowcase and tossed them into a storm drain en route to the dealership, where he arrived at around six a.m.

DeFeo indicated he had no idea why his father was not at work. By noon, he left the dealership to visit friends, drink, and do drugs, while hoping to manufacture an alibi for his whereabouts once the truth came out about his horrible deed.

At about six-thirty that evening, DeFeo showed up at Henry's Bar in Amityville, where he voiced in apparent distress: "You got to help me! I think my mother and father are shot!"[8]

Accompanied by some friends, DeFeo went back to the family residence where the group confirmed the deaths of his parents. An emergency call was made to the Suffolk County Police Department. Officers and detectives arrived at the horrific scene and discovered that six members of the DeFeo family had been executed in bed, with each victim lying on their stomach. Evidence would later show that Louise and Allison DeFeo were awake when they were murdered.[9]

* * *

Ronald DeFeo, Jr. was brought in for questioning by Suffolk County police officers. DeFeo had initially indicated that the mass murder had been perpetrated by a hit man for the mob, suggesting there was bad blood between them and the DeFeos regarding the car dealership. DeFeo was placed in protective custody as the police followed up on his story and investigated.

However, a further search of the DeFeo residence turned up an empty box in Butch DeFeo's room that was for the .35 caliber Marlin 336C rifle that he had purchased of late. When pressed by the detectives regarding the sequence of events and estimated time of deaths with the victims still in their pajamas, DeFeo's story about the murders quickly fell apart.

The next day, he admitted to being the shooter in the massacre of his own family, in which he claimed: "Once I started, I just couldn't stop. It went so fast."[10]

At the time, DeFeo was on probation and under surveillance as a drug user. According to the confessed killer, after the slaughter he had bathed, put on fresh clothing, and gotten rid of the evidence, including his blood-soaked clothing, the murder weapon, and cartridges. He would later lead authorities to the storm drain where he had discarded the evidence of his mass killing.

The six dead DeFeo family members were laid to rest in Saint Charles Cemetery in Farmingdale, New York.

* * *

On October 14, 1975, Ronald DeFeo, Jr. went on trial for the mass slaying of his family. Representing the State was Suffolk County Assistant District Attorney Gerard Sullivan. In his opening statement, Sullivan was candid when saying:

Ladies and gentlemen of the jury, each of you will be changed to some degree by this case. You will leave this courtroom after rendering a verdict, perhaps a month from now, carrying with you an abiding memory of the horror that occurred in that house at 112 Ocean Avenue in the dead of night eleven months ago.[11]

He made it clear that any suggestion to the contrary regarding the defendant's mental state at the time of the murders would not hold up under scrutiny. "If you will keep your minds open, carefully evaluate and assess all the proof," he stated, "I'm confident that at the end of the case you will come back into this courtroom and find Ronald DeFeo, Jr. guilty of six counts of murder in the second degree."[12]

In fact, DeFeo did use an insanity defense, testifying that he was possessed by Satan in committing the unconscionable crimes, while indicating that his actions were in self-defense because family members were conspiring against him, according to the voices he heard in his head.

Representing DeFeo was defense attorney William Weber, who called his client to the stand and asked pointblank if he killed his father.

DeFeo responded, "Did I kill him? I killed them all. Yes, Sir. I killed them all in self-defense."[13]

When asked why, the defendant stuck to his position of insanity, answering, "As far as I'm concerned, if I didn't kill my family, they were going to kill me.... What I did was self-defense and there was nothing wrong with it."[14]

While defense psychiatrist Dr. Daniel Schwartz argued in support of DeFeo's claims of insanity, suggesting that he was "neurotic and suffered from dissociative disorder," prosecution psychiatrist Dr. Harold Zolan asserted that DeFeo abused LSD and heroin and suffered from antisocial personality disorder, but was certainly able to distinguish right from wrong when he callously murdered his entire family.[15]

On November 21, 1975, the insanity defense failed to convince the jury, as with a unanimous vote, Ronald "Butch" DeFeo, Jr. was convicted on six counts of murder in the second degree.

On December 4, 1975, he was sentenced by Judge Thomas Stark to six concurrent terms of twenty-five years to life behind bars to be served at the Green Haven Correctional Facility, a maximum security penitentiary in Beekman, New York.

Since his conviction, DeFeo has changed his story about the murders a number of times, each seemingly more inventive than the last. In an interview with *Newsday* in 1986, the convicted killer stated that, in fact, it was his eighteen-year-old sister Dawn who actually murdered their father. Hysterical, their mother then murdered Dawn and her other children, after which DeFeo supposedly shot to death Louise DeFeo.[16]

DeFeo would later claim that Dawn and another attacker murdered their parents and Dawn shot and killed her younger sister and brothers. According to DeFeo, in this scenario while battling Dawn for control of the rifle, he accidentally shot and killed his sister.

With this contention, a 440 motion was filed by DeFeo as he sought to have the conviction set aside. The motion was denied by Judge Stark, who wrote:

I find the testimony of the defendant overall to be false and fabricated.... Another reason for my disbelief of the defendant's testimony is demonstrated by consideration of several portions of the trial testimony...he signed a lengthy written statement describing in detail his activities.... Defendant's testimony that he did not shoot and kill the members of his family is likewise incredible and not worthy of belief.[17]

Ronald "Butch" DeFeo's claims since have largely fallen on deaf ears. Now sixty-three, the convicted mass killer continues to serve his time behind bars, with the parole board rejecting every appeal up to now.[18]

What remains clear is that a family was slaughtered for reasons that may never be fully known, though the prosecution argued during his trial that DeFeo was financially motivated in an attempt to collect on life insurance policies.

* * *

Since Ronald DeFeo's incarceration, the subject of the shocking familicide in Amityville has been the inspiration for a number of books and movies.

The Amityville Horror by Jay Anson, published in September 1977, set the tone for these.[19] It chronicles a twenty-eight day span starting in December 1975—a year after the DeFeo tragedy—from the time new residents George and Kathy Lutz, along with their three children, lived at the DeFeo's house on 112 Ocean Avenue to when they moved out after being terrorized by a "house possessed by evil spirits, haunted by psychic phenomena almost too terrible to describe."[20]

The notion of a "haunted house" and "demonic possession" in Amityville was called into question by Dr. Stephen Kaplan, a paranormal investigator, in his 1995 book, *The Amityville Horror Conspiracy*. He referred to *The Amityville Horror* book as "packed with every sort of ghost, ghoul, poltergeist, and demon, all of which employed every trick in the book to terrorize the Lutz family, but could not scare them into leaving for an entire month."[21] Similarly discrediting the Lutz's account of a house of horrors were the Amityville Police Department and the Roman Catholic Diocese of Rockville Centre, among others.[22]

A 1979 movie adaptation, *The Amityville Horror*, starred James Brolin and Margo Kidder as George and Kathy Lutz.[23] Other films followed, including a 2005 remake with Ryan Reynolds and Melissa Gorge playing the Lutz's;[24] and the 1982 *Amityville II: The Possession*, which is based on the 1979 novel, *Murder in Amityville*, by Hans Holzer, a parapsychologist.[25]

The 2002 book, *The Night the DeFeos Died: Reinvestigating the Amityville Murders*, by Ric Osuna was about the actual murders of the entire DeFeo family, based largely on an interview with Ronald DeFeo, Jr.'s ex-wife, Geraldine Gate.[26] The author met as well with DeFeo, who claimed he "immediately left the interview and did not speak to Osuna about anything substantive."[27] Whether fact or fiction, a docudrama based on the book *Shattered Hopes: The True Story of the Amityville Murders* came out in 2011, with actor Ed Asner narrating it.[28]

In 2008, the bloodbath in Amityville was explored again in the Will Savive book, *Mentally Ill in Amityville: Murder, Mystery, & Mayhem at 112 Ocean Ave.*[29]

* * *

As unnerving as the tale is of the DeFeo family's untimely demise at the hands of one of their own, tales of familial mass murder can sadly be found in American society throughout history. On May 26, 1896 in Santa Clara Valley, California, James Durham totally lost it and murdered four members of his family on that tragic day. He used an axe, a .45 caliber revolver, and a .38 caliber pistol to do his dirty deeds, which included killing his twenty-five-year-old wife Hattie, as well as his brother, mother-in-law, and stepfather. Unfortunately, Durham managed to dodge a posse by escaping on his brother-in-law's horse, never to be apprehended.[30]

On August 1, 1967, in another case of familicide that eerily mirrors that of the DeFeo family, sixteen-year-old James Wolcott, armed with a .22 caliber long-barrel rifle, gunned down his whole family in the living room of their home in Georgetown, Texas, a suburb of Austin. The victims included his parents, Gordon and Elizabeth Wolcott, and his seventeen-year-old sister, Libby.

Wolcott, who had been sniffing airplane glue for weeks prior to the bloodbath, and apparently believed his family was trying to drive him crazy, was diagnosed as suffering from paranoid schizophrenia. This was enough to convince a jury that the confessed killer was not guilty by reason of insanity. After spending six years at a psychiatric facility, Wolcott was released.

On July 9, 1985, in yet one more example of familial mass murder in Naples, Florida, Steven Wayne Benson used two pipe bombs to murder his wealthy widow mother, Margaret Benson—heiress to the Lancaster Leaf Tobacco Company fortune—and her twenty-one-year-old adopted son Scott, as they sat in a van outside the family home. Seriously injured in the explosion was Margaret's daughter, Carol Lynn. Benson, who had been stealing from the family company, was being threatened by his mother to be disinherited. He was convicted of his heinous crimes and sentenced to two consecutive life terms of imprisonment.[31]

What these all too often unfortunate cases of familicide illustrate is that, though stranger danger is present around every corner, where it concerns murder, family can often be your worst enemy and the home a death trap.

#

THE PICKAXE KILLERS
Karla Faye Tucker and Daniel Garrett

In the wee hours of the morning in Houston, Texas, on June 13, 1983, twenty-three-year-old Karla Faye Tucker and her boyfriend, thirty-seven-year-old Daniel Ryan Garrett, broke into the apartment of Jerry Lynn Dean, an acquaintance with whom Tucker held a grudge. Both Tucker and Garrett were under the influence of alcohol and drugs as they made their way into the residence. What followed was one of the most horrendous and violent crimes in modern times. Dean, twenty-seven, and a companion, Deborah Thornton, thirty-two, were the victims of a vicious assault with a pickaxe.[1] The crime would prove consequential to all four persons involved and galvanize the world itself on matters of life and death...

* * *

Karla Faye Tucker's road to infamy began in the state of Texas. Born in Houston on November 18, 1959 to parents Larry and Carolyn Tucker, she was the youngest of three girls. Kathi Lynne was two years old and Kari Ann was one. Karla's father was a longshoreman, working on the Gulf of

Mexico; while her mother was a stay-at-home mom. A German Shepherd completed what seemed like the picture perfect family—including owning a cottage in the city of Brazonia, Texas, nearly sixty miles from Houston, where they often spent time.

Years later, Karla would look back fondly on those days of boating, fishing, water skiing, and other family activities, before things began to go downhill. Her parents' marriage started to fall apart due to infidelity and trust issues. Karla was ten when her parents divorced. It was during that time that she learned she was the product of an extramarital affair.

Up until that time, Karla had been little more than curious as to why with brunette hair and brown eyes, she didn't quite measure up to the blonde hair and blue eyes of her older siblings.

In spite of this, Karla's father stood by her as his daughter, and gained custody of all three girls. But Karla would forever see herself as different from Kari and Kathi and, as such, not a real Tucker. Given that sentiment, not too surprisingly, she preferred to be with her mother in the post-divorce era.

In a 1990 interview with the magazine, *Lifeway Church*, Karla indicated that all three sisters wanted to live with their mother—noting that their father was unable to control them or adequately discipline them.[2]

When she was ten, Karla began smoking marijuana, following in the footsteps of her sisters. By age eleven she was injecting herself with heroin. In an interview with the Christian Broadcasting Network during the 1990s, Karla discussed peer pressure and her drug use. "My sisters were into drugs and they had a friend who was older; they always hung around with older people. There was a lot of drugs."[3]

Most of those Karla and her sisters hung out with were bikers, many belonging to a local gang known as the Banditos who were known to party hard, including drugs and sexual activity.

By the age of twelve, Karla was having sex. Her first sexual experience was with a biker who supplied her with drugs while breaking the pre-teen's virginity.

With an overworked, single father in no position to keep his daughters in line, Karla dropped out of school at fourteen and went to live with her mother. By that time, Carolyn Tucker was supporting herself as a call girl prostitute and living in an apartment.

Karla took up the sex trade, becoming a teenage prostitute. She would later testify that she did so in order to please her mother. "[She] took me to a place where [the] men wanted to school me in the art of being a call girl.... I wanted her to be proud of me. So, instead of saying no, I just tried to do as she asked."[4]

That included using drugs. According to Karla, in describing the close bond with her mother and substance abuse, "We used to share drugs like lipstick."[5]

Since her mother was also a rock groupie, Karla often traveled with her on concert tours with the likes of such groups as the Allman Brothers, Eagles, and Marshall Tucker Band, while involving herself in whatever activities her mother engaged in.

When she was sixteen, Karla met a mechanic named Stephen Griffith. They married and the relationship was volatile practically from the start. In an interview with the *Houston Chronicle*, Griffith said, "We fist-fought a lot. I've never had men hit me as hard as she did."[6]

The couple also drank and did drugs together, but could not stay in love, if in fact they ever were. The marriage ended nearly as quickly as it began.

* * *

Karla was in her early twenties when she returned to spending much of her time with the biker crowd. It was during this period that she met and became close to a woman by the name of Shawn Dean, who was married to Jerry Lynn Dean, who did work as a cable television installer. In 1981, Shawn would introduce Karla Faye Tucker to

Daniel Ryan Garrett, a thirty-seven-year-old Vietnam vet. The two quickly became romantically involved.

Garrett allegedly bragged about his army exploits and indicated he could train Karla to be the Mafia's first hired assassin. Whether or not she bought into any of that, the petite, five-foot-three Karla Faye's relationship with Garrett was soon to take a deadly turn for which neither would be able to escape its implications.

* * *

On the Sunday evening of June 12, 1983, a party had been underway practically nonstop for several days at the home on McKean Street in the Quay Point neighborhood of Houston that Karla Faye Tucker shared with her biker boyfriend, Daniel Garrett. It was partly a birthday party for Karla's sister, Kari. Whisky, beer, and tequila were the drinks of choice, often in combination with illicit drugs such as marijuana, cocaine, and methamphetamines, and illegal use of prescription drugs such as valium, dilaudids, and mandrex.

According to Karla in an interview, "On top of all this I had been doing a considerable amount of coke and bathtub speed...heroin and downers was my preference because I am a very hyper person and doing speed always 'skitzed' me out, made me go crazy.... We were cooking speed, and started shooting it because it was there, and I loved the needle in my arm...what one would call a needle freak."[7]

One big topic of discussion at the party was the breakup of Shawn and Jerry Lynn Dean's marriage. Shawn, who was at the party, had left Dean the previous week and appeared to have been the victim of domestic violence with bruises on her face. This didn't set well with Karla as her best friend.

"I saw what he had done to her," Karla recalled later, "and I was really mad [because] I was really protective of her. I thought, 'Yeah, I'll get even with him!' My idea of getting even with him meant confronting him, standing toe to toe, fist to fist."[8]

Indeed, Karla's loathing of Jerry Lynn Dean had begun months earlier. Aware that Shawn had married him on a lark,

Dean had found ways to get under Karla's skin, intentionally or not—such as parking his Harley Davidson in her living room, dripping oil and releasing fumes in its wake; picking on her, and showing a general disdain for her.

According to Karla, "One time he was sitting in his car outside and I punched him in the eye for just being there."[9]

The incident caused Dean, who was wearing glasses that day, to seek medical attention to have glass extracted from an eye.

It was with this contentious relationship in mind, and while under the influence of a heavy dose of alcohol and drugs, that Karla Faye Tucker's thoughts began to turn darker than the norm toward Dean.

After driving Daniel Garrett to a nearby tavern where he worked as a bartender, Karla returned to the house for more boozing and drug using, while continuing to console Shawn and express dismay over the way Jerry Dean had treated her.

Karla and a friend named James Leibrant went to pick up Garrett as he closed down the tavern at two a.m. During the drive back to the house, the three discussed robbing Jerry Lynn Dean, perhaps stealing his motorcycle and making away with any money he had, along with teaching him a lesson he wouldn't soon forget for his attitude and abuse of Shawn, along with any other pent up hostility Karla had toward Dean.

The idea picked up steam at Karla and Garrett's house. Determined to see it through, Karla Faye quietly took the keys to Dean's apartment from Shawn, who may or may not have been the wiser to the plan in motion. Karla, Garrett, and Leibrant changed into black clothing as camouflage and armed themselves with a shotgun and a .38 caliber pistol Garrett kept.

The trio had nearly reached a point of no return as they embarked on their mission.

* * *

Somewhere around three-thirty a.m. on Monday, June 13, 1983, Karla Faye Tucker, Daniel Garrett, and James Leibrant arrived at the apartment building that Jerry Lynn Dean lived in. While Leibrant went in search of Dean's 1974 blue El Camino, Karla and Garrett gained access to the ground floor unit in the dark of night, using the keys Karla had taken from Shawn Dean.

They found Jerry Dean in his bedroom and as he was roused awake by the noise, the intruders immediately went on the attack. While Karla sat on him and spewed profanities, Garrett grabbed a hammer off the floor and began bludgeoning Dean in the back of the head. Dean apparently put up some effort to ward off the blows while begging for his life. The pleas fell on deaf ears as the violent assault continued.

Once the battered and bloody victim appeared helpless, Garrett stopped and exited the bedroom to take motorcycle parts from the residence to his Ranchero. Karla stayed behind and watched as the badly injured Dean made eerie gurgling sounds. Feeling unnerved by this and wanting it to cease, she grabbed a three foot long, fifteen pound pickaxe and proceeded to strike him with it relentlessly as all her frustrations came out in wanting to make Dean pay mightily for the wrongs she believed he'd done to Shawn and her.

When Garrett came back into the room, he finished Dean off with a vicious and fatal bludgeon to the chest, before resuming the theft of motorcycle parts to load into his own vehicle.

With the lights on, Karla spotted movement under some blankets by the wall. She realized there was someone else in the room. A witness. She quickly discovered that it was a woman hiding. Apparently it hadn't taken Dean long to move on from his estranged wife.

In fact, Dean had met thirty-two-year-old Deborah Thornton, a married office worker, earlier that very night at a party. If Karla Faye Tucker saw her as just another victim of Dean, she no longer cared at this point, wanting only to silence her permanently.

She went after Thornton with the pickaxe. Though Thornton attempted to defend herself, it proved to be futile as Karla was relentless in her attack—bypassing Garrett who had reappeared and made only a halfhearted effort to come between the two. Karla struck Thornton repeatedly and mercilessly, before leaving the axe fatally lodged inside the victim's heart.

Karla went on to reveal to friends and in testimony that the experience with the pickaxe was akin to having powerful and multiple orgasms with each blow delivered. She would later try to retract this deplorable claim, though it was on the record from the wiretap.

Leibrant came into the bedroom at the tail end of Karla's brutal assault on Deborah Thornton. He would later testify to hearing gurgling sounds coming from Thornton even as Karla pulled the pickaxe out of her smiling, before striking her with it again and again.

Shocked at the bloodshed, James Leibrant fled the scene on foot, leaving Karla Tucker and her boyfriend Daniel Garrett to deal with the fallout of the double murder.

Leibrant would return later that night to help the killers get rid of Dean's El Camino.

* * *

Jerry Lynn Dean and Deborah Thornton's bodies were discovered that morning of June 13th by Gregory Scott Traver, who was a co-worker of Dean's and was supposed to get a ride to work with him. Traver walked to Dean's apartment and found the door partially open. After getting no response from anyone, he entered the apartment. Traver found Dean's and Thornton's bloody corpses in the spare bedroom. A pickaxe was embedded in Thornton's chest. Traver also noted that Dean's bike and El Camino were missing, while a television and stereo were misplaced.

The authorities were notified and it was now a crime scene with the killer or killers on the loose.

Upon their arrival, the police found the decedents identified as Jerry Lynn Dean and Deborah Ruth Thornton in the spare bedroom. Dean was on a mattress and Thornton on the floor. Both had been the victims of multiple stab wounds—with the injuries apparently inflicted with the pickaxe, still lodged in the body of the deceased female.

In the room, police also observed boxes of items stacked haphazardly, garden tools, and dirty clothes lying around.

It was determined that in addition to Dean's motorcycle and El Camino, also missing were Dean's and Thornton's wallets.

A search for the killers and thieves came up empty.

Autopsies performed on the decedents illustrated the especially heinous and violent nature of their deaths. Jerry Lynn Dean had been the victim of blunt force trauma to the head, resulting in a skull fracture, and multiple stab wounds. His intimate mate, Deborah Thornton, had also been subject to a multitude of stab wounds and blunt force trauma to her back. In all, both victims had more than twenty injuries consistent with stabbing. A pickaxe recovered at the scene was thought to be the primary murder weapon.

* * *

"We offed Jerry Dean last night!" Karla Faye Tucker bragged hours after the double killing to Douglas Garrett, Daniel Garrett's brother, after they wound up at his residence, where the killer couple and James Leibrant unloaded the frame of a motorcycle from Dean's El Camino.[10]

That evening, Karla and Daniel entertained themselves while watching on television as the story of the murders unfolded, seemingly unconcerned or affected by the ramifications of their actions for the victims' families and themselves.

Five weeks after the murders of Jerry Lynn Dean and Deborah Thornton, Karla Faye Tucker and Daniel Garrett were arrested for the crimes after Karla's sister, Kari, and Garrett's brother, Douglas, turned the killers in to authorities. Detectives had talked Douglas Garrett into wearing a wire while discussing the murders with Daniel and

Karla. The nearly two hours long recorded conversation resulted in the arrest of Karla Faye Tucker, Daniel Garrett, James Leibrant, and Ronnie Burrell. Burrell, who was the ex-husband of Karla's sister, Kari, had picked up Leibrant after he fled the double homicide scene. The recording would later be admitted into evidence at Tucker's trial.

Douglas Garrett, who had earlier contacted homicide detective J. C. Mosier in fingering James Leibrant and his involvement in the crimes, would also lead authorities to some of the stolen motorcycle parts taken by Karla and Daniel during the commission of the homicides, which Douglas had gotten rid of.

* * *

On July 20, 1983, Karla Faye Tucker and Daniel Ryan Garrett were charged with capital murder in the slayings of Jerry Lynn Dean and Deborah Ruth Thornton, allegedly set into motion by the longtime dislike Tucker had for Dean.

In September of 1983, the accused killers were indicted and faced separate trials for the murders. Karla Faye Tucker was indicted in Harris County, Texas for murdering Jerry Lynn Dean in the process of robbery and attempted robbery. She entered a plea of not guilty.

Shortly after her confinement, Tucker began reading a Bible in her cell that she had stolen from the prison ministry program. She would say later, "I didn't know what I was reading. Before I knew it, I was in the middle of my cell floor on my knees. I was just asking God to forgive me."[11]

In October 1983, Karla Faye Tucker became a born again Christian.

On March 2, 1984, Tucker's trial began in Harris County's 180th District Court before Judge Patricia Lykos and a jury of eight women and four men. Testimony started on April 11th with the prosecution presenting a strong case against the defendant, including her own damning words, eyewitness testimony of James Leibrant to the heinous nature of the killings, and a pickaxe as a weapon of violence and death.

This gave the defense—who called no witnesses—little to stand on, aside from Tucker being heavily under the influence of alcohol and drugs during the commission of the crime and claiming temporary insanity, considering the acrimony between her and one of the victims, Jerry Lynn Dean.

Finding this unacceptable or believable in deciding her fate, on April 19, 1984, it took the jury just over an hour to deliberate before finding Karla Faye Tucker guilty of capital murder in the cruel death of Jerry Lynn Dean.

During the penalty phase on April 25th, a female psychiatrist for the defense testified as to Tucker's long history of drug abuse, including becoming addicted to heroin at the age of ten, and how on the night in question, Tucker was under the influence of alcohol and drugs and had gone without sleep for three days. The psychiatrist further stated that, in her view, it was unlikely that Karla Faye Tucker had achieved sexual gratification from the murders, in spite of the convicted killer's assertion to the contrary.

Tucker testified in her own defense, seemingly seeking to distance herself from her violent crimes. "I did not see the bodies," she claimed. "I do not remember seeing any holes or any blood."[12]

Nevertheless, Tucker did appear to own up to her part in the murders, stating that were she herself the victim of a pickaxe attack, it would not be enough to compensate for the crimes she committed.

The jury concurred, deliberating for three hours, before sentencing Karla Faye Tucker to be put to death by lethal injection.

* * *

The trial of Daniel Garrett for the murder of Jerry Lynn Dean commenced in Harris County, Texas in September 1984. In spite of her own conviction, Karla Faye Tucker became the State's star witness in testifying against her former lover Garrett. As a result of this, on November 2, 1984, the capital murder charge Tucker faced for the death of Deborah Thornton was dropped by Harris County officials.

On November 22, 1984, Daniel Garrett was found guilty of capital murder in Jerry Lynn Dean's death. Just over a week later, Garrett was sentenced to death.

On January 13, 1993, Garrett's conviction would be overturned by the Texas Court of Criminal Appeals relating to improper jury selection. A new trial was ordered. However, before he could get another day in court, Daniel Garrett died as an inmate at a hospital in Houston on June 14, 1993 of internal bleeding and cirrhosis of the liver.

His death came just beyond the ten year anniversary of the Jerry Dean and Deborah Thornton pickaxe murders.

In spite of the ghastly death of Deborah Thornton—who had clashed with her husband before ending up at the party and then leaving with Dean to go to his house—which Karla Faye Tucker admitted to and perpetrated with Daniel Garrett as her accomplice, neither would ever be tried for her murder.

* * *

Upon her conviction, Karla Faye Tucker was transferred to the Texas Department of Criminal Justice's Mountain View Unit's Death Row for female prisoners in Gatesville, Texas where she became inmate #777.

Her cellmate, Pam Perillo, who became a close friend, would ultimately have her sentence commuted to life imprisonment. This did little to quell Tucker's fears about her own pending execution while being isolated from the general prison population and surrounded by the walls of death.

As Tucker began to get in touch with her newfound Christianity, she appeared to accept her fate while, at the same time, fought tooth and nail through her lawyers to have her life spared.

From 1984 to 1992, various early legal maneuvers fell flat, including appeals and seeking a retrial. On February 27,

1992, Tucker's hope for an evidentiary hearing was denied by State District Judge Patricia Lykos.

On May 29, 1992, the judge set a date for Karla Faye Tucker's execution of June 30th of that year.

On June 22, 1992, Tucker appeared to have caught a break when her execution was stayed by the Texas Court of Appeals, who ordered an evidentiary hearing into allegations that Tucker's former friend and co-defendant James Leibrant had perjured himself as a prosecution witness during Tucker's trial. Leibrant, who faced burglary charges at the time, wound up serving no jail time after his testimony.

The evidentiary hearing was held on July 6th and 7th before Judge Lykos as both sides made their case. More than three months later, on November 19th, Judge Lykos submitted a Supplemental Findings of Fact and Conclusions of Law and Order to the Texas Court of Appeals in responding to issues raised by Tucker—particularly with respect to Leibrant's testimony.

In spite of the stay of execution remaining in effect from the Court of Appeals, more than a year later, on October 21, 1993, Judge Lykos set a new execution date for Karla Faye Tucker of November 19th.

On November 9, 1993, the Texas Court of Appeals stepped in, reinstating an indefinite stay of execution for Tucker. However, on January 30, 1995, the Court of Criminal Appeals lifted the stay and Tucker's date with death for her violent crimes seemed all but a foregone conclusion.

Though her life and times were on a public stage and time was running out to spare her life, Karla Faye Tucker managed to find love along with faith while on death row.

On June 25, 1995, in a proxy service outside the prison, Tucker married Dana Lane Brown, a prison ministry worker. However, prison policy denied the newlyweds contact visitation.

On December 8, 1997, Karla Faye Tucker's attempt to have her case reviewed was rejected by the U.S. Supreme Court. And on December 18th, State District Judge Debbie

Stricklin set an execution date for Tucker of February 3, 1998.

* * *

On January 14, 1998, in an attempt to present herself in a favorable light as a reformed killer, Karla Faye Tucker gave a death row interview to CNN's Larry King.

Recalling her days as a school dropout, teenage prostitute, and heavy drug user who hung out with a tough crowd whom she tried to impress as belonging, Tucker indicated that with respect to the killings, inevitably "something like that was going to happen in my life. I not only didn't walk around without any guilt, I was proud of thinking that I had finally measured up to the big boys."[13]

But she saw herself as a totally different person today, noting her religious conversion and being a model prisoner. As such, Tucker contended that she no longer posed a threat to society, a key factor when handing out a death sentence in Texas.

"If there is a change for the positive, and it's proven, and it's factual, why can't that be considered?" Tucker posed the question as to why she should not be put to death.[14]

She spoke of wanting to counsel and serve as a role model to other inmates who were as troubled as she once was when entering the system—indicating that prior to having God in her life, she put practically no value in human life, including her own. "I didn't care about anybody. I didn't care about myself," Tucker confessed to King.[15]

Tucker now rejected the taking of life—including the death penalty, abortion, and euthanasia. Regarding her current plight, she said hopefully, "It's a blessing to be a part of it and it's exciting to know that God has a plan for this."[16]

Tucker went on to say to King, "What I firmly believe is, if God is going to allow this to happen, he has a purpose for it. If he has a purpose for my life to continue on, he'll change the hearts of the governor and the parole board. He will help them to see what can be done through a commutation."[17]

As reality perhaps further began to set in for her prospects of evading the death sentence, Tucker gave a final interview on The 700 Club, hosted by Pat Robertson on the Christian Broadcasting Network. She reflected on her thoughts while lying on the gurney. "I am going to be thinking certainly about what it's like in heaven," Tucker said. "I'm going to be thinking about my family and my friends and the pain. I am going to be thankful for all the love."[18]

* * *

Though the window to staving off the execution was fast closing for Karla Faye Tucker, her attorneys frantically sought to save her life. On January 20, 1998, the Court of Criminal Appeals was asked to postpone the execution in order to give attorneys further time to contest the state's clemency process.

It took just over a week, on January 28th, for the Texas Court of Criminal Appeals to reject Tucker's petition, arguing that rulings on clemency "are not the business of the courts; they belong solely to the executive branch."[19]

However, in spite of concurring with the majority ruling, it appeared as though Judge Morris Overstreet felt that there was perhaps some merit to Karla Faye Tucker's argument, writing: "I would say that clemency law in Texas is a legal fiction at best. It is within the Legislature's prerogative to enact laws to correct some of these problems. Yet it has chosen not to do so. Thus the people of Texas, acting through the elected Legislature, must be satisfied with the current clemency process, or lack thereof."[20]

* * *

On January 22nd, Tucker had also appealed to the Texas Board of Pardons and Paroles to commute her sentence to life behind bars, as well as a postponement of the execution.

In her plea to the board, Karla Faye Tucker offered a heartfelt apology for the murders of Jerry Lynn Dean and Deborah Thornton, perpetrated by her and ex-boyfriend, Daniel Garrett.

"I am truly sorry for what I did," she expressed. "I will never harm another person again in my life, not even trying to protect myself. I pray God will help you believe all that I have shared and will help you decide to commute my sentence to life in prison."[21]

Perhaps in considering the odds against her, Tucker went on to say, "If you decide you must carry out this execution, do it based solely on the brutality and heinousness of my crime. But please don't do it based on me being a future threat to society, because I am definitely no longer a threat to our society, and in fact I believe I am a positive contributor to our society and helping others."[22]

On Monday, February 2, 1998, in spite of the sincerity in Tucker's heartfelt words, the Texas Board of Pardons and Paroles was unmoved, showing her no mercy in voting 16-0 with two abstentions to deny Tucker her plea for clemency. It had been more than a decade since the last request for clemency had been granted by the board.

According to the pardons board chairman Victor Rodriguez, "It's final. It's done with. That's the decision of the board. Frankly, there's nothing that anyone can do or tell me that would change my vote otherwise."[23]

It appeared as though the convicted killer and death row inmate's fate was sealed.

* * *

The onus for keeping Karla Faye Tucker from becoming the first woman in Texas to be executed in 135 years fell on the shoulders of then Governor George W. Bush, whom Tucker had also petitioned on January 22nd to delay her execution, which was less than two weeks away.

Bush, with presidential aspirations, was under pressure from both sides as opponents and proponents weighed in on perhaps the most highly charged execution the country had known since convicted killer Gary Gilmore was put to death by a firing squad in Utah in January 1977. Gilmore was the first inmate to be executed in the United States since the Supreme Court reinstated the death penalty the prior year.[24]

The American Civil Liberties Union condemned the pending execution, stating, "The A.C.L.U. opposes the execution of Karla Faye Tucker, not because she is a woman, not because she is a born again Christian, but because the death penalty is wrong. The fact that a white woman has now drawn a ticket in this deadly lottery does not make the system any less racist or unfair."[25]

Opposing forces were just as vociferous. According to Dianne Clements, the president of a Houston victims' rights group, Justice for All, "There is a public campaign to spare the life of Karla Faye Tucker. This campaign is based on fraud, lies, ignorance, and sexism."[26]

The public as well weighed in on the Karla Faye Tucker case and death penalty. According to a CBS poll, 54 percent of those who were familiar with the case believed Tucker's death sentence should be carried out; while 37 percent felt that it was more appropriate that she should receive a commutation of life behind bars.[27]

In a poll by the *Houston Chronicle*, 48 percent of the respondents believed the execution should go on as planned, with 24 percent preferring that Tucker receive a life sentence instead. Twenty-seven percent of those polled felt they were not knowledgeable enough on the case to form an opinion.[28]

According to the *Chronicle* poll, 61 percent of Texans favored capital punishment overall; while a *Dallas Morning News* poll estimated that 75 percent of those living in the state supported the death penalty.[29]

* * *

With time fast running out for Karla Faye Tucker, her hopes to evade execution were dashed on her day of reckoning as two appeals to the U.S. Supreme Court were rejected as well as one to the governor of Texas.

In seeking a thirty-day reprieve from George W. Bush, Tucker faced an uphill battle. During his time in office since 1995, Bush had neither postponed nor commuted a single death sentence. This case would be no exception, in spite of the fact that his office reported that the governor had been inundated with calls and faxes as the execution drew near, the majority of which sought mercy for Karla Faye Tucker. Included amongst those seeking clemency for Tucker was Pope John Paul II.

In a press conference held by the governor on February 3, 1998, he spoke about his decision:

"When I was sworn in as the Governor of Texas, I took an oath of office to uphold the laws of our state, including the death penalty.... I have concluded judgment about the heart and soul of an individual on death row are best left to a higher authority.... Karla Faye Tucker has acknowledged she is guilty of a horrible crime. She was convicted and sentenced by a jury of her peers.... The state must make sure each individual sentenced to death has opportunity for access to the court and a thorough legal review. The courts, including the United States Supreme Court, have reviewed the legal issues in this case, and therefore I will not grant a 30-day stay."[30]

And so ended Karla Faye Tucker's last chance at a reprieve, as the sentence for her crimes was now set to be carried out.

* * *

On February 2, 1998, Karla Faye Tucker was transported by state officials aboard a Texas Department of Criminal Justice aircraft from Gatesville's Mountain View Unit to the Texas State Penitentiary at Huntsville, Texas, which housed the state's execution chamber.

Just hours before she would meet her Maker, Tucker gave a handwritten letter to the chairman of the Texas Board of Criminal Justice, Allan B. Polunsky, who routinely met with death row inmates prior to their executions. The letter titled, "Rehabilitation Plan for Inmates," suggested that prisoners should receive monetary payment for work, which would be returned to the state to pay for inmates' food, medical care, clothing, and housing.

According to Tucker in the letter, "When a person enters, they are fed three square meals a day, have a roof over their head, are given clothes to wear, schooling, medical, and many other things free.... Everything is handed to us on a silver platter free! Having everything given to us free and told how to do everything has a big tendency to condition a person to be irresponsible and become very dependent upon the people in care of them.... Show them that one must work to eat in here just like one must work to eat out in the normal world. If an inmate refuses to work, I say put them in segregation and put them immediately on a food loaf! No TV, no recreation, just a food loaf and showers."[31]

The recommendations, meant to help inmates become more responsible and better prepared for when released, was believed to have been passed along to the entire board.

Tucker's last meal included a banana, peach slices, and a tossed salad with ranch dressing. She wore a white prison uniform and tennis shoes, as she lay strapped upon a gurney, a catheter inserted into each arm.

Witnessing the execution at Karla's request were her attorney, her husband prison minister Dana Brown, her sister Kari Weeks, close friend Jackie Oncken, and Ronald Carlson, the brother of one of Tucker's victims, Deborah Thornton. Carlson, a Houston machinist, who had at one time been in favor of the execution, changed his opinion on executions in general following a religious conversion and had lobbied at the state Capitol in Austin to have Tucker's life spared.

Those in attendance in a separate room on behalf of the victims were Richard Thornton, the husband of Deborah Thornton, her son, William Joseph Davis and stepdaughter Katie Thornton.

Other witnesses included prison warden Pamela S. Baggett and other officials from the Texas Department of Criminal Justice and members of the media.

As her head turned in the direction of the witness chamber, Karla Faye Tucker's final words were:

"Yes sir, I would like to say to all of you—the Thornton family and Jerry Dean's family—that I am so sorry. I hope

God will give you peace with this. Baby, I love you. Ron, give Peggy a hug for me. Everybody has been so good to me. I love all of you very much. I am going to be face to face with Jesus now. Warden Baggett, thank all of you so much. You have been so good to me. I love all of you very much. I will see you all when you get there. I will wait for you."[32]

At that point, "a lethal dose of sodium thiopental began dripping into the veins of [Tucker's] arm[s], along with pancuronium bromide, which is a muscle relaxant, and potassium chloride, which stops the heartbeat."[33]

Within minutes, Karla Faye Tucker was pronounced dead at 6:45 p.m. According to witnesses, "she coughed twice shortly after the injection was administered, groaned, and soon stopped breathing. Her eyes remained open throughout."[34]

In the process of being put to death, Karla Faye Tucker became the first woman to be executed in Texas since 1863 when Josefa Chipita Rodriguez died by hanging during the Civil War for murdering a horse trader with an axe.[35]

Tucker was just the second woman to be executed in the United States since the reinstatement of the death penalty in 1976. Margie Velma Barfield, who confessed to killing her lover who died from arsenic poisoning; as well as two husbands, her mother, and others, was put to death by lethal injection in North Carolina in 1984.[36]

Karla Faye Tucker was laid to rest at the Forest Park Lawndale Cemetery in Houston, Texas.

* * *

Even after Karla Faye Tucker was executed, the debate over her death and the death penalty in general continued.

"Justice for Deborah Thornton is complete," Richard Thornton declared. "I want to say to every victim in the world, demand this. Demand this. This is your right."[37]

Similarly, victims' rights advocate Dianne Clements spoke of the strong message Tucker's execution sent: "Regardless of your gender, those who are convicted and given that punishment can expect that punishment to be carried out."[38]

Others, however, took real issue with Tucker being put to death.

David Botsford, a lawyer representing Karla Faye Tucker, strongly criticized the execution, saying, "Texas has no mercy. The clemency process in this state is a farce.... It should concern all of the United States. It should concern the world. Because there is no mercy in Texas. Rehabilitation, religious conversion, that's meaningless in this state."[39]

The director of the Southern Center for Human Rights, Stephen Bright, argued in opposition to the death penalty: "People know that there often is such a thing as redemption. People are more than the worst thing they ever did in their life."[40]

The religious aspect of the debate also tended to side with Tucker, a born again Christian, and the notion of governments and humans deciding who lives and dies. According to Joaquin Navarro-Valls, the then chief spokesman for the Vatican in Rome, "It is always the same principle: only God is the lord of life and death."[41]

With respect to a "higher authority" passing judgment on a death row inmate's "heart and soul," as indicated by the former Texas governor, George Bush, according to University of Florida sociology professor, Mike Radelet, "The experts on higher authority are the nation's religious leaders, the vast majority of whom strongly oppose the death penalty."[42]

* * *

Many saw the media event and great interest that Karla Faye Tucker's case created as a reflection of the humanizing aspects of the convicted killer through frequent interviews and positive stories written about her and her religious conversion. Though many death row inmates have similar tales of repentance, transformation, faith, and perhaps genuine rehabilitation, few ever have a similar spotlight to plead their case for escaping a date with death.

According to University of Houston law professor, David Dow, Karla Faye Tucker possessed five characteristics to set her apart from other prisoners on death row insofar as having been given a platform for pleading her case. "She was a woman, white, attractive, articulate and a Christian," Dow pointed out. "A lot of people on death row have three of those characteristics; some have four. But very few have all five, and I simply don't see another case commanding this amount of attention."[43]

In spite of the debate on whether or not clemency should have been granted to a double murderer, the fact that it was not in Karla Faye Tucker's case was largely a foregone conclusion to most criminologists. Franklin Zimring, director of the criminal justice research program at the University of California at Berkeley based Earl Warren Legal Institute, contended, "Getting clemency from an American death-penalty-state governor is right up there statistically with winning the lottery as an unlikely event."[44]

Since Karla Faye Tucker's execution, there have been ten other females put to death in the United States, including two other killers in Texas, Betty Lou Beets and Frances Newton. Among the other women executed during the span was the 2002 death by lethal injection of Aileen Wuornos in Florida, a serial killer and prostitute whose case was also sensationalized.[45]

Though Daniel Garrett managed to avoid a similar fate as Karla Faye Tucker, due to dying of natural causes while incarcerated, between January 1998 and the end of March 2013, there were 346 men executed by the state of Texas—indicating that true justice for Jerry Lynn Dean and Deborah Thornton would likely have been carried out in equal measure.[46]

* * *

The fascination with the Karla Faye Tucker and Daniel Garrett case and its outcome has inspired a number of television documentaries (such as the 1998, *A Question of Mercy: The Karla Faye Tucker Story* and in 1999, an episode of the American Justice series, *Dead Woman Walking: The Karla Faye Tucker Story*).

Tucker was also the basis for several movies, including *Crossed Over*, made in 2002 starring Diane Keaton, Jennifer Jason Leigh, and Sean Bell, and *Karla Faye Tucker: Forevermore*, a 2004 release, starring Karen Jezek and Kenneth Jezek.

# # #

MURDEROUS TANDEM
James Gregory Marlow and Cynthia Coffman

James Gregory Marlow and Cynthia Coffman were cold-blooded serial killers and their killing spree occurred over a relatively short period of time before the reign of terror ended. During a several month stretch in 1986, Coffman who was nicknamed "Sinful," and Marlow, who called himself "Folsom Wolf," murdered at least four women and one man.[1] As with most serial killer couples, they abducted, sexually assaulted, and robbed victims before slaying them.

James Marlow, a white supremacist and career criminal, had little problem with antisocial behavior all by himself. But, together, Coffman and Marlow, who both had troubled pasts, were even more toxic. They mostly went after women, targeting them for death, showing no mercy in their thirst for forced sexual gratification and brutal murders.

* * *

Cynthia Lynn Coffman was born January 19, 1962 in St. Louis, Missouri. Raised Catholic, Coffman characterized her childhood and family life as resembling *Leave it to Beaver*, a popular sitcom from the 1950s and 1960s.[2]

Things began to change when she became pregnant at age seventeen and was forced to get married. After five years, she ended the marriage and sought further escape from family issues by moving to Arizona. In early 1985, while waitressing, Coffman met a man. Shortly after that, she was living with him and got involved with alcohol and drugs. Before the year was through, the two were evicted from their residence following "wild parties," along with other issues, and became vagabonds. Soon they were charged with felony drug possession.

While Coffman managed to get the charges against her dropped, her boyfriend ended up in the county jail. In spite of their tumultuous relationship, she stood by him and visited him in jail. During one such visit, Cynthia Coffman met James Marlow, who happened to be the cellmate of her boyfriend. There was an instant attraction and Coffman found a reason to break away from her lover and form a new and deadly bond with Marlow, who was six years older, more seasoned with a criminal background, and more than ready to take her on a journey for which there would be no return.

* * *

Born in 1956, James Gregory Marlow had a difficult childhood, growing up in eastern Kentucky's coal mining region. According to Marlow's public defender attorney, Leonard Gumlia, he was the victim of child abuse by his mother, which led to "a deep and powerful anger, a rage that [was] carried for a lifetime."[3] Marlow and his sister later relocated to California with their grandmother. Marlow would go on to have a swastika tattooed on his arm and join the Aryan Brotherhood.

By the time Marlow met Cynthia Coffman, he was already a seasoned violent criminal. Only now he had a partner in crime who would prove only too willing to follow his lead. The two traveled across the South, living off relatives and money they obtained through theft and robbery.

During a stop in Kentucky on July 26, 1986, Coffman and Marlow broke into a residence where they stole money, jewelry, and weapons, among other things before fleeing to Tennessee and getting married. In an indication of their deep and dangerous bond, Coffman had the words, "Property of Folsom Wolf," tattooed on her buttocks, reflecting the nickname Marlow had while he was incarcerated in California.[4]

The couple's criminality became murderous while in Kentucky when they killed a twenty-eight-year-old man described as an informant in a murder-for hire.[5]

Marlow and Coffman focused their attention from that point on to targeting young women to kill. On October 11, 1986, in Costa Mesa, California, they accosted a thirty-two-year-old woman at an ATM, assaulting, robbing, and strangling her until she died. The victim's body was dumped in Riverside County and would not be found for weeks.

On October 28th, Marlow and Coffman were in Arizona again, where they killed a second woman, age thirty-five, who was also at an ATM. They battered, robbed, and strangled her to death.

The relative ease of the killings, cash acquired, and lack of connection to other killings by the authorities perhaps emboldened the couple to continue on their path as serial killers by targeting other young women.

* * *

On November 7, 1986, Corinna Novis, a twenty-year-old insurance clerk, had just completed an ATM transaction in a shopping center in Redlands, California and offered a ride to the couple. Novis could not have conceived that an act of kindness would prove to be a horrifying and deadly experience for her.

Marlow and Coffman kidnapped the young woman and took her to a home in San Bernardino where the killer duo was staying with relatives of Marlow. Novis was sexually assaulted and tortured. Then she was handcuffed and taken to Fontana, where Marlow and Coffman strangled her, then buried the victim in a shallow grave. Coffman would later lead authorities to the remains of Corinna Novis in a San Bernardino County vineyard.[6]

But before such time, the serial killer team of Marlow and Coffman would strike again. On November 12th, just five days after the murder of Corinna Novis, Coffman and Marlow perpetrated the armed robbery of nineteen-year-old college student Lynell Murray and then kidnapped her from a dry cleaner where she worked in Huntington Beach, California.

Murray was handcuffed and driven in a stolen car (that belonged to Novis) to an oceanfront motel. There, like Novis, she was raped, beaten, and strangled with a towel till she died at the hands of the couple. Murray's remains were found the same day.

It seemed as if the killing spree of Marlow and Coffman would continue nonstop.

* * *

As it was, the couples' overconfidence and sloppiness as killers would lead to their downfall. According to Seattle psychologist Judy Mahoney, "Marlow and Coffman were careless in the aftermath of their crimes, while basking in their sense of glory...leaving evidence in their wake."[7]

The police, in fact, were able to track down the suspects because of the trail they left behind. A credit card belonging to Corinna Novis was used by Marlow and Coffman to pay their motel bill and other charges. In addition, belongings of the victims, such as checks and credit cards, were discovered in a dumpster in Laguna Beach along with identification papers belonging to Marlow and Coffman. Moreover, Cynthia Coffman's fingerprint showed up on Novis's vehicle that was stolen by the killers and an earring belonging to Murray was found in Coffman's purse. The matching earring was still in the victim's ear when her remains were found.

With the identities of the serial killer suspects no longer a mystery, the media assisted in spreading the news in hopes of capturing the killers.

On November 14, 1986 James Marlow and Cynthia Coffman were captured in Big Bear, California. The couple had chosen to use their real names when registering at a nearby motel, helping to lead to their arrest.

And so their homicidal crime spree had come to an end and the process for justice was just beginning.

* * *

In July 1989, James Marlow and Cynthia Coffman went on trial together in San Bernardino, California for the kidnapping, rape, and murder of Corinna Novis. The case against the suspects was solid, with evidence often leading directly to them. Coffman testified that she was a battered woman and Marlow forced her to participate in the murders. Superior Court Judge Don Turner did not buy this, believing that she was "in this thing up to the hilt and enjoyed it up to the last minute."[8]

On August 30, 1989, Marlow and Coffman were sentenced to death. In the process, Coffman became the first woman put on death row in California since its reinstatement of the death penalty in 1977. The previous women sentenced to death in the state were Charles Manson followers Patricia Krenwinkel, Leslie Van Houten, and Susan Atkins, whose sentences were later commuted to life in prison when executions were halted by the California Supreme Court in 1972.[9]

The serial killers were tried separately for the kidnapping, rape, and murder of Lynell Murray, due to apparently conflicting defenses.

But the similarities in the killings of Novis and Murray were described by the prosecutor, who noted that "both victims were attractive young women with bright red fingernails [and] actually resembled each other."[10]

James Marlow was again found guilty and sentenced to death in the gas chamber. He currently sits on death row at San Quentin State Prison.

* * *

Cynthia Coffman's trial for the murder of Lynell Murray commenced in Orange County, California's Superior Court on May 14, 1992. As in her first trial, Coffman tried to blame the killing of Murray solely on lover, Marlow, whom her attorney referred to as "a master manipulator[,] cunning and smart. He knew all of the buttons to push in Cyndi Coffman."[11] Marlow was alleged to have battered Coffman, used a cigarette to burn her face, stabbed her, and hurt or humiliated her in other ways.

The prosecution countered, arguing that Coffman "played a major role" in the kidnapping and murder of Murray. According to Deputy District Attorney Robert Gannon Jr., rather than merely a passive partner in murder, Coffman had actually "instigated" Murray's death and that there was "more than ample evidence" of Coffman's intent.[12] Gannon insisted that Coffman was not a frightened woman, tormented by Marlow, but rather "a murderess hunting for the next victim."[13]

Indeed, during cross-examination, Coffman admitted to initiating the strangulation of Murray in a room at the Huntington Beach motel where she was taken. The defendant also confessed, "Yes, it was more important," when asked if her involvement with Marlow meant "more to her than the people they killed together."[14]

Cynthia Lynn Coffman was found guilty as charged and on September 26, 1992, sentenced to life behind bars without the possibility of parole. She remains on death row in the California Department of Corrections Central California Women's Facility, located in Chowchilla.

* * *

As with some other infamous serial killer couples, the story of Cynthia Coffman and James Gregory Marlow was covered on the Investigation Discovery channel's *Wicked Attraction* series in an episode titled "The Folsom Wolf," first shown on July 23, 2009.[15]

# # #

MURDER IN MISSION HILL
The Disturbing Tale of Carol Stuart and Charles Stuart

On the evening of October 23, 1989, Charles Stuart committed one of the most heinous crimes imaginable when he shot to death his thirty-year-old wife, Carol Stuart, who was seven months pregnant, while the couple sat in their car in the Mission Hill district of Boston, Massachusetts.[1] The thirty-year-old Stuart then shot himself in the abdomen and used his car phone to call 911, deceitfully reporting that he and his wife had just been the victims of a carjacking. The perpetrator was described as a "raspy-voiced" African American man wearing a jogging suit. The false accusation by Stuart, who, along with his wife, was white, caused a countrywide manhunt for the purported suspect, dividing the nation, mostly along racial lines.

Once the frightening truth was exposed, law enforcement closed in on the actual killer, Charles Stuart, who had a number of reasons for wanting his wife dead—including his apparent involvement with another woman, worries about starting a family, and an insurance payment. However, before he could be arrested and held accountable for his shocking actions, Stuart committed suicide by jumping off the Tobin Bridge and into the Mystic River in Massachusetts.

Christopher, his son, who was born two months premature shortly after the death of Stuart's wife, had died earlier from complications related to the shooting of Carol Stuart. Charles Stuart's brother, Matthew Stuart, was convicted of helping him to cover up the crime and sentenced to prison.

The case was yet another tragic example, such as with child killer Susan Smith, of how playing the race card manipulatively could easily ignite already underlying racial tensions in society, while leading the authorities awry as a cunning killer sought but failed to commit the perfect crime of murder.

* * *

Charles "Chuck" Stuart, Jr., was born on December 18, 1959 in Boston, Massachusetts. His father was an insurance salesman and made money on the side as a bartender. The Stuarts resided in a Cape Cod style red home and Charles Stuart, along with his brothers, went to a Roman Catholic elementary school.

As a teenager, Stuart participated in sports—baseball and basketball, but not football as he had claimed—and was considered average at best, according to his former coaches.

In 1977, upon graduating from vocational school, Stuart worked as a cook at an Italian restaurant called the Driftwood, in Revere, a city some five miles outside of downtown Boston. He met attractive Boston College student Carol DiMaiti there, where she had a job as a waitress. Carol was also born in Boston, on March 26, 1959.

According to former coworker Rosemarie Bartolo, Stuart "was very popular with the women, and [Carol] fell madly in love with him."[2] However, Carol's father did not like him, Bartolo claimed, noting that at the time Carol had been dating a college student who was Italian-American, as was she.

Stuart soon became disinterested in cooking, and in 1981 he applied for and got a job at Edward F. Kakas & Sons' furs on Newbury Street. One of the co-owners, Ted Kakas, recalled of Stuart in an interview with the *Boston Globe*, "He was just an all-around terrific guy. I think I can say he was loved by all of our employees."[3] The furrier would later close on the day of Carol Stuart's funeral so Stuarts' coworkers could attend.

In 1985, Charles Stuart and Carol DiMaiti were married and moved into a house in the upscale town of Reading, Massachusetts in Middlesex County. By most accounts, the couple seemed to be a good match. According to Mali Sheikhi, Carol's hairdresser, she "was so happy and sweet and I was always telling her, you never seem to have any problems."[4]

But apparently looks could be deceiving. A neighbor of the Stuarts would later recall Carol griping about Stuart going out alone and not returning until late.[5] It would eventually be discovered that he was developing feelings for someone other than his wife.

* * *

On that fateful night of October 23, 1989, Charles Stuart was making $100,000 a year as the general manager for Edward F. Kakas & Sons' furs on Newbury Street. It was a big jump from the $4.00 an hour he was bringing in as a short-order cook a decade earlier. His wife, Carol DiMaiti Stuart, was a tax attorney and seven months pregnant with the young couple's first child.

As one article put it, Stuart's current life was a "long journey from his hometown of Revere, a blue-collar community best known for its dog track and neighborhood bars, to the affluent environs of Newbury Street, with its fashionable boutiques and crowded restaurants in Boston's Back Bay."[6]

Add to that a lawyer for a wife, a phone in his car, and "a slate-blue house in a comfortable suburb with a swimming pool and Jacuzzi," and it appeared as though Stuart had everything he could want.[7] But apparently it was not enough, as some who knew him suggested that he had become "consumed by his own rapid financial success."[8]

This led him down a dangerous and deadly path of no return.

* * *

That Monday night, the Stuarts were driving home through Boston's Roxbury district after attending a birthing class at Brigham and Women's Hospital, when they were purportedly the victims of a violent carjacking. The perpetrator, described by Charles Stuart as a raspy-toned black man wearing a red-striped black jogging suit, was said to have forced his way into the couple's car while at a stoplight on Huntington Avenue. The carjacker supposedly sought money and made them drive to the nearby neighborhood of Mission Hill. It was there that the alleged gunman then shot Charles Stuart once in the stomach and his wife, Carol, once in the head, before fleeing on foot. A wounded Charles then claimed to have driven off and used his car phone to call 911.

Boston broadcast journalist Delores Handy recalled, "On Oct[ober] 23, 1989, the story was all over the nightly news.... The images were gripping. Carol DiMaiti Stuart slumped over in the front seat of her car, her husband in the driver's seat."[9]

According to Handy, "At that time of night, Huntington Avenue was a fairly busy street—why had no one seen this man with a gun forcing his way into the car?"[10]

In spite of this early skepticism, others were more prone to give a perceived grieving husband the benefit of the doubt as a town sat on edge with a possible killer on the loose.

* * *

As Carol Stuart lay critically wounded in the hospital, her baby boy was delivered by Cesarean section two months prematurely and named Christopher. Shortly thereafter, at about three a.m. Carol passed away from her injuries. Her son, who was baptized in the neonatal intensive care unit at

Brigham and Women's, died seventeen days later after suffering trauma and oxygen deprivation due to Carol's shooting.

On Saturday, October 28, 1989, while Charles Stuart remained hospitalized recovering from his injuries, funeral services were held for his wife Carol. Hundreds of mourners flocked to the church to pay their last respects, including then Governor Michael Dukakis, Boston's Mayor Raymond Flynn, the Police Commissioner Francis Roache, and Cardinal Bernard F. Law.

A message from Charles Stuart was read out loud: "Good night sweet wife, my love. God has called you to his hands. Not to take you away from me, but to bring you away from the cruelty and the violence that fills this world."[11]

On November 20, 1989, a private funeral service was held for Christopher Stuart.

The brazen and senseless shooting that destroyed a family left the city on edge and touched nerves nationwide as race relations were strained and racial stereotypes floated to the surface.

* * *

As the investigation ensued into the murder mystery, law enforcement authorities considered early on the possibility that the injuries suffered by Charles Stuart may have been self-inflicted and, consequently, that he may have been responsible for the death of his wife and son. This angle was rejected, more or less, with the general consensus being that the severity of Stuart's wound was such that it seemed highly improbable that he would have shot himself and tried to make it look like someone else had done it. This therefore let him off the hook for the time being as a plausible family murderer.

The police concentrated their efforts instead on trying to locate the alleged African American carjacker described by Charles as the assailant. Mayor Flynn even went on television promising to "'get the animals responsible'," Handy remembered. "Police stepped up their 'Stop and Frisk' program. Mothers in the Mission Hill neighborhood complained of their sons being targeted; stopped on the street and forced to drop their pants as police searched for a suspect."[12]

Thousands of possible suspects were questioned by law enforcement. They zeroed in particularly on the predominantly black housing projects of Mission Hill, where officers from the Boston Police Department "systematically stopped and searched just about every young black man they could find."[13] As a result, many there rightfully accused the police of "indiscriminately harassing black men."[14]

Though African Americans believed they were being unfairly singled out with no concrete evidence to back up Charles Stuart's story, his account resonated with many "suburban whites, reinforc[ing] perceptions that the inner city had become a savage and dangerous place."[15] Whereas for African-Americans "and others who live in neighborhoods where crime is an everyday occurrence often ignored by the public and media, the unprecedented manhunt for the killer of an affluent [white female] lawyer only added to long-festering bitterness in a metropolitan area that has long been troubled by racial divisiveness."[16]

The police brought in Willie Bennett, a thirty-nine-year-old African American with a criminal record, on suspicion of being the perpetrator in this deadly apparent robbery gone wrong. Bennett immediately claimed he was being set up, but few outside his family and neighborhood believed him.

On December 28, 1989, when Charles Stuart picked Bennett out of a police lineup as the man who carjacked and shot him and his wife, it became more or less a foregone conclusion by many that Willie Bennett was guilty of this heinous crime.

The city of Boston breathed a collective sigh that the nightmare was behind them.

It was not.

* * *

On January 3, 1990, the seemingly airtight case against Willie Bennett took a dramatic turn when Charles Stuart's twenty-three-year-old brother, Matthew Stuart, identified Stuart as the actual shooter and admitted to helping him cover up the murder. According to Matthew, he had "driven to meet Stuart that night to help him commit what he'd been told was to be an insurance fraud."[17] When he arrived, Matthew claimed that "Carol had been shot, and that his brother had shot himself to make it appear as a carjacking."[18]

According to John Perenyi, Matthew Stuart's attorney, his client had prearranged meeting his brother close to the hospital, even going through a "practice run" with Stuart days earlier. Matthew had "picked up a silver snub-nose .38-caliber revolver as well as Carol Stuart's jewelry and handbag," as allegedly a "jewelry insurance scam."[19]

Matthew admitted to taking "the gun and a bag of valuables, including the couple's wedding rings, and [throwing] them off the Pines River Bridge in Revere," a city in Suffolk County, about five miles from Boston. Authorities recovered the items.[20]

In a *New York Times* article, it was reported that a family conspiracy to commit murder went beyond Charles and Matthew Stuart, with another brother, Michael Stuart, allegedly being asked by Stuart weeks before the murder to help him kill his wife, according to the brother's lawyer.[21] The twenty-seven-year-old Michael, a firefighter, supposedly turned down the request.

The article indicated that other family members of Charles Stuart, including "three brothers and two sisters, as well as their spouses and friends, either participated in part of the crime, wittingly or unwittingly, or learned about it at various points without telling the police."[22]

The bombshell revelation hit the DiMaiti family hard. According to an interview given by Carol Stuart's brother, Carl DiMaiti, to WLVI-TV in Boston shortly after the news broke on the siblings' connection to the crime, "Can you believe that they came over to our house to comfort my parents? It is just mind-boggling that they could sit with us, or allow us to visit Chuck, to cry over him and pray for his recovery, knowing that Chuck was responsible for what happened to Carol."[23]

* * *

Equipped with this startling new information, the police dug further into Charles Stuart's background looking for possible motives for the murder, which began to surface. The police discovered that he was unhappy that Carol was pregnant and would not get an abortion. Stuart feared that his wife might want to be a stay at home mother. This would cause them to lose her significant part of their joint income, which in turn, could affect the affluent lifestyle he had grown accustomed to.

Stuart apparently had even bigger plans that required capital. According to neighbors, he had high hopes of opening up a restaurant and had taken a course earlier in the year at the Boston Center for Adult Education called "Buying and Operating a Restaurant Successfully."[24] This grand idea was in jeopardy with Carol Stuart possibly bowing out of the work force for the foreseeable future.

Stuart was also reportedly engrossed with a fellow employee of Kakas & Sons, Deborah Allen. He took the attractive twenty-two-year-old graduate of Brown University out for some meals and gave her gifts. Prior to the shooting, Allen was said to have showed Stuart around the prep school she attended.

While Stuart was in Boston City Hospital recovering from his injuries sustained in the shooting, Allen allegedly phoned him often. Her attorney, Thomas Dwyer, contended in a statement on her behalf that Stuart asked that she call, using his telephone credit card to charge the calls. Allen claimed that when Stuart sought to have a more romantic relationship upon his discharge from the hospital, she ended things between them.[25]

It was reported that shortly after his release in December, Charles Stuart began purchasing women's jewelry, including a "$999 pair of diamond solitaire earrings [and] a $250 14-karat gold brooch."[26]

Though the police suspected that Stuart may have bought the jewelry as a gift for Deborah Allen in hopes of perhaps starting a relationship, she denied having been given any of the jewelry.

* * *

As with many cases of uxoricide, or when a wife is murdered by her husband, the killer typically has a financial motive. That appeared to be a key factor in the murder of Carol Stuart, as authorities learned that Charles Stuart was the beneficiary of several insurance policies taken out on his wife totaling a few hundred thousand dollars.[27] Moreover, the couple's joint estate was valued at more than half a million dollars, including the posh home they owned in Reading.

After processing their new evidence and revelations, Suffolk County District Attorney Newman Flanagan revealed to the stunned residents of Boston and the nation itself, who had been riveted to the case, that the "entire drama had been an elaborate ruse on the part of Stuart."[28]

With Willie Bennett suddenly exonerated, to the surprise of many and delight of others, the arrest of Charles Stuart was ordered for the murders of Carol and Christopher Stuart.

* * *

With the authorities in hot pursuit, Charles Stuart managed to elude them temporarily as he checked into a Braintree Sheraton motel, where he asked for a 4:30 a.m. wake-up call. That early morning of January 4, 1990, shortly after Charles Stuart allegedly confessed to his attorney about the horrible crime, and before an arrest could be made, Stuart took his own life by jumping off the Tobin Bridge in Chelsea, Massachusetts and into the Mystic River's icy waters some 145 feet below. His new Nissan Maxima, with the hazard lights on and hood up, was found abandoned on the bridge. On the car's front seat were his driver's license and a note that indicated he was distraught over the allegations about him that had come to light.

Charles Stuart's body was recovered from Boston Harbor the following day.

Authorities discovered that the revolver used to commit the crime had been taken from an unlocked cabinet at Stuart's employer, Edward F. Kakas & Sons, after he had apparently been unable to get hold of a gun elsewhere.

Investigators would also conclude that Stuart had talked about wanting to murder his wife previously to others, inside and outside his family; such was his twisted desire to end her life and that of the child she was carrying.[29]

According to Harvard University psychiatrist Robert Coles, Charles Stuart represented an "extreme example of a psychopath, an antisocial personality with little sense of remorse, a propensity to lie and often an ability to deceive others into believing his fantasies."[30] Coles added, "In most psychopaths there is cruelty and callousness, but Stuart outdoes that."[31]

In committing suicide, Stuart took to his grave the senseless impetuses within that led him to murder and deprived his young wife and child of a future, which had seemed so bright before tragedy struck.

* * *

In September 1991, Matthew Stuart was indicted by a grand jury on charges of "conspiracy to obstruct justice and compounding a felony," along with insurance fraud, for participating with his brother Charles in the cover up of Carol Stuart's murder.[32]

In November 1992, Matthew pleaded guilty to fraud, possession of a firearm, and additional charges, and was sentenced to three to five years behind bars.[33] After being released on probation in 1997, he was arrested again for trafficking in cocaine and returned to prison for violating probation. The charges were eventually dropped for insufficient evidence.

On September 3, 2011, Matthew Stuart, now forty-five, was found dead at a Cambridge homeless shelter, the apparent victim of a drug overdose.[34]

His death brought mixed feelings for the family of Willie Bennett, the initial suspect in the murder of Carol Stuart. In an interview with the *Boston Globe*, a still somewhat embittered Diane Bennett, Willie Bennett's sister, said of Matthew Stuart, "I'm sorry for him. He got my brother off the hook and I appreciate that. But at the same time, that was after helping his brother kill his wife and his baby. My brother didn't do it, but got blamed. Twenty-one years later, I feel we've never gotten the recognition we deserve."[35]

Though Willie Bennett was very nearly railroaded with a carefully orchestrated murder by Charles Stuart, who used the race card to tap into stereotypes and hysteria, the plot failed at the end of the day when the truth came out. It happened too late to save Carol Stuart and her baby boy, but not Willie Bennett.

* * *

In October 1992, Carol DiMaiti Stuart's family filed a wrongful death lawsuit against Edward F. Kakas & Sons, former employer of Charles Stuart, charging that the Back Bay furrier "carelessly stored a revolver allegedly used by Charles Stuart to kill his pregnant wife and unborn son."[36] In December 1996, the case was dismissed by a Superior Court.[37]

On January 25, 1990, the Carol DiMaiti Stuart Foundation was established by Carol Stuart's family, providing scholarships to residents of Mission Hill. Nearly $1.4 million was awarded to 230 students by the foundation over a twenty year span.[38] According to Marvin Gellar, the attorney for the DiMaitis, "Carol would not want to be remembered as the victim of a sensational murder, but rather as a woman who left behind a legacy of healing and compassion."[39]

* * *

The dynamics of uxoricide, infanticide, racism, family cover up, and a rush to judgment in the shocking murder of Carol Stuart and her newborn child by Charles Stuart, inspired a number of television projects on the crime.

In the 1990 movie on CBS, *Good Night Sweet Wife: A Murder in Boston*, Ken Olin played Charles Stuart and Annabella Price was in the role of Carol Stuart;[40] while the *Law & Order* franchise did episodes, "Happily Ever After" and the "Tangled" that were apparently based on the Carol Stuart murder.[41] The case also was profiled in the A&E documentary series, *City Confidential*, in the episode, "Boston: Betrayal in Beantown."[42]

# # #

MURDER IN BELLEVUE
The Killing of Alan and Diane Johnson

In the early morning on September 2, 2003, the affluent community of Bellevue, Idaho, was rocked by the murder of residents Alan Scott Johnson and Diane Johnson in their home. Both had been shot to death.[1] Their sixteen-year-old daughter, Sarah Marie Johnson was in the house when the murder occurred. She ran from the house hysterically shouting that someone had killed her parents.

The tale that emerged was far different, as Sarah Johnson became the chief suspect in her parents' murder in a case of misplaced love, family discord, betrayal, revenge, and violent rage.

As with similar cases of teen familicide (killing of family), parricide (killing of father or mother), patricide (killing of father), and matricide (killing of mother) across the country, this one was no less shocking for its sheer brutality. Few who knew the Johnsons could make sense of the crime or how things could reach such a tragic point within the family.

* * *

By most accounts, in the summer of 2003, Alan Johnson, forty-six, and his wife of twenty years, Diane, fifty-two, had a great life together. They had two children: Matt, twenty-two (Diane's son from a previous relationship), and Sarah Marie, sixteen. The Johnsons had a nice home in Bellevue, Idaho in Blaine County's Wood River Valley, just south of the resort city of Sun Valley. Alan co-owned a landscaping business and Diane was employed by a medical clinic.

But their storybook life ended tragically when Alan and Diane Johnson were shot to death in their home just after Labor Day on September 2, 2003. Diane was shot in the head while she lay sleeping in bed. Then Alan was shot in the chest above his heart, his body still wet after just leaving the shower.

As police arrived and took in the ghastly site of two adults dead from gunshots, the crime scene was quickly secured for possible evidence and to perhaps catch a killer.

According to Blaine County Sheriff Walt Femling, the crime scene was the worst he could remember ever seeing, noting, "There was blood and hair on the carpet. It was on the ceiling. It was on all the walls. There was part of a skull cap in the hallway."[2]

Investigators "found a trail of blood spatters, tissue, and bone fragments that went from the Johnson's bedroom into the hall, and across to [their daughter] Sarah Johnson's bedroom," which was about twenty feet away.[3]

The police went into full investigation mode, blocking off the street and searching a garbage truck that had just picked up trash from the house. In it was a treasure trove of DNA evidence on "a bloody bathrobe, a left-handed leather glove, and a right-handed latex glove."[4]

More evidence was found inside, including in the master bedroom where a .264 Winchester Magnum rifle, along with two butcher knives were situated at the bottom of the victim's bed. In Sarah's room, authorities also discovered an ammunition magazine.

An important item that detectives noted was the lack of any sign of forced entry in the Johnson's home, suggesting that the killer either had a key or was let in.

They turned their attention to Alan and Diane Johnson's sixteen-year-old daughter, Sarah.

* * *

Sarah Marie Johnson was born in 1987. Those who knew her described her as a sweet girl. This depiction seemed to change during the summer of that year when she began dating Bruno Santos Dominguez, a nineteen-year-old illegal immigrant from Mexico. Dominguez was a high school dropout who lived on the poor side of town and was said to be mixed up with drugs. Sarah appeared to become smitten and fixated with him.

This didn't set well with her parents, who believed she was headed in the wrong direction by dating him. The relationship between Sarah and her boyfriend became a real source of contention in the Johnson household, and even amongst some of Sarah's friends. According to one friend, "I felt she could do a lot better. He was a high school dropout and was selling drugs and she was from a nice family. It just didn't seem like it was right."[5]

But Sarah thought otherwise, falling head over heels for the older bad boy. Not long before the death of her parents, she told friends that she and Bruno Dominguez were engaged to be married, showing off a ring to that effect.

The stress and strain over this unwelcome romance and possible engagement threatened to boil over on the Saturday of Labor Day weekend when Alan and Diane learned that Sarah was staying over at Dominguez's place. After going to his apartment to get her, Alan warned Dominguez not to see Sarah anymore or he would have him charged with having sexual relations with a minor.

Sarah was grounded by her parents for the remainder of the holiday weekend. They also took away their daughter's car keys to help ensure she stayed put.

On the night before Alan and Diane Johnson were gunned down, Diane and Sarah both called Matt at the college he attended, in which they vented about their respective points of view on her relationship with Bruno Dominguez.

The following Tuesday morning, Alan and Diane Johnson were found murdered.

* * *

Authorities were eager to interview the lone survivor in the house when the double homicide occurred, Sarah Johnson. According to the teenager, she was awakened at about 6:15 a.m. when she heard the shower in her parents' bathroom running. While still in bed, she heard what sounded like two gunshots. Racing to her parents' bedroom, she saw that the door was closed. Terrified as to what she might find inside, she resisted opening the door, instead running from the home crying out to neighbors for assistance.

Not sold on her account of the events, detectives continued to question Sarah and inconsistencies began to develop in her story, such as whether or not the door to her parents' bedroom was open or closed. As forensic evidence was found in both the hallway and Sarah's bedroom, police had concluded that the doors were open to both bedrooms.

When questioned about the bloodstained bathrobe uncovered in the trash, Sarah conceded that it was hers, but had no idea how it ended up there.

At one point, she had suggested that a former maid employed by the Johnsons had killed them after being fired for theft. She also had indicated that an intruder may have murdered her parents, in spite of no indication that the killer forced his or her way into the house.

* * *

Police discovered that the murder weapon was owned by Mel Speegle, who was a renter of the garage apartment in the Johnsons' guesthouse. But it was established that he was elsewhere during the weekend of Labor Day and, as such, was not present at the time the murders were committed. When he was tracked down, he admitted to authorities that his rifle had been in a closet in his apartment that was not locked.

Investigators would learn that Sarah kept a key to Speegle's apartment, and had been in the guesthouse a number of times.

Though authorities were suspicious that Sarah may have been involved in her parents' murder, given the contentious nature of her relationship with her parents of late, the number one suspect was Bruno Dominguez, given the fact that the Johnsons had insisted Sarah break off their relationship, while also threatening to charge the nineteen-year-old with statutory rape.

However, when the forensic evidence failed to match Bruno's DNA, the focus turned squarely toward Sarah Marie Johnson who, along with her changing stories during police interrogation, appeared to those who knew her to be less than convincing about her sorrow and more interested in keeping her "hair and nail appointments."[6]

Investigators got the "smoking gun" they were looking for after the state lab found Sarah's DNA inside the latex glove. Also, the leather glove had gunshot residue on it and police found the matching glove in Sarah's bedroom. Finally, Diane Johnson's DNA was found on Sarah's bathrobe and the socks the teenager wore the morning of her parents' murder.

On October 29, 2003, upon failing to extract a confession from her, Sarah Johnson, a junior in high school, was arrested and charged with two counts of first degree murder. She pled not guilty.

* * *

In February 2005, Sarah Marie Johnson's trial began. Though the lead prosecutor, Jim Thomas, was confident the forensic evidence was powerful enough to get a conviction, his concern was being able to convince the jury "that a bright, athletic high school girl suddenly became a killer."[7]

Sarah's defense attorney, Robert Pangburn's strategy was to focus on the lack of blood on the defendant at the time of the killing. He argued that, "Her mother's head literally exploded in a spherical fashion. The gun itself had blood on it. Yet there was none on her. Absolutely none."[8] The clear implication was that Sarah was not the person who fired the deadly shots into her parents.

Indeed, Pangburn believed that Bruno Dominguez was behind the double homicide, arguing, "Bruno very easily could have recruited cohorts of his."[9] However, the defense lawyer chose not to call Dominguez to the stand.

In testifying for the prosecution, Matt Johnson spoke of the often volatile relationship between his mother and sister. "Her and my Mom didn't get along. It was fairly rocky. Constant fighting, bickering back and forth!"[10]

The defendant was also described by her brother as a "drama queen and a good actor who had a propensity to lie."[11]

Sarah Johnson's aunt, Linda Vavold, who along with her husband, Jim, became the teenager's legal guardians upon the death of her parents, testified against her as well. Vavold cited examples of what she considered to be behavior unbecoming by her niece, making her believe Sarah could be guilty of a double homicide. "When we would be discussing Alan and Diane and someone would be upset, [Sarah] would roll her eyes and act disgusted," Vavold said on the witness stand.[12]

According to Vavold—who was the eldest sister of Diane Johnson—at the memorial service for the Johnsons, Sarah appeared "more concerned with who was there," while asking "to attend a volleyball game later that evening."[13] Vavold claimed as well that a day prior to the service, she heard her niece tell a person at a beauty salon while having her nails manicured that she only wished to "get on with her life."[14]

Further damaging to Sarah Johnson was testimony by witnesses who knew her from jail. One in particular was

Malinda Gonzales, a convicted felon and former cellmate. She testified that Sarah spoke openly about the case against her while awaiting trial. "I would ask her questions over and over again," Gonzales claimed. "One time, [Sarah] said, 'When I killed....' Then she stopped herself and was like, 'When the killers...'"[15]

Gonzales also talked about Sarah's volatile relationship with her mother and jealousy over her brother being the apple of her mother's eye. According to the witness, "[Sarah] said she'd have knock-down, drag-out fights with her mom because she favored her brother and would give him anything."[16]

Strangely, Gonzales indicated that Sarah had a much more favorable view of her father, testifying, "[Sarah] loved her dad; she was a daddy's girl. She said her father had changed the life insurance and she was going to get everything because her brother was not really his kid."[17]

This affection was in stark contradiction to the fact that Sarah Johnson was on trial for murdering her father, Alan Johnson, along with her mother, Diane.

* * *

The trial lasted five weeks before going to an Ada County, Idaho jury. By then, most family members and others who knew the Johnsons were strongly behind the prosecution in believing that Sarah Johnson had cold-bloodedly taken the lives of her parents.

Pat Dishman, Sarah's grandmother, would later say, "It takes a lot of evidence to convince a grandma that her granddaughter killed her daughter. I mean, it had to be overwhelming."[18]

The jury agreed, for on March 16, 2005, after eleven hours of deliberation, they came back with a verdict of guilty for the defendant on two counts of murder in the first degree in the deaths of Diane and Alan Johnson. Sarah Johnson received a sentence of two concurrent life terms, along with fifteen years for the use of a firearm to murder her parents. She was given no possibility of parole.[19] The convicted killer was fined $10,000 as well, with $5,000 of this allotted to her brother, Matt.

The conviction was upheld by the Idaho Supreme Court.[20]

In 2011, attorneys Dennis Benjamin and Deborah Whipple and the Idaho Innocence Project started to work on Sarah Johnson's case pro bono, arguing that some of the DNA evidence gathered from the crime scene was not tested and that the convicted killer's counsel was "ineffective."[21] Moreover, Idaho Innocence Project head and ex-FBI agent Robert Kerchusky contended that fingerprints found at the crime scene indicated that someone else murdered Alan and Diane Johnson.[22]

The request by Benjamin and Whipple for Sarah Johnson to get a new trial was denied by Fifth District Court Judge G. Richard Bevan in 2011. However, in November 2012, a hearing was granted based on the attorneys' belief that new testing procedures for DNA and fingerprints could lead to other possible suspects and exonerate Sarah of her parents' murder.[23]

The Deputy Attorney General, Kenneth Jorgensen, dismissed this argument as "frivolous."[24]

* * *

The tragedy of Alan and Diane Johnson's deaths and the conviction of their teenage daughter as the killer sparked public outrage and fascination. As opposed to teen juvenile parent killers, parricide involving girls is relatively rare, with a study recently finding that just four such incidences have occurred in the United States during a span of two decades.[25]

The Johnson family tragedy resulted in a number of crime investigation documentaries and reenactments of the case on television. These include episodes of such popular crime series as ABC's *Primetime Crime*, Investigation Discovery's *Deadly Women* and *Solved*, Oxygen's *Snapped*, and TruTv's *Forensic Files*.[26] The tale also ranked number nine in the E! Documentary, *Too Young to Kill: 15 Shocking Crimes*.[27]

\# \# \#

MURDER OF A STAR QUARTERBACK
The Tragic Tale of Steve McNair and Sahel Kazemi

Sahel Kazemi was a twenty-year-old waitress who went from anonymity to the subject of national attention and interest when she shot her thirty-six-year-old lover, former NFL star quarterback Steve McNair, multiple times with a 9-millimeter semiautomatic pistol, fatally wounding him in a rented condominium in downtown Nashville, Tennessee on July 4, 2009.[1] Reportedly distraught over money issues and the belief that the married McNair had another mistress, Kazemi then turned the gun on herself and, with a single shot to the head, completed a murder-suicide. This type of tragedy typically involves a love triangle, jealousy, financial problems, depression, and/or desperation. In this case, the evidence points toward Kazemi setting a course in motion designed to end her life and that of the man she loved and apparently could not bear to see with anyone else.

* * *

Sahel Kazemi was born in Iran on May 29, 1989. Growing up in Tehran as one of five children, tragedy struck the family early in Sahel's life when her mother, Ghodsyeh, was murdered in a home invasion robbery. Sahel was only nine years old. According to her sister, Azadeh, there was no real investigation of the murder because the family belonged to the Baha'i faith rather than Muslim.[2] Iranian Bahá'ís had been historically marginalized in Iran, as a reflection of the religious minority's persecution by Muslim clergy.

After moving from Iran to Turkey, Sahel lived there for two and a half years, before relocating to the United States as an Iranian refugee on August 29, 2002. The thirteen-year-old spoke no English when she took up residence in Jacksonville, Florida with her sister, Soheyla, who became her guardian.

According to those who knew her, Sahel adjusted with relatively few problems to the American culture and teen lifestyle. She quickly became fluent in English, along with Turkish and Farsi. However, she had difficulty getting along with other students at school, some of whom bullied her, and moved from one high school to another.

Her life seemed to get better after Sahel met Keith Norfleet. She dropped out of school at sixteen and moved from Jacksonville to Nashville, Tennessee with him to live together. The on and off relationship lasted for four years and was described by some as "volatile."

According to Norfleet's stepmother, Trudie Norfleet, "They had a lot of jealousy in their relationship and they'd fight and break up a lot."[3]

Things between the two reached a breaking point in January 2009 when nearly six months after the couple had broken up, Sahel called 911 to report that Norfleet was displaying aggression toward her in the course of an argument between them.

"My boyfriend just threw my phone right in my face, and he's going crazy, and I don't want him here," Sahel, who went by the name "Jenni," as she called herself to friends and colleagues, told the 911 operator.[4]

After being asked if she had been assaulted by Norfleet, Sahel responded, "No, he just threw a phone in my face."[5]

Because she was never actually struck by the phone otherwise during the incident, Norfleet was not charged with any crime.

Sahel Kazemi met Steve McNair in December 2008, at Dave & Buster's, a bustling restaurant on Opry Mills Drive where she worked as a waitress. McNair, the former Tennessee Titans star quarterback who was now retired, frequented the place and was known as a big tipper with an eye for attractive ladies. He and Sahel hit it off right away and soon after began dating.

The romance between McNair and the nineteen-year-old impressionable waitress would come to a shocking and violent end.

* * *

Stephen (Steve) LaTreal McNair, with the nickname of Air McNair, was born in Mount Olive, Mississippi on February 14, 1973. After excelling in multiple sports at Mount Olive High School, particularly football, he went to Alcorn State, a historically black university in Lorman, Mississippi. There, he joined the Omega Psi Phi fraternity and soon became a star quarterback. As a senior, McNair racked up almost 6,000 yards passing and rushing, as well as fifty-three touchdowns, breaking over a dozen records and named an All-American. He also won the Walter Payton Award in 1994 as the NCAA Division 1-AA top player, while finishing third in the Heisman Trophy voting.[6]

As the third pick in the 1995 NFL Draft, McNair went to the Houston Oilers. In 1997, he became the team's regular starting quarterback in their first season as the Tennessee Oilers/Titans. He led the team to four playoff appearances, and quarterbacked the Titans to Super Bowl XXXIV, where they narrowly lost 23-16.

In June 2006, McNair was traded to the Baltimore Ravens, leading the team to the playoffs that year with a 13-3 record, along with an NFC North Championship.

He retired in April 2008, after playing thirteen seasons in the NFL, which included three trips to the Pro Bowl.

In June 1997, Steve McNair married his college sweetheart, Mechelle McNair, with whom he had two boys; and had two other sons with different mothers. He was dividing his time between Nashville and a 45-acre farm he owned in Mount Olive, Mississippi, when in December 2008, the thirty-five-year-old McNair met and became smitten with the dark-haired, attractive Sahel Kazemi who was sixteen years his junior.

* * *

It wasn't long after Steve McNair and Sahel Kazemi started dating that the couple split much of their time between Kazemi's Cherry Creek apartment in Hermitage, a Nashville suburb in Davidson County, and a downtown Nashville condominium at 105 Lea Avenue that McNair rented with his good friend Wayne Neely. The condo, just six miles away from the 14,000 square foot Green Hills mansion that McNair occupied with his wife and children, overlooked Titans stadium and was perhaps for McNair homage to his glory days as an NFL star.

McNair's generosity toward his young mistress did not end there. The couple parasailed together while on vacation and took trips to such places as Key West, Florida, Las Vegas, and Mississippi. For Kazemi's twentieth birthday, McNair also put a nice down payment on a 2007 black Cadillac Escalade for her to drive, but Kazemi still reportedly found herself "swallowed up in the massive payments."[7]

That notwithstanding, being treated like a queen by the former star quarterback was something Kazemi found hard to turn away from. Farzin Abdi, her nephew, would later comment, "She just had it made, you know, this guy taking care of everything."[8]

The two became so involved that Kazemi apparently believed McNair would divorce his wife, giving her one less person to compete with for his affection and money.

But as the months rolled by, Kazemi would come to suspect that she wasn't the only one McNair was involved in an extramarital affair with.

In June 2009, the seeds of jealousy and resentment by Kazemi were firmly planted when she caught another female coming out of the condominium. Following her to an apartment, Kazemi became convinced that McNair was cheating on her. According to her sister Azadeh, who lived in Australia, Kazemi complained that the Britney Spears song, "Womanizer," made her think of McNair and how she viewed him.[9]

In a police report released months later, Kazemi's former roommate, Emily Andrews, revealed to authorities that Kazemi had told her about finding a tampon in a bathroom wastebasket in the condominium on Lea Avenue, giving more credence to her suspicion that McNair was seeing someone else.[10]

The same police report would confirm that McNair did indeed have another mistress at the time by the name of Leah Ignagni, an attractive twenty-five-year-old, who acknowledged the affair with McNair. Ignagni also stated that a car that matched the description of the black Cadillac Escalade that Kazemi drove had once followed her home from the condo and a woman was behind the wheel.

In her taped interview with police detectives, Ignagni claimed she had never even heard of Kazemi until the day before the murder-suicide, when McNair called her and mentioned that a "good friend of his named Jenni got a DUI."[11]

According to Ignagni, McNair had indicated his deep affection for her and his desire to be with her, as opposed to any other woman. "He said that he loved me and that he was going to make everything work so that he could be with me, and he had some things to handle and to wait for him."[12]

Perhaps to get back at McNair and her belief that he was seeing other women, Kazemi reportedly began having affairs of her own that summer. "She was cheating, too," her sister

Azadeh claimed. "She said, 'I was faithful to him. If he's going to do that, I'm going to do the same.'"[13]

Emily Andrews also confirmed that Kazemi was seeing other men. These reportedly included a Tennessee Titans player and a member of Vanderbilt University's football team.[14]

In spite of her infidelity, Sahel Kazemi's heart apparently still belonged with Steve McNair. And she was having trouble letting go...

* * *

Two days before the fatal encounter, Kazemi was pulled over by police on Broadway and Ninth Avenue in Nashville while driving the 2007 Cadillac Escalade that was registered in her name and McNair's name. McNair was in the passenger seat. A chef who worked at McNair's Jefferson Street restaurant called Gridiron 9, located near Tennessee State University, was in the back. An arrest affidavit indicated that Kazemi's eyes were bloodshot and there was alcohol on her breath. She was arrested and charged with driving under the influence and refusal to submit a breath test.[15] Kazemi reportedly told police she was high, not drunk.

McNair, who was not arrested, bailed Kazemi out of jail, unaware of the deadly plan she was about to set in motion. It was upon her release that she purchased a fully loaded Bryco Jennings 9-millimeter gun for $100 from Adrian Gilliam, Jr. in the parking lot of Opry Mills Shopping Center, where the Dave & Busters restaurant Kazemi worked at was located. Kazemi had met Gilliam a few weeks earlier outside a nightclub in downtown Nashville. Gilliam, thirty-three, was convicted of second-degree murder and armed robbery in 1993 in Dade County, Florida.[16]

* * *

On Saturday, July 4, 2009 at around one p.m., Wayne Neely and Robert Gaddy, a teammate of Steve McNair's at Alcorn State, found the former gridiron star and his girlfriend, Sahel Kazemi, shot dead in the downtown condominium McNair and Neely co-rented, and called 911.

According to Gaddy, "When I walked in I knew it immediately (something was wrong).... I called 911 and told them they needed to get there.... It was like something you might imagine seeing on TV or in the movies, but never imagine you would see it first-hand, to have that happen to someone you love. I am still shook up..."[17]

Steve McNair had been shot multiple times while sitting on the sofa, including twice in the head. Sahel Kazemi had been shot a single time in the head and was lying face down on the floor in front of the sofa. A pistol was found beneath her.

The macabre death scene was described as being devoid of warmth and individuality by the *Tennessean* newspaper days after the tragedy. There were bloodstains on what was left of the couch after investigators removed parts of it for evidence, and a blood saturated carpet—both indicative of where the victims were shot. Investigators had removed pieces of dry wall from behind the couch and written the words: "strike mark #1," "strike mark #2" and "stain #1" alongside what was apparently bullet holes.[18] Fingerprint dust was present everywhere in the condo. There were around a dozen or so liquor bottles left on a kitchen countertop and a mound of men's sneakers sitting on the floor in the kitchen.

* * *

Once the news spread about the shocking death of NFL great Steve McNair, grief-stricken fans made their way to his Lea Avenue condominium in downtown Nashville. In a testament to McNair's enduring popularity, one teary-eyed supporter commented, "I think all of Nashville is pretty heartbroken over this.... He built the Titans organization."[19]

Over the course of the day, many of McNair's fans swapped their Independence Day attire of red, white, and blue with simply blue and white, the colors of the Tennessee Titans.

The sad occasion upstaged what was supposed to be a day of celebration, capped off with a fireworks display downtown.

Though a rainstorm caused some fans and bystanders to disperse from the area around the condo, once the rain stopped, the gathering grew once more as the reality of Steve McNair's unexpected death and that of the woman he was with, Sahel Kazemi, began to sink in.

McNair's fans also showed up at his restaurant, Gridiron 9, to be close to him in spirit and grieve with other supporters of the former star quarterback.

In response to his untimely death, a statement was issued by McNair's family through his agent, James "Bus" Cook: "The families of Steve McNair in Mississippi and Tennessee appreciate the concern, thoughts, and prayers during this difficult time of our loss of a husband, father, and son. The family requests everyone would allow them time to mourn."[20]

* * *

According to the autopsy report, Steve McNair and Sahel Kazemi died early Saturday morning on Independence Day in 2009. McNair's death, as the result of being shot at close range twice in the head and twice in the chest as he sat on the living room couch, was ruled a homicide. Kazemi's death, which came from a single shot to the head, was ruled a suicide. Her corpse was found on the carpet near the sofa. A semiautomatic handgun was lodged beneath her body.[21]

Ballistics and gunshot residue tests indicated that Sahel Kazemi fired the weapon that led to the deaths of both victims. There was a trace amount of gunshot residue found on Kazemi's left hand. Dr. Feng Li, the assistant medical examiner who performed the autopsies on McNair and Kazemi, reported that the findings were consistent with a murder-suicide.[22]

According to a toxicology report, Steve McNair had a blood alcohol level that was twice the Tennessee legal limit at the time of his death; while a trace amount of marijuana was found in Sahel Kazemi's body.[23]

* * *

In the course of their investigation into the deaths of Steve McNair and Sahel Kazemi and what led up to it, detectives interviewed family and friends of the victims. It was reported that the football star's wife of a dozen years, Mechelle McNair, had apparently been oblivious to his affair with Kazemi up until being told how he died. The widow was described as being "crushed," and "blindsided," with "her whole world shattered" as a result of the news.[24]

Some others close to McNair appeared just as shocked, indicating they had no knowledge of Kazemi or his involvement with her prior to the shootings.

However, apparently this wasn't the case among those who were close to Sahel Kazemi. In an interview with the *Florida Times-Union*, Kazemi's sister, Soheyla, believed that Kazemi was going to become McNair's new wife, stating, "She said they were planning to get married."[25]

This was backed up by Kazemi's ex-roommate Emily Andrews who, according to a police report, claimed that McNair had said he was seeking to divorce his wife in order for him and Kazemi to get married.[26]

Similarly, Sepideh Salmani, Kazemi's aunt, told the *Tennessean* that her niece was under the impression that McNair had already begun divorce proceedings.[27]

An examination of county records revealed that there was no indication that McNair had filed for divorce.

* * *

The police brought in Sahel Kazemi's ex-boyfriend, Keith Norfleet, for questioning. He confirmed that they had dated for several years and had not been together as a couple for about five months. In spite of their rocky history, Norfleet claimed that Kazemi had told him that she planned to break off things with McNair, making him believe they would resume their relationship soon. Norfleet also reportedly expressed his concern that Kazemi was involved with a married man, stating, "He was making her believe they were going to be together and everything would be perfect."[28]

Norfleet alleged that on that fateful Saturday morning of July 4th, Kazemi had knocked on his apartment door, but had left by the time he opened it; and that he had tried to locate her that afternoon, concerned that she might have been the female found dead with McNair.

Norfleet was not considered a suspect at that point, with the evidence pointing squarely at Sahel Kazemi as the shooter in taking both her life and McNair's.

* * *

In a news conference held at Titans headquarters two days after McNair's death, team coach Jeff Fisher spoke maudlinly, "The Steve McNair I knew would want me to say, 'Celebrate my life for what I did on the field, for what I did in the community, for the kind of teammate that I was.' That's what the Steve I knew would want me to say."[29]

On the morning of Thursday, July 9th, there was a heavy turnout at the Lewis & Wright Funeral Home in north Nashville, where mourners got a look at a closed silver casket that held Steve McNair's body. That day, a public memorial service for McNair was held at the Tennessee Titans stadium, LP Field, to allow the former NFL great's fans to pay their final respects. Thousands of people—many of whom wore blue jerseys with McNair's number 9 on them—were in attendance. The same was true for another memorial service that was held in the evening at Mount Zion Baptist Church in White Creek, Tennessee, where McNair was remembered not only as a football star, but for his charity work in the local community.

On Saturday, July 11th, a week after his death, funeral services for Steve McNair were held in Hattiesburg, Mississippi at Reed Green Coliseum on the University of Southern Mississippi's campus. McNair was laid to rest at Griffith Cemetery in Prentiss, Mississippi, not far from his hometown of Mount Olive.

A day earlier, the funeral of McNair's killer and victim of suicide, Sahel Kazemi, took place in Jacksonville, Florida, after authorities released the twenty-year-old's body. Following a half hour service, Kazemi was laid to rest at Jacksonville Memory Gardens.

* * *

On Friday, July 17th, Bureau of Alcohol, Tobacco, Firearms, and Explosives agents arrested Adrian Gilliam, Jr.—the man who sold the gun to Sahel Kazemi that she used to shoot Steve McNair to death before turning the weapon on herself. Gilliam was arrested at his residence in LaVergne, Tennessee. According to the unsealed criminal complaint, he was charged with illegal possession of a firearm as convicted felon.[30]

Gilliam had previously been interviewed by Metro Nashville police investigators on July 5th, the day after the McNair-Kazemi murder and suicide. It was then that Gilliam admitted to selling the murder weapon to Kazemi for $100, supposedly for personal protection after she indicated concern with prowlers in the neighborhood. The 9-millimeter semiautomatic pistol had been traced to the convicted killer, who served nine years in prison. The gun had originally been purchased in January 2002 from a pawn shop in Nashville, before Gilliam bought the gun in early 2008.

Though authorities did not believe Adrian Gilliam was directly involved in the murder-suicide, he did apparently have a romantic interest in Sahel Kazemi, as indicated through text messages the two exchanged. A CBS News report would later reveal that Gilliam and Kazemi made hundreds of phone calls to one another, which included nearly fifty calls and texts just a day before Kazemi killed Steve McNair and herself.[31]

Aside from the murder-suicide, Metro Police Chief Ronal Serpas stressed the seriousness local and federal law enforcement attached to ex-con Gilliam's illegal possession of the firearm and its deadly potential thereof, stating, "If you remove this from the McNair tragedy, this is still a felon trafficking a weapon on the streets of Nashville, Tennessee in contradiction to federal law."[32]

* * *

In spite of the belief by police that Sahel Kazemi committed murder and suicide, some who knew her portrayed Kazemi as a happy, vivacious, outgoing, and fun person, not prone to suicide or perpetrating a homicide.

According to a CBS News investigation, video taken at the jail upon Kazemi's DUI arrest appeared to indicate that she was "in good spirits."[33] Also a copy of her bank statement obtained on the day she died revealed that there was over $2,500 in Kazemi's checking account, which appears to contradict the belief that she was over her head in debt.[34]

"She wasn't angry enough to do something like that," her sister Azadeh insisted in an interview, rejecting the murder-suicide conclusion.[35]

Similarly, another sister, Soheyla, also refused to believe Kazemi could have killed McNair, telling the *Florida Sun-Times*, "It's not true. She love[d] Steve too much."[36]

However, Kazemi's friend, Antonio Watson, challenged the notion that Kazemi loved and wanted a future with McNair, telling a Nashville television station that Kazemi had indicated she planned to move in with ex-boyfriend Keith Norfleet.[37]

This appeared to support Norfleet's belief to that effect. Furthermore, Norfleet had described the Kazemi he knew as "a very strong, independent girl" and a "hard worker," who had "a huge heart" and "was very caring," which seemed to also point to a self-sufficient, loving, and stable woman who would not have committed murder and suicide.[38]

* * *

The authorities painted a very different picture of Sahel Kazemi and her final days. From their investigation, it was clear that Kazemi "had become very distraught and on two occasions told friends and associates that her life was all messed up and that she was going to end it all."[39]

Kazemi's problems were said to include jealousy over McNair's involvement with a second mistress, Leah Ignagni, as well as perhaps the painful realization that McNair was not going to divorce his wife Mechelle and marry her. She was also having difficulty making payments on two cars and was about to be left paying the entire monthly rent for her Hermitage apartment, as Kazemi's roommate Emily Andrews was planning to move out.

More grief came when Sahel Kazemi was allegedly stood up by Steve McNair in Las Vegas a couple of weeks before the tragedy. Then perhaps the final straw was that Thursday morning, two days before the fateful 4th of July, while when driving in downtown Nashville a police officer pulled Kazemi over and charged her with driving under the influence.

According to the police, the evidence clearly indicated that "she was spinning out of control," when Sahel Kazemi decided to take her own life and Steve McNair's.[40]

Authorities released text messages between Kazemi and McNair the day before the murder-suicide that seemed to illustrate her deteriorating mental state and financial struggles. For example, a text message sent from Kazemi on Friday, July 3rd at 10:05 a.m., read: "Baby I might have a break down im so stressed;" then there was the suggestion that she may have to pay "the cell phone bills n the hospital."[41]

At one point, Kazemi texted McNair requesting he transfer to her account $2,000, which he agreed to do. A little later, she talks about money owed by her, complaining that she "can hardly breathe," along with: "I just want this pain in my chest to go away."[42] By 4:04 p.m. that day, Kazemi, in an apparent desperate attempt to draw McNair to her, texted, "Baby I have to be w u 2nite. I dnt care where."[43]

"The totality of the evidence clearly points to a murder-suicide," concluded Police Chief Serpas, noting that no evidence was uncovered at the condominium to indicate that anyone else was present at the time the deaths occurred sometime after one a.m. on Saturday, July 4, 2009.[44]

The police conclusion of murder-suicide was supported by the assistant medical examiner working the case, Dr. Feng Li, who reported that all the evidence backed up the belief that Sahel Kazemi "killed Mr. McNair and killed herself.... It's almost an assured thing. We have to be convinced otherwise."[45]

Detectives believe that Steve McNair made the rounds at a couple of Nashville hotspots—Loser's Bar & Grill and Blue Moon Lagoon Restaurant—in the hours before his death on Saturday, July 4th. James Weathers, manager of the Blue Moon Lagoon, stated that McNair entered the establishment by himself, meeting a couple at about ten-thirty p.m., before leaving alone around one a.m.

According to a witness, McNair arrived at the condo at 105 Lea Avenue sometime between one-thirty and two a.m. Kazemi's car was parked, indicating she was present and, unbeknownst to McNair, armed, with deadly plans already in the works for the former star quarterback and herself.

During a police press conference, Serpas described the victims and nature of their deaths. "McNair was seated on the sofa and likely was asleep, and we believe that Kazemi shot him in the right temple, then shot him twice in the chest, and then shot him a final time in the left temple."[46] He went on to say, "Kazemi then positioned herself next to McNair on the sofa and shot herself once in the right temple and expired.... We do believe she tried to stage that when she killed herself, she would fall in his lap."[47]

A 9-millimeter pistol, determined to be the weapon used in the fatal shootings, was found beneath Kazemi's body. Tests established that there was a trace of gunshot residue on her left hand.[48]

Metro Police homicide detective Sergeant Pat Postiglione would later say in describing Sahel Kazemi's mental state in deciding to murder Steve McNair: "I think she had her mind set on killing the man that she...could not live without. She figured if she couldn't have him, then nobody would."[49]

In December 2009, the case was officially closed by the Metropolitan Nashville Police Department as a murder-suicide.[50]

On December 18, 2009, Adrian Gilliam, Jr. was sentenced to two and a half years behind bars after pleading guilty to selling to Sahel Kazemi the gun used to kill Steve McNair and herself.[51] He was released from prison on September 23, 2011.[52]

* * *

Notwithstanding the official conclusion of the deaths of Steve McNair and Sahel Kazemi, there are still lingering doubts about the case for some people.

"There are a bunch of inconsistencies that would cause me to go back and investigate it further," argued former police detective Wayne Black.[53]

Similarly, another ex-cop, Vincent Hill, questioned why Steve McNair, a big spender who reportedly often kept a money roll of a couple of grand or more on him, had less than ten dollars on his person the day he died, according to the police report, suggesting robbery as a possible motive in his murder.[54]

Hill also pointed out discrepancies in statements given by Adrian Gilliam, such as when he and Kazemi first met. Furthermore, Hill pondered why McNair's friend Wayne Neely, who discovered the retired football player and his lover dead, supposedly phoned several people, including another McNair friend, Robert Gaddy, who called 911 to report the incident about forty-five minutes later.

Hill went to a Davidson County grand jury, seeking to have the McNair-Kazemi case reopened. The grand jury declined for insufficient new evidence to justify such a move.[55]

This came as no surprise to Metropolitan Nashville Police Department spokesperson Don Aaron, who said the department stood by both the investigation and its outcome.

He explained that in spite of Adrian Gilliam's connection to Sahel Kazemi, he was never considered a suspect in the crime because no evidence surfaced to indicate his involvement. Aaron went on to say, "When it all comes down to the science of the crime scene, and a detailed analysis of the crime scene, we concluded that she killed him then killed herself."[56]

The now Metro Police Chief Steve Anderson, reiterated the department's position, pointing out the "hundreds of hours" the department had put in to solve the case, with Sahel Kazemi seen as fatally shooting Steve McNair, before turning the gun on herself. "Without any doubt, I remain confident in the murder-suicide conclusion," Anderson stated.[57]

Echoing this sentiment as well was Davidson County District Attorney Torry Johnson, who said, "While we have continued to review information brought to us about the murder of Mr. McNair, nothing we have been presented has changed the results of our findings. We've seen nothing to refute the fact that anyone other than Sahel Kazemi fired the fatal shots."[58]

* * *

The tragedy of Steve McNair's death went well beyond the murder-suicide itself. McNair, who was only thirty-six when he died, did not leave a will. At the time of his death, the ex-NFL quarterback's estate was valued at $19.6 million, excluding unconnected stocks and bonds, his Mississippi farm, and his 80 percent stake in the Gridiron 9 restaurant. McNair's widow, Mechelle McNair, was named the estate's administrator, and most of his assets were frozen amidst tax and other implications.[59]

In April 2010, she was given $3.72 million from the estate to pay state and federal taxes. On October 15, 2010, Mechelle McNair's request to a Nashville judge to unfreeze $2.5 million—or $500,000 each for her and McNair's four children—from his estate pending the probate case being resolved, was granted.[60]

McNair's restaurant, Gridiron 9, which had remained empty since his death, was purchased from his estate in August 2010, after a Nashville probate court judge had authorized the sale of McNair's stake in the establishment in October 2009.[61]

In February 2010, artist Patricia Thompson was granted $5,000 by a judge after suing Steve McNair's estate for $12,000 for nonpayment on a life-sized painting McNair had commissioned for his restaurant. She testified that she delivered the collage of the former gridiron star to him only two days before McNair was murdered.[62]

In May 2012, Steve McNair's Green Hills home in Nashville, which the late quarterback bought in 2004 for a little less than $1.6 million, was put up for sale for the second time since his tragic death. It was sold by McNair's widow in February 2013 for $1.7 million.[63]

According to Nashville's WSMV-TV, in May 2011, nearly two years after Steve McNair's death, his mother, Lucille McNair, was reportedly forced by the former NFL star's estate to leave the 45-acre ranch he had built for her in Collins, Mississippi on Air McNair Road. This came after she had called it home for thirteen years at no cost to her, because she could not afford to pay a newly required monthly rent of $3,000 and McNair had failed to take the necessary legal steps to avoid this misfortune before his ill-timed passing.[64]

The Hattiesburg, Mississippi offices of the Steve McNair Foundation, which started in 2001 and raised hundreds of thousands of dollars for at-risk youth, the Boys & Girls Clubs, and victims of natural disasters in Mississippi and Tennessee, were now occupied by a company specializing in electric vehicles and alternative fuel.[65] According to the foundation's website, its last event was on July 10th, 2009.[66]

* * *

The shocking murder-suicide perpetrated by Sahel Kazemi, a woman barely out of her teens with seemingly her whole life ahead of her, also left things unsettled with Kazemi's estate upon her death.

In November 2009, the Probate Court of Davidson County ruled that her sister, Soheyla Kazemi, could collect on Kazemi's $10,000 life insurance policy issued by The Hartford Group, after filing a claim the previous month.[67] The company's standard group life insurance policy does not have a suicide exclusion provision. Apparently there were no further claims filed against the estate of Sahel Kazemi.

Following the murder of Steve McNair, Sahel Kazemi's family became the victims of threats and contempt as mourning fans of the much beloved ex-gridiron star lashed out in trying to come to grips with the senseless tragedy. Those who knew Kazemi were also left to deal with the aftermath of a tragic life—from her mother's violent death to her own—while wondering what went so horribly wrong.

The unlikely and fortuitous crossing paths of Steve McNair and Sahel Kazemi, along with a volatile mixture of money, romance, infidelity, jealousy, and hopelessness, seemed to all but seal their sad fate.

# # #

The following is a bonus excerpt from R. Barri Flowers'
bestselling true crime book

THE SEX SLAVE MURDERS
The True Story of Serial Killers Gerald and Charlene Gallego

It began as a fairly quiet early Sunday morning on November
2, 1980 in California's capitol city. By the end of the day, two
lives would be lost forever and many others changed
indelibly.

A gateway between the bustle of the San Francisco Bay
area, the idyllic beauty of the Sierra Nevada and the gambling
meccas of Lake Tahoe and Reno, Sacramento offered
perhaps the best of all worlds. It retained much of its cultural
and rural past while steadily becoming an urban and
suburban center with an eye on the future.

Arden Fair was an indication of Sacramento catering to
its middle class and modernization with nice homes, popular
stores, and new businesses popping up. On this tepid
Saturday night, the Arden Fair shopping center was the place
to be, particularly if you happened to be a fraternity or
sorority member at California State University, Sacramento
(CSUS). The Carousel restaurant, located on the east end of

the shopping center, had been transformed for the night/morning into a Founder's Day dinner-dance celebration, courtesy of Sigma Phi Epsilon.

Among those attending were CSUS seniors Craig Miller, twenty-two, and Mary Elizabeth Sowers, twenty-one. The attractive, All-American couple was engaged to be married on New Year's Eve 1981. For Sowers and Miller, hope seemed eternal.

Mary Beth Sowers fit all the adjectives of admiration or envy: beautiful, bright, outgoing, ambitious, warm, sensitive, in love with the world around her and the man she planned to marry. "She was somebody that had a lot of bubble and a lot of sparkle in the way she talked," said a close friend and fellow member of Alpha Chi Omega, the sorority Sowers joined in 1979. "You got more than just words when she talked. You got her feelings and her thoughts."

Mary Beth graduated from Sequoia High School in Redwood City in 1978. Her father was a nuclear physicist at ITEL Corporation in Palo Alto. Following graduation, she moved to Redding, California to attend junior college. There she won the title of runner-up in the Miss Shasta County contest.

Sowers began her junior year at CSUS, majoring in finance. Despite a full course load, she worked during the week at Arco Financial Services and on weekends at J.C. Penney to support herself. Later, she worked as a ski instructor on weekends at Boreal Ridge, a ski area east of Sacramento. Her talents also included being an expert seamstress, one weekend tailoring three suits.

Mary Beth began dating Craig Miller in late fall of 1979. Theirs was described by friends as a relationship of equals. Noted one friend: "It's so hard to find two people in the same relationship who are that much alike. So dynamic, outgoing, and personable."

Craig Miller graduated from La Sierra High School in 1976. Two years later, he graduated from American River College before attending CSUS, where he was on the dean's list. Like Sowers, he seemed tireless with the sky the limit. Aside from being an accounting executive at Miller Advertising, Miller was vice president of the campus chapter of Sigma Phi Epsilon and the 1979 Man of the Year.

When Mary Beth turned twenty-one on October 21, 1980, she and Craig Miller had been dating for nearly a year. With a spring graduation coming up, marriage plans did not seem premature. New Year's Eve 1981 seemed the perfect wedding day for the couple because New Year's Eve was Mary Beth's favorite day.

* * *

On the night of the Sigma Phi Epsilon fraternity function, Craig and Mary Beth arrived late, favoring some quiet time together over the dinner that started three hours prior to their arrival.

That didn't mean they weren't looking to make the most of their outing in the spirit of true fraternity and sorority members. From every indication, Miller and Sowers were happy and content on this night. According to dance attendee Sheryl Arkin, neither shied away from attention. "She had barely gotten in the door," said Arkin of Sowers, "and five of the Alpha Chi pledges were around her in a circle. She was just talking away."

Nevertheless, Craig and Mary Beth's stay was relatively short. They left the Carousel restaurant just after midnight. Shortly thereafter, a fraternity brother happened by chance to notice them in the back of an Oldsmobile Cutlass rather than Mary Beth's red Honda.

After an exchange of words between the fraternity brother and the front seat occupants of the car—a woman was in the driver's seat with a man beside her—the Oldsmobile sped off with Craig and Mary Beth still in the back seat.

That was the last time they were ever seen alive.

* * *

That afternoon, Craig Miller's body was discovered alongside a gravel road twenty miles from Placerville, near

Bass Lake in El Dorado County, California. He had been shot three times at point blank range. An autopsy performed the following day revealed that Miller had been shot once above the right ear, once in the back of the neck, and once at the right cheekbone—apparently at the site.

Mary Beth Sowers was still missing.

* * *

As with many non-domestic crimes of violence, solving such crimes often takes a combination of painstaking police investigative work and a bit of luck. In this instance, the luck came with a license plate number taken down by a concerned friend who thought it unusual that Craig Miller and his fiancée, Mary Beth Sowers, would take off with strangers in the wee hours of the morning of November 2, 1980 from the Arden Fair shopping center parking lot, leaving her Honda behind.

When the couple failed to return to the Honda by that afternoon, the friend and fellow member of Miller's fraternity reported them missing. Tracing the license number of the car Miller and Sowers disappeared in, the police discovered that the car—a silver 1977 Oldsmobile Cutlass— was registered to Charlene A. Williams or Charles Williams, her father. This was the second big break.

In the meantime, Miller's mother worried that her usually dependable son and future daughter-in-law were missing. A friend of Sowers had phoned Miller's mother early Sunday morning looking for Miller. "I don't want you to worry," the friend had said, "but something really strange is going on. Nobody has seen Mary Beth or Craig since last night."

When Miller failed to show up for his 10:00 A.M. shift at a paint store in Carmichael, his mother telephoned police.

* * *

After learning from the Department of Motor Vehicles that the Oldsmobile Cutlass belonged to Charlene A. Williams or Charles Williams, Detective Lee Taylor and Detective Larry Burchett drove to the home of Charles and Mercedes Williams on Berrendo Drive in Arden Park.

The parents told the detectives that the Cutlass was their daughter Charlene's, and that she had left home about 6:30 P.M. Saturday to go to a movie theater with her boyfriend, Stephen Robert Feil. During the conversation, Charlene drove up in her silver Cutlass. This was the third big break, although it did not seem like it at the time.

Charlene, twenty-four, was blonde, pretty, petite, and seven months pregnant. She coolly denied any knowledge of the disappearance of Sowers or Miller. She allowed the detectives to search the Cutlass. They found no indication of foul play or otherwise incriminating evidence that a crime had been committed.

Charlene complained of being sick because of her pregnancy and suffering from a hangover. She gave few details about her boyfriend, Stephen Feil.

The detectives, unaware that Miller's body was soon to be discovered and having no other reason to detain the ill Charlene further, promised to return later that day to photograph her. She, in turn, hoped to have recovered somewhat and be more cooperative.

* * *

It was not until the following day that Charles and Mercedes Williams admitted to the detectives that their daughter was married to Stephen Feil and that this was actually an alias used by Gerald Gallego, thirty-four, who was wanted on incest and other sex charges.

Suddenly some frightening pieces of a bizarre puzzle began to fall into place. Not only had the Gallegos become the chief suspects in the murder of Craig Miller and disappearance of Mary Beth Sowers, but neighboring Yolo County authorities were also investigating the connection of a Stephen Feil to the kidnapping-murder of Virginia Mochel, a local bartender.

Unfortunately, by now the Gallegos, sensing trouble, had fled to parts unknown. On November 5, 1980, El Dorado County filed charges of kidnapping and murder against Gerald and Charlene Gallego. The following day, a federal fugitive warrant of unlawful flight to avoid prosecution was issued against the Gallegos to allow the FBI to join in a nationwide search for the fugitive couple on the run.

That search came to an uncomplicated end twelve days later. On Monday, November 17, 1980, Gerald and Charlene Gallego were captured by FBI agents in Omaha, Nebraska while they were attempting to pick up money that had been wired to them by Charlene's parents at a Western Union office in downtown Omaha.

The arrest came without incident and brought to an end what was later discovered to be a twenty-six month reign of sex-motivated brutality and cold-blooded murder.

Yet this was only the beginning of a bizarre tale of sexual fantasies, domination, and sheer terror that was to unravel and take three and a half more years to bring to a conclusion.

* * *

Read the entire THE SEX SLAVE MURDERS, available in print, eBook, and audio.

# # #

The following is a bonus excerpt from R. Barri Flowers'
bestselling true crime book

SERIAL KILLER COUPLES
Ian Brady and Myra Hindley

This murderous British couple was involved in pornography
and had a fascination with sex and murder, leading them to
act out their dark fantasies in the early 1960s.

In what became known as the Moors Murders, Brady and
Hindley murdered five children, sexually assaulting most of
them, and burying four of them in Saddleworth Moor, an
area that is now Greater Manchester, England. Brady was
characterized by a forensic psychiatrist as a "sexually sadistic
psychopath," while the British press referred to Hindley as
"the most evil woman in Britain."[1] This dangerous mix put
the couple on a deadly path as they pursued vulnerable
victims in carrying out their brutal crimes.

* * *

Ian Brady was born as Ian Duncan Stewart in Glasgow,
Scotland on January 2, 1938 to an unwed mother. Unable to
support her son, she gave him up to a local married couple,
while still keeping in touch. The seeds for Brady's antisocial
and violent behavior were planted early in life as he

developed a predilection for the torture of animals. These included breaking "the hind legs of one dog, [setting] fire to another, and decapitat[ing] a cat."[2]

By his teenage years, Brady was attending Shawlands Academy, a school for students who were considered above average. It was there that his deviant behavior now included harming smaller youths and burglary. Before turning seventeen, Brady had threatened a girlfriend with a knife and was in court for various other crimes committed.

After moving to Manchester to live with his mother, who had remarried while he was on probation, trouble continued to follow Ian Brady, including theft, and he spent time in juvenile detention.

In January 1959, Brady went to work in a clerical capacity for a wholesale chemical distribution plant called Millwards Merchandising in the Gorton district of Manchester. It was there where he would meet his future partner in crime and murder, Myra Hindley.

* * *

Born on July 23, 1942, Myra Hindley grew up in the working class Gorton district. Her father, who had served his country in North Africa and Italy during World War II, was an alcoholic and child batterer intent upon hardening his first of two daughters. At the age of eight, Hindley returned home in tears after being scratched and bloodied in the face by a boy.

Her father ordered her to "Go and punch him [the boy], because if you don't I'll leather you!" Hindley did as she was told and felt a sense of triumph. She recalled later that, at eight, "I'd scored my first victory."[3]

This particular scenario between daughter and father would be described by forensic psychiatrist Malcolm MacCulloch as instrumental in understanding the role Hindley played in the Moors murders: "The relationship with her father brutalised her[....] She was not only used to violence in the home but rewarded for it outside. When this happens at a young age it can distort a person's reaction to such situations for life."[4]

As a teenager, Hindley, who had been baptized in infancy as a Catholic, became more involved with the church following the drowning death of a friend, taking the confirmation name Veronica in late 1958. She also started bleaching her hair and working. At seventeen, she got engaged briefly, but broke it off, believing her fiancé was too immature and unable to give her the life she wanted.

Hindley dyed her hair pink and took judo lessons. A job at an engineering company was short-lived due to missing work too often. In 1961, at the age of eighteen, Hindley found work as a typist at Millwards where she met Ian Brady.

* * *

It didn't take long for the two to hit it off. Hindley became enthralled with Brady, in spite of knowing about his criminal record and perhaps because of it, detailing this in a diary. They began dating, watching pornography, drinking German wine, and reading about Nazi acts of violence.

Hindley soon started emulating the notion of Aryan perfection, including dying her hair blonde and wearing red lipstick. She also became more risqué in her attire, wearing short skirts, leather jackets, and high boots. Hindley's obsession with Brady kept her following his lead.

She would later say about Brady, in a letter sent to the Home Secretary in an attempt at parole: "Within months he had convinced me that there was no God at all. He could have told me that the earth was flat, the moon was made of green cheese and the sun rose in the west, I would have believed him, such was his power of persuasion."[5]

Brady and Hindley visited the library often, reading books on crime, torture, and philosophy. They also spent time at shooting ranges, with Hindley purchasing a .22 caliber rifle, a .38 Smith and Wesson, and a .45 Webley. Plans to rob banks fizzled.

The pair also took an interest in photography. Brady bought darkroom supplies and lights to go with his Brownie camera, and they took explicit pictures of one another and of Hindley's dog.

* * *

According to Hindley, it was during the summer of 1963 that Brady first spoke of committing "the perfect murder." He was apparently fixated on the story of American teenage killers, Richard Loeb and Nathan Leopold, who planned the so-called perfect crime in the kidnapping and murder of fourteen-year-old Bobby Franks in Chicago during the 1920s.[6]

Hindley and Brady were living with her grandmother at the time. On July 12, 1963, the couple set their sights on the first person they would murder.

Pauline Reade was sixteen and had gone to school with Myra Hindley's younger sister, Maureen. Reade had also dated David Smith, a local fifteen-year-old with a criminal record, including violence, who would eventually become a pivotal player in bringing an end to the homicides of Brady and Hindley.

But not before Brady and Hindley had already ended a number of lives.

* * *

Read the entire SERIAL KILLER COUPLES, available in print, eBook, and audio.

# # #

NOTES

MURDER AT THE PENCIL FACTORY

1. R. Barri Flowers and H. Loraine Flowers, *Murders in the United States: Crimes, Killers and Victims of the Twentieth Century* (Jefferson, NC: McFarland, 2004), pp. 13-14, 73.

2. Wikipedia, the Free Encyclopedia, "Leo Frank," http://en.wikipedia.org/wiki/Leo_Frank. *See also* Mary Phagan Kean, *The Murder of Little Mary Phagan* (Far Hills, NJ: New Horizon Press, 1989), p. 111.

3. Donald E. Wilkes Jr., "Wrongly Accused, Falsely Convicted, Wantonly Murdered," *Flagpole Magazine*, (May 5, 2004), p. 7, http://www.law.uga.edu/dwilkes_more/his38_wrongly.html.

4. *Ibid.*; Flowers and H. Loraine Flowers, *Murders in the United States*, pp. 13-14.

5. "Leo Frank."

6. *Ibid.*

7. Charles Pou, "The Leo Frank Case," Georgia Info, http://georgiainfo.galileo.usg.edu/leofrank.htm.p

8. Cited in Wilkes Jr., "Wrongly Accused, Falsely Convicted."

9. Pou, "The Leo Frank Case."

10. *Ibid.*

11. Quoted in *Ibid.*

12. "Leo Frank."

13. *Ibid. See also* Steve Oney, *And the Dead Shall Rise: The Murder of Mary Phagan and the Lynching of Leo Frank* (New York, NY: Pantheon Books, 2003), pp. 129-32.

14. Pou, "The Leo Frank Case."

15. Oney, *And the Dead Shall Rise,* pp. 134-36.

16. "Leo Frank."

17. *Ibid.*

18. Oney, *And the Dead Shall Rise,* pp. 139-40.

19. "Leo Frank."

20. Wilkes Jr., "Wrongly Accused, Falsely Convicted."

21. "Leo Frank."

22. *Ibid.*

23. Famous Trials: The Leo Frank Trial 1913, "Testimony of Leo Frank," http://law2.umkc.edu/faculty/projects/ftrials/frank/testimonyleofrank.html.

24. *Ibid.*

25. *Ibid.*

26. Oney, *And the Dead Shall Rise*, p. 303.

27. Pou, "The Leo Frank Case."

28. Wilkes Jr., "Wrongly Accused, Falsely Convicted."

29. Pou, "The Leo Frank Case."

30. *Ibid.*

31. *Ibid.*

32. "Leo Frank."

33. *Ibid.*

34. *Ibid. See also* Eugene Levy, "Is the Jew a White Man?" in Maurianne Adams and John H. Bracey, eds., *Strangers & Neighbors: Relations Between Blacks & Jews in the United States* (Amherst, MA: University of Massachusetts Press, 2000).

35. "Leo Frank."

36. *Ibid.*

37. "Begin Last Frank Appeal to Governor," *New York Times* (June 13, 1915).

38. "A Political Suicide," *Time* (January 24, 1955).

39. Wilkes Jr., "Wrongly Accused, Falsely Convicted."

40. Tribal Theocrat, "The Leo Frank Murder: Semitism Birthing Anti-Semitism," (April 2011), http://tribaltheocrat.com/2011/04/the-leo-frank-murder-semitism-birthing-anti-semitism/.

41. Quoted in Wilkes Jr., "Wrongly Accused, Falsely Convicted."

42. *Ibid.*

43. Comer Vann Woodward, *Tom Watson: Agrarian Rebel.* (New York: Oxford University Press, 1963), p. 432.

44. Pou, "The Leo Frank Case."

45. "Leo Frank."

46. *Ibid.*; Flowers and H. Loraine Flowers, *Murders in the United States*, pp. 13-14, 73.

47. Wilkes Jr., "Wrongly Accused, Falsely Convicted."

48. Cited in "Leo Frank."

49. Kean, *The Murder of Little Mary Phagan*; Wilkes Jr., "Wrongly Accused, Falsely Convicted;" Elaine M. Alphin, *An Unspeakable Crime: The Prosecution and Persecution of Leo Frank* (Minneapolis, MN: Carolrhoda Books, 2010), p. 117.

50. Quoted in Allison Gaudet Yarrow, "The People Revisit Leo Frank," *Jewish Daily Forward* (May 13, 2009), http://forward.com/articles/105936/the-people-revisit-leo-frank/.

51. Wikipedia, the Free Encyclopedia, "Anti-Defamation League," http://en.wikipedia.org/wiki/Anti-Defamation_League.

52. "Leo Frank."

53. Cited in Wilkes Jr., "Wrongly Accused, Falsely Convicted."

54. Quoted in *New Georgia Encyclopedia*, History and Archeology, "Leo Frank Case," (August 3, 2009), http://www.georgiaencyclopedia.org/nge/Article.jsp?id=h-906&hl=y.

55. Wilkes Jr., "Wrongly Accused, Falsely Convicted."

56. *Ibid.*

57. Pou, "The Leo Frank Case."

58. Wilkes Jr., "Wrongly Accused, Falsely Convicted."

59. "Death Witness Says Lynch Victim Innocent," *Bangor Daily News* (March 8, 1982), http://news.google.com/newspapers?nid=2457&dat=19820 308&id=EBE0AAAAIBAJ&sjid=YSMIAAAAIBAJ&pg=28 60,2563887.

60. *Ibid.*

61. Pou, "The Leo Frank Case."

62. *Ibid.*

63. *Ibid.*; "Leo M. Frank: The 1913 Leo Frank Case and Trial Research Library," http://www.leofrank.org/alonzo-mann/.

64. Pou, "The Leo Frank Case."

65. "The 1913 Leo Frank Case and Trial Research Library"

66. *Ibid.*

67. *Ibid.*

THE "GOLD SPECIAL" TRAIN ROBBERY

1. R. Barri Flowers and H. Loraine Flowers, *Murders in the United States: Crimes, Killers and Victims of the Twentieth Century* (Jefferson, NC: McFarland, 2004), p. 18.

2. "Siskiyou Outrage," *Slabtown Chronicle* (May 5, 2006), http://portlandcrime.blogspot.com/2006/05/siskiyou-outrage.html; Wikipedia, the Free Encyclopedia, "Industrial Workers of the World," http://en.wikipedia.org/wiki/Industrial_Workers_of_the_World.

3. Paul Fattig, "D'Autremonts' Bungled Train Robbery in 1923 Left 4 Dead," *The Mall Tribune* (October 11, 1998), http://www.angelfire.com/wa/andyhiggins/Greattrainrobbery.html.

4. Edward H. Smith, "Worldwide Man Hunt Started by a Chemist," *New York Times* (April 24, 1927).

5. "Siskiyou Outrage."

6. "Worldwide Man Hunt Started."

7. Paul Fattig, "Great Train Robbery," http://tunnel13.com/history/robbery.html.

8. *Ibid.*

9. "Siskiyou Outrage."

10. Wikipedia, the Free Encyclopedia, "D'Autremont Brothers," http://en.wikipedia.org/wiki/DeAutremont_Brothers. *See also* Michael Newton, *The Encyclopedia of Robberies, Heists, and Capers* (New York: Facts On File Inc., 2002), pp. 78-79.

11. "Worldwide Man Hunt Started."

12. *Ibid.*

13. *Ibid.*

14. "D'Autremont Brothers."

15. "Worldwide Man Hunt Started."

16. Flowers and Flowers, *Murders in the United States*, p. 18.

17. "D'Autremont Brothers;" "Chemist Turns Detective," *New York Times* (June 10, 1927).

18. "Worldwide Man Hunt Started."

19. *Ibid.*

20. *Ibid.*

21. *Ibid.*

22. "Siskiyou Outrage;" "Earn $15,000 Reward. Solider and Cripple Get Shares for D'Autremonts' Capture," *New York Times* (July 8, 1928).

23. "Worldwide Man Hunt Started."

24. "D'Autremont Brothers;" "Siskiyou Outrage;" "Earn $15,000 Reward."

25. "Fugitive Bandits Caught," *New York Times* (June 9, 1927); "Twin Bandits Held Under Heavy Guard," *New York Times* (June 10, 1927); "D'Autremonts' Bail Put at $50,000 Each," *New York Times* (June 11, 1927).

26. Flowers and Flowers, *Murders in the United States*, p. 18; "Hugh D'Autremont Convicted in Oregon," *New York Times* (June 22, 1927).

27. News Watch 12 Staff, "Oregon Trails: D'Autremont Train Robbery," KDRV.com (October 18, 2013), http://www.kdrv.com/oregon-trails-dautremont-train-robbery/.

28. "Siskiyou Outrage."

29. Fattig, "D'Autremonts' Bungled Train Robbery."

30. Newton, *The Encyclopedia of Robberies, Heists, and Capers*.

31. "Last of Train Robbers Dies in Oregon at 84," *Record-Journal* (December 22, 1984), p. 2.

32. Mark Freeman, "Tunnel 13," *Mail Tribune* (November 18, 2003), http://www.mailtribune.com/apps/pbcs.dll/article?AID=/20031118/BIZ/311189998&cid=sitesearch; Paul Fattig, "Tunnel Smoke Blocks Access, *Mail Tribune* (November 19, 2003), http://www.mailtribune.com/apps/pbcs.dll/article?AID=/20031119/BIZ/311199998&cid=sitesearch.

33. Sam Wheeler, "Return of the Rails: Grant for Railroad Repairs Likely to Bring Financial Benefits to Rogue Valley," *Ashland Daily Tidings* (June 26, 2012), http://www.dailytidings.com/apps/pbcs.dll/article?AID=/20120626/NEWS02/206260305.

34. "Reopening Siskiyou Rail," *Moving Ahead* (September 28, 2012), http://www.odotmovingahead.com/2012/09/.

35. IMDb, *The Crime of the D'Autremont Brothers*, (2012), http://www.imdb.com/title/tt2357389/?ref_=fn_al_tt_1.

36. Ted P. Yeatman, *Frank and Jesse James: The Story Behind the Legend* (Nashville, TN: Cumberland House, 2nd ed., 2003); Frank Triplett, *Jesse James: The Life, Times, and Treacherous Death of the Most Infamous Outlaw of All Time* (New York: Skyhorse Publishing, 2013); Marley Brant, *The Outlaw Youngers: A Confederate Brotherhood* (Lanham, MD: Madison Books, 2014).

37. Wikipedia, the Free Encyclopedia, "The James–Younger Gang," http://en.wikipedia.org/wiki/James%E2%80%93Younger_Gang.

38. Brant, *The Outlaw Youngers*.

39. "Jesse James Shot Down. Killed By One Of His Confederates Who Claims To Be A Detective," *New York Times* (April 4, 1882).

40. "Frank James Dies at 72," *New York Times* (February 19, 1915).

41. Editorial from the *Seattle Daily Times* (July 3, 1902). *See also* Stan Flewelling, "The Dauntless Desperado: Harry Tracy," *White River Journal* (April 1998), http://www.wrvmuseum.org/journal/journal_0498.htm; Christine Clarridge, "A Plan to honor 130 Years of Fallen Seattle Officers, *Seattle Times* (September 14, 2014), http://seattletimes.com/html/localnews/2017162440_mem orialsigns05m.html; Wikipedia, the Free Encyclopedia, "Harry Tracy," http://en.wikipedia.org/wiki/Harry_Tracy.

42. Alan J. Stein, HistoryLink.org Essay 5375, Timeline Library (March 5, 2003), http://www.historylink.org/index.cfm?DisplayPage=output. cfm&file_id=5375; "Where Convict Tracy Made his Last Stand," *Seattle Post-Intelligencer* (August 7, 1902); Bill Gulick, *Manhunt: the Pursuit of Harry Tracy* (Caldwell, ID: Caxton Press, 1999).

43. IMDb, *Harry Tracy, Desperado* (1082), http://www.imdb.com/title/tt0084052/?ref_=nm_flmg_act _70.

MURDER OF THE BANKER'S DAUGHTER

1. R. Barri Flowers and H. Loraine Flowers, *Murders in the United States: Crimes, Killers and Victims of the Twentieth Century* (Jefferson, NC: McFarland, 2004), pp 19-21.

2. Grave Spotlight, Marion Parker, http://www.cemeteryguide.com/gotw-parker.html.

3. Wikipedia, the Free Encyclopedia, "Marion Parker," http://en.wikipedia.org/wiki/Marion_Parker. *See also* Flowers and Flowers, *Murders in the United States,* pp. 19-21.

4. Grave Spotlight.

5. *Ibid.*; Mark Gribben, "The Murder of Marion Parker," The Malefactor's Register: Crime, Punishment, Law, Writing, http://malefactorsregister.com/wp/?p=779.

6. Grave Spotlight.

7. Gribben, "The Murder of Marion Parker."

8. *Ibid.*

9. Grave Spotlight.

10. Gribben, "The Murder of Marion Parker;" "Los Angeles Killer Eludes All Pursuit," *New York Times* (December 22, 1927).

11. "Let Murderer's Hang," *Los Angeles Times* (December 21, 1927).

12. Grave Spotlight.

13. "Ex-Bank Messenger Positively Named Los Angeles Killer," *New York Times* (December 21, 1927).

14. *Ibid.*

15. *Ibid.*

16. *Ibid.*

17. Flowers and Flowers, *Murders in the United States,* pp. 19-21; Grave Spotlight.

18. "Ex-Bank Messenger Positively Named."

19. Grave Spotlight; "Los Angeles Killer Eludes All Pursuit," *New York Times* (December 22, 1927).

20. "Ex-Bank Messenger Positively Named."

21. *Ibid.*

22. Grave Spotlight.

23. *Ibid.*

24. "Hickman Made Way as Far as Seattle," *New York Times* (December 23, 1927).

25. "Cramer Refutes Hickman. Police Reconstruct Crime with Kidnapper as Sole Killer," *New York Times* (December 24, 1927).

26. Associated Press, "Hickman Confused as Alibi of Cramer Proves He Is Lying," *New York Times* (December 24, 1927).

27. Associated Press, "Hickman Attempts Twice to End Life Before Start South," *New York Times* (December 26, 1927).

28. "Hangman Captured, Admits Kidnapping," *New York Times* (December 23, 1927).

29. *Ibid.*

30. "Text of Hickman's Confession in Los Angeles Crime," *New York Times* (December 23, 1927).

31. Grave Spotlight.

32. "Marion Parker;" Gribben, "The Murder of Marion Parker."

33. Grave Spotlight.

34. "Find Hickman Sane, Guilty of Murder," *New York Times* (February 10, 1928).

35. "Hickman Admits Second Murder; Companion Jailed," *New York Times* (December 30, 1927).

36. *Ibid.*

37. "Assert Hickman Said He Killed Toms," *New York Times* (March 18, 1928).

38. Flowers and Flowers, *Murders in the United States*, pp. 19-21; "Hickman to Invoke Leopold-Loeb Plea," *New York Times* (January 10, 1928).

39. "Hickman to Invoke Leopold-Loeb Plea."

40. "Hickman Rejected by Juvenile Court," *New York Times* (January 12, 1928).

41. "Try to Prove Kin of Hickman Insane," *New York Times* (January 31, 1928).

42. *Ibid.*; "Hickman's Father Goes to His Aide," *New York Times* (February 1, 1928).

43. Grave Spotlight.

44. "Marion Parker."

45. "Find Hickman Sane, Guilty of Murder," *New York Times* (February 10, 1928).

46. *Ibid.*; Flowers and Flowers, *Murders in the United States*, pp. 19-21.

47. "Find Hickman Sane, Guilty of Murder."

48. *Ibid.*

49. "Hickman Convicted of Second Murder," *New York Times* (March 11, 1928).

50. "Assert Hickman Said He Killed Toms."

51. *Ibid.*

52. "Hickman Conviction Upheld on Appeal," *New York Times* (July 6, 1928).

53. Grave Spotlight.

54. "Hickman Confesses Murder and Robberies, *New York Times* (October 14, 1928).

55. Flowers and Flowers, *Murders in the United States*, pp. 19-21; "Hickman Hanged as He Collapses," *New York Times* (October 20, 1928).

56. "Hickman Hanged as He Collapses."

57. *Ibid.*

58. Grave Spotlight.

59. *Ibid.*

60. IMDB, "Edward Hickman (1908-1928)," http://www.imdb.com/name/nm1489218/.

61. Cited in Grave Spotlight.

62. *Ibid.*

MASS MURDER IN THE SKY

1. R. Barri Flowers and H. Loraine Flowers, *Murders in the United States: Crimes, Killers and Victims of the Twentieth Century* (Jefferson, NC: McFarland, 2004), pp. 30-31. *See also* Al Nakkula, "44 Killed in Airliner Explosion," *Rocky Mountain News* (November 2, 1955).

2. Mark Gado, "Sabotage: The Downing of Flight 629," TruTV Crime Library, http://www.trutv.com/library/crime/notorious_murders/mass/jack_graham/index.html.

3. *Ibid.*

4. *Ibid.*

5. *Ibid.*

6. Federal Bureau of Investigation, Famous Cases and Criminals, "Jack Gilbert Graham,". http://www.fbi.gov/about-us/history/famous-cases/jack-gilbert-graham.

7. *Ibid.*

8. *Ibid.*; Flowers and Flowers, *Murders in the United States.*

9. Gado, "Sabotage: The Downing of Flight 629.

10. *Ibid.*

11. Federal Bureau of Investigation, "Jack Gilbert Graham."

12. *Ibid.*

13. *Ibid.*

14. *Ibid.*

15. Gado, "Sabotage: The Downing of Flight 629."

16. Federal Bureau of Investigation, "Jack Gilbert Graham."

17. Wikipedia, the Free Encyclopedia, "Jack Gilbert Graham," http://en.wikipedia.org/wiki/Jack_Gilbert_Graham.

18. *Ibid.*

19. *Ibid.*

20. *Ibid.*

21. Federal Bureau of Investigation, "Jack Gilbert Graham."

22. Gado, "Sabotage: The Downing of Flight 629.

23. Federal Bureau of Investigation, "Jack Gilbert Graham." *See also* R. Barri Flowers, *Murder, at the End of the Day and Night: A Study of Criminal Homicide Offenders, Victims, and Circumstances* (Springfield, IL: Charles C Thomas, 2002).

24. *Ibid.*; Flowers and Flowers, *Murders in the United States.*

25. Gordon Gauss, "Graham Spurns Appeal and is Sentenced to Die," *Longmont-Times-Call* (May 15, 1956).

26. Wikipedia, the Free Encyclopedia, "Jack Gilbert Graham."

27. Warner Bros. Pictures, *The FBI Story* (1959), http://www.imdb.com/title/tt0052792/.

THE AMITYVILLE MASSACRE

1. R. Barri Flowers and H. Loraine Flowers, *Murders in the United States: Crimes, Killers and Victims of the Twentieth Century* (Jefferson, NC: McFarland, 2004), p. 75.

2. "Ronald DeFeo Biography," Bio (September 17, 2014), http://www.biography.com/people/ronald-defeo-580972#synopsis.

3. Douglas B. Lynott, "The Real Life Amityville Horror," Crime Library: Criminal Minds & Methods, http://www.crimelibrary.com/notorious_murders/family/a mityville/2.html.

4. "Ronald DeFeo Biography."

5. Lynott, "The Real Life Amityville Horror."

6. *Ibid.*

7. Flowers and Flowers, *Murders in the United States.*

8. Quoted in Wikipedia, the Free Encyclopedia, "Ronald DeFeo, Jr.," http://en.wikipedia.org/wiki/Ronald_DeFeo%2C_Jr.

9. *Ibid.*

10. *Ibid.*

11. Quoted in Lynott, "The Real Life Amityville Horror."

12. *Ibid.*

13. *Ibid.*

14. *Ibid.*

15. "Ronald DeFeo Biography."

16. Bob Keeler, "DeFeo's New Story," *Newsday* (March 19, 1986).

17. Thomas J. Stark, *People v DeFeo Memorandum Denying Motion to Vacate Conviction* (January 6, 1993), pp. 3-4.

18. "Ronald DeFeo Biography."

19. Jay Anson, *The Amityville Horror* (Englewood Cliffs, NJ: Prentice-Hall, 1977).

20. *Ibid.*

21. Lynott, "The Real Life Amityville Horror." *See also* Stephen Kaplan, Ph.D. and Roxanne Salch Kaplan, *The Amityville Horror Conspiracy* (Laceyville, PA: Belfry Books, 1995).

22. Cited in Lynott, "The Real Life Amityville Horror."

23. IMDb, *The Amityville Horror* (1977), http://www.imdb.com/title/tt0078767/?ref_=nv_sr_2.

24. *Ibid.*; *The Amityville Horror* (2005), http://www.imdb.com/title/tt0384806/?ref_=nv_sr_1.

25. *Ibid.*; *Amityville II: The Possession* (1982), http://www.imdb.com/title/tt0083550/?ref_=fn_al_tt_1;

Hans Holzer, *Murder in Amityville* (New York: Belmont Tower Books, 1977).

26. Ric Osuna, *The Night the DeFeos Died: Reinvestigating the Amityville Murders* (Bloomington, IN: Xlibris, 2002).

27. "Ronald DeFeo, Jr."

28. IMDb, Shattered Hopes: The True Story of the Amityville Murders—Part I: From Horror to Homicide (2011), http://www.imdb.com/title/tt1786665/?ref_=fn_al_tt_3. *See also* Shattered Hopes: The True Story of the Amityville Murders—Part II: Mob, Mayhem, Murder (2012), http://www.imdb.com/title/tt2150455/?ref_=fn_al_tt_2; Shattered Hopes: The True Story of the Amityville Murders—Part III: Fraud & Forensics (2014), http://www.imdb.com/title/tt2295444/?ref_=fn_al_tt_1.

29. Will Savive, *Mentally Ill in Amityville: Murder, Mystery, & Mayhem at 112 Ocean Ave.* (Bloomington, IN: iUniverse, 2008).

30. Flowers and Flowers, *Murders in the United States.*

31. *Ibid.*

THE PICKAXE KILLERS

1. R. Barri Flowers and H. Loraine Flowers, *Murders in the United States: Crimes, Killers and Victims of the Twentieth Century* (Jefferson, NC: McFarland, 2004), p. 167.

2. Joseph Geringer, "Karla Faye Tucker: Texas' Controversial Murderess," Crime Library: Criminal Minds and Methods, http://www.trutv.com/library/crime/notorious_murders/women/tucker/2.html.

3. Quoted in *ibid.*

4. *Ibid.*

5. "Special Report 1998: Karla Faye Tucker: Portrait of a Repentant Killer," *BBC News* (January 30, 1988), http://news.bbc.co.uk/2/hi/special_report/1998/karla_faye_tucker/48816.stm.

6. Quoted in Geringer, "Karla Faye Tucker."

MURDER CHRONICLES

7. *Ibid.*

8. *Ibid.*

9. *Ibid.*

10. Texas Department of Criminal Justice, "Fact Sheet on Karla Faye Tucker," (February 3, 1998), http://www.clarkprosecutor.org/html/death/US/tucker437.htm.

11. CNN Interactive, "Profile: Facing Death with Memories of Murder," (February 1998), http://www.cnn.com/SPECIALS/1998/tucker.execution/profile/.

12. American Female Executions 1900-2010, "Karla Faye Tucker, Justice Delayed?" http://www.capitalpunishmentuk.org/karla.html.

13. "Profile: Facing Death with Memories of Murder."

14. *Ibid.*

15. *Ibid.*

16. *Ibid.*

17. *Ibid.*

18. Quoted in Sue A. Pressley, "Two Cases, Two States: Appeals Fail, Texas Executes Woman," *Washington Post* (February 4, 1998), http://articles.sun-sentinel.com/1998-02-04/news/9802040006_1_karla-faye-tucker-death-house-death-penalty.

19. Sam H. Verhovek, "Texas, in First Time in 135 Years, Is Set To Execute Woman," *New York Times* (February 3, 1998), http://www.nytimes.com/1998/02/03/us/texas-in-first-time-in-135-years-is-set-to-execute-woman.html?ref=karlafayetucker.

20. Quoted in *ibid.*

21. *Ibid.*

22. *Ibid.*

23. *Ibid.*

24. Flowers and H. Loraine Flowers, *Murders in the United States,* pp. 41-54.

25. Quoted in Sam H. Verhovek, "Execution in Texas: The Overview Divisive Case of a Killer of Two Ends as

Texas Executes Tucker," *New York Times* (February 4, 1998), http://www.nytimes.com/1998/02/04/us/execution-texas-overview-divisive-case-killer-two-ends-texas-executes-tucker.html?ref=karlafayetucker.

26. *Ibid.*

27. Cited in Verhovek, "Texas, in First Time in 135 Years."

28. *Ibid.*

29. *Ibid.*

30. "Execution in Texas; Texas Governor Refuses to Intervene," *New York Times* (February 4, 1998), http://www.nytimes.com/1998/02/04/us/execution-in-texas-texas-governor-refuses-to-intervene.html?ref=karlafayetucker.

31. Sam H. Verhovek, "Near Death, Tucker Gave Suggestions to the Prison," *New York Times* (February 8, 1998), http://www.nytimes.com/1998/02/08/us/near-death-tucker-gave-suggestions-to-the-prison.html?ref=karlafayetucker.

32. "Karla Faye Tucker, Justice Delayed."

33. Pressley, "Two Cases, Two States: Appeals Fail."

34. Verhovek, "Execution in Texas."

35. Wikipedia, the Free Encyclopedia, "Chipita Rodriguez," http://en.wikipedia.org/wiki/Chipita_Rodriguez.

36. Flowers and H. Loraine Flowers, *Murders in the United States,* p. 110.

37. Quoted in Verhovek, "Execution in Texas."

38. Sam H. Verhovek, "Karla Tucker Is Now Gone, But Several Debates Linger," *New York Times* (February 5, 1998), http://www.nytimes.com/1998/02/05/us/karla-tucker-is-now-gone-but-several-debates-linger.html?ref=karlafayetucker.

39. Verhovek, "Texas, in First Time in 135 Years."

40. Verhovek, "Karla Tucker Is Now Gone."

41. "Execution in Texas; Europeans Call Penalty Barbaric," *New York Times* (February 4, 1998),

http://www.nytimes.com/1998/02/04/us/execution-in-texas-europeans-call-penalty-barbaric.html?ref=karlafayetucker.

42. Quoted in Verhovek, "Karla Tucker Is Now Gone."

43. *Ibid.*

44. *Ibid.*

45. Flowers and H. Loraine Flowers, *Murders in the United States,* pp. 144-45; R. Barri Flowers, *The Dynamics of Murder: Kill or Be Killed* (Boca Raton, FL: CRC Press, 2013), p. 201.

46. Wikipedia, the Free Encyclopedia, "List of Individuals Executed in Texas, 1990–99," http://en.wikipedia.org/wiki/List_of_individuals_executed_in_Texas,_1990%E2%80%931999; Wikipedia, the Free Encyclopedia, "List of Individuals Executed in Texas, 2000–09," http://en.wikipedia.org/wiki/List_of_individuals_executed_in_Texas,_2000%E2%80%932009; Wikipedia, the Free Encyclopedia, "List of People Executed in Texas, 2010–" http://en.wikipedia.org/wiki/List_of_people_executed_in_Texas,_2010%E2%80%93.

MURDEROUS TANDEM

1. R. Barri Flowers and H. Loraine Flowers, *Murders in the United States: Crimes, Killers and Victims of the Twentieth Century* (Jefferson, NC: McFarland, 2004), p. 163; Mark I. Pinsky, "Defendant Chose Love Life Over Victims' Lives. Courts: Woman Already Sentenced to Death for One Murder Describes Starting Strangulation of Huntington Beach Student at Ex-Convict's Request," *Los Angeles Times* (January 5, 1992), http://articles.latimes.com/1992-06-05/local/me-695_1_huntington-beach.

2. Jennifer Furio, *Team Killers: A Comparative Study of Collaborative Criminals* (New York: Algora, 2001), p. 53; IMDb, *Leave it to Beaver* (TV Series: 1957-63), http://www.imdb.com/title/tt0050032/.

3. Mark I. Pinsky, "2nd Coffman Murder Trial Opens. Crime: Woman Already Under Death Sentence for Rampage

With Lover Faces Similar Charges in College Student's Rape-Slaying in a Huntington Beach Hotel," *Los Angeles Times* (March 14, 1992), http://articles.latimes.com/1992-05-14/local/me-3208_1_death-sentence.

4. Pinsky, "Defendant Chose Love Life Over Victims'."

5. "Execution Ordered for Pair Linked to Kentucky Slayings," *Daily News* (August 31, 1989), http://news.google.com/newspapers?id=8rQaAAAAIBAJ&sjid=HEgEAAAAIBAJ&pg=6842,6967599&dq=killers+cynthia+coffman+and+james+gregory+marlow&hl=en.

6. Pinsky, "2nd Coffman Murder Trial Opens."

7. Furio, *Team Killers*, pp. 55-56.

8. "Execution Ordered for Pair."

9. Flowers and Flowers, *Murders in the United States*.

10. Mark I. Pinsky, " Guilt Conceded in Motel Murder: Trial: Attorney is Trying to Spare Convicted Killer James Gregory Marlow from the Death Penalty in a Huntington Beach Strangling," *Los Angeles Times* (March 5, 1992), http://articles.latimes.com/1992-03-05/local/me-4877_1_huntington-beach.

11. Pinsky, "2nd Coffman Murder Trial Opens."

12. David Reyes, Coffman 'Instigated' Killing, Prosecutor Says : Trial: Deputy District Attorney Disputes Defense Contentions that She Acted Out of Fear, Saying in Closing Arguments that She Played a Major Role in the Crime**,** *Los Angeles Times* (June 23, 1992), http://articles.latimes.com/1992-06-23/local/me-970_1_closing-arguments.

13. *Ibid.*

14. Pinsky, "Defendant Chose Love Life Over Victims' Lives."

15. Investigation Discovery, *Wicked Attraction*, "The Folsom Wolf," (July 23, 2009), http://www.imdb.com/title/tt1481516/.

MURDER IN MISSION HILL

1. R. Barri Flowers and H. Loraine Flowers, *Murders in the United States: Crimes, Killers and Victims of the Twentieth Century* (Jefferson: McFarland, 2004), pp. 50-51.

2. Fox Butterfield and Constance L. Hays, "Boston Tragedy: The Stuart Case – A Special Case; Motive Remains a Mystery In Deaths That Haunt a City," *New York Times* (January 15, 1990), http://www.nytimes.com/1990/01/15/us/boston-tragedy-stuart-case-special-case-motive-remains-mystery-deaths-that-haunt.html?pagewanted=all&src=pm.

3. *Ibid.*

4. *Ibid.*

5. *Ibid.*; R. Barri Flowers, *The Dynamics of Murder: Kill or Be Killed* (New York: CRC Press, 2012), pp. 265-71.

6. Butterfield and Hays, "Boston Tragedy: The Stuart Case."

7. *Ibid.*

8. *Ibid.*

9. Delores Handy, "The Murder That Forced A Divided Boston To Reflect," *90.9 WBUR* (October 23, 2009), http://www.wbur.org/2009/10/23/charles-stuart-anniversary.

10. *Ibid.*

11. "Boston Mourns Pregnant Woman Killed by Robber," *United Press International* (October 29, 1989), http://articles.latimes.com/1989-10-29/news/mn-501_1_boston-police.

12. Handy, "The Murder That Forced A Divided Boston."

13. Adam Smith, "Remembering Carol Stuart DiMaiti 1959-1989," *Daily Kos* (October 24, 2008), http://www.dailykos.com/story/2008/10/24/640950/-Remembering-Carol-Stuart-Dimaiti-1959-1989#.

14. Flowers, *The Dynamics of Murder*, pp. 265-71; Karen Tumulty and David Treadwell, "Suicide of Man Whose Wife Was Slain Stuns Boston," *Los Angeles Times* (January 5, 1990),

http://articles.latimes.com/1990-01-05/news/mn-204_1_charles-stuart.

15. Tumulty and Treadwell, "Suicide of Man Whose Wife Was Slain."

16. *Ibid.*

17. Wikipedia, the Free Encyclopedia, "Charles Stuart (murderer),"
http://en.wikipedia.org/wiki/Charles_Stuart_(murderer) (May 7, 1912).

18. *Ibid.*; Flowers and Flowers, *Murders in the United States*, pp. 50-51.

19. Butterfield and Hays, "Boston Tragedy: The Stuart Case."

20. "Charles Stuart (murderer)."

21. Butterfield and Hays, "Boston Tragedy: The Stuart Case."

22. *Ibid.*

23. *Ibid.*

24. *Ibid.*

25. *Ibid.*

26. *Ibid.*

27. Elizabeth Mehren, Civil Suit Is Filed in Boston Murder Case : Courts: Carol Stuart's Family Wants to Bar Her Husband's Heirs From Inheriting Any of Her Estate. They Claim 'Public Policy' Prevents Profiting From Her Death," *Los Angeles Times* (January 10, 1991),
http://articles.latimes.com/1991-01-10/news/vw-11239_1_carol-stuart.

28. Flowers, *The Dynamics of Murder*, p. 267; Tumulty and Treadwell, "Suicide of Man Whose Wife Was Slain Stuns Boston."

29. Butterfield and Hays, "Boston Tragedy: The Stuart Case;" Flowers, *The Dynamics of Murder*, p. 268.

30. Butterfield and Hays, "Boston Tragedy: The Stuart Case."

31. *Ibid.*

32. "Nation in Brief: Massachusetts: Brother Charged in Stuart Slaying." *Los Angeles Times* (September 27, 1991), http://articles.latimes.com/1991-09-27/news/mn-2919_1_charles-stuart.

33. Christopher B. Daly, "Young Stuart Pleads Guilty To Fraud; Alleged Wife Killer's Brother Gets 3 to 5," *Washington Post* (November 3, 1992), http://www.highbeam.com/doc/1P2-1033002.html.

34. Associated Press, "Mass. Man Convicted of Aiding In-Law Killing Dies," *Seattle Times* (September 4, 2011), http://seattletimes.nwsource.com/html/nationworld/2016108848_apusstuartbrotherdeath.html; John M. Guilfoil and Meghan Irons, "Stuart Found Dead in Shelter," *Boston.com* (September 4, 2011), http://www.boston.com/news/local/massachusetts/articles/2011/09/04/brother_of_charles_stuart_found_dead_at_cambridge_homeless_shelter/.

35. Adrian Walker, "No Solace for Scapegoat," *Boston.com* (September 5, 2011), http://www.boston.com/news/local/massachusetts/articles/2011/09/05/stuart_death_brings_no_relief_to_bennetts/.

36. Doris S. Wong, "Kakas Furs is Sued Over Gun in Stuart Slaying," *Boston Globe* (October 22, 1992), http://www.highbeam.com/doc/1P2-8764877.html.

37. The Free Library, "DiMaiti Family Files Appeal," http://www.thefreelibrary.com/DiMaiti+family+files+appeal.-a018949219 (December 16, 1996).

38. "Devoted Husband or Sick Psychopath," *Dark Deeds* (February 11, 2012), http://darkdeeds.susanfleet.com/blog_1.php?tag=carol+dimaiti.

39. "Charles Stuart (murderer)."

40. Arnold Shapiro Productions, *Goodnight Sweet Wife: A Murder in Boston* (September 25, 1990), http://www.imdb.com/title/tt0099684/.

41. "Charles Stuart (murderer)."

42. Flowers, *The Dynamics of Murder*, p. 269.

MURDER IN BELLEVUE

1. R. Barri Flowers, *The Dynamics of Murder: Kill or Be Killed* (Boca Raton, FL: CRC Press, 2012), pp. 273-76.

2. Elizabeth R. Grodd and Jeffrey L. Diamond, "Primetime Crime: Teen Charged With Parents' Gruesome Murder," *ABC Primetime* (August 13, 2008), http://abcnews.go.com/TheLaw/story?id=3451371&page=1.

3. Charles Montaldo, "Profile of Idaho Teen Killer Sarah Johnson," *About News*, http://crime.about.com/od/juvenile/a/sarah_johnson.htm.

4. Grodd and Diamond, "Primetime Crime."

5. *Ibid.*

6. *Ibid.*

7. *Ibid.*

8. Quoted in Flowers, *The Dynamics of Murder*, p. 274.

9. Grodd and Diamond, "Primetime Crime."

10. *Ibid.*

11. Montaldo, "Profile of Idaho Teen Killer."

12. Emanuella Grinberg, "Aunt Testifies Against Teen Niece Accused of Parents' Murder," CNN.com (February 21, 2005), http://www.cnn.com/2005/LAW/02/21/johnson/index.html?eref=sitesearch.

13. *Ibid.*

14. *Ibid.*

15. *Ibid.*

16. *Ibid.*

17. *Ibid.*

18. Grodd and Diamond, "Primetime Crime."

19. Flowers, *The Dynamics of Murder*, pp. 275-76.

20. *Idaho v. Johnson*, Opinion 89 (2008).

21. Nastacia Leshchinskaya, "Is Convicted Parent Killer Sarah Johnson Innocent?" Crime Library: Criminals Minds & Methods (December 28, 2012), http://www.crimelibrary.com/blog/2012/12/28/is-

convicted-parent-killer-sarah-johnson-innocent-lawyers-say-yes/index.htm.

22. *Ibid.*

23. *Ibid.*

24. Quoted in Montaldo, "Profile of Idaho Teen Killer."

25. Cited in Grodd and Diamond, "Primetime Crime."

26. Flowers, *The Dynamics of Murder*, pp. 275-76; Wikipedia, the Free Encyclopedia, "Murder of Diane and Alan Scott Johnson," http://en.wikipedia.org/wiki/Sarah_Marie_Johnson (May 3, 2012).

27. IMDb, E! Entertainment Television, *Too Young to Kill: 15 Shocking Crimes* (January 10, 2010), http://www.imdb.com/title/tt1686119/.

MURDER OF A STAR QUARTERBACK

1. R. Barri Flowers, *The Dynamics of Murder: Kill or Be Killed* (New York: CRC Press, 2012), pp. 253-57.

2. Elizabeth Merrill, "The Woman Forever Tied to Steve McNair," *ESPN.com* (July 4, 2010), http://sports.espn.go.com/espn/otl/news/story?id=5347315.

3. Quoted in Tim Ghianni and Jonathan Lemire, "Steve McNair's Wife was Unaware of Affair with Sahel Kazemi Until Husband's Death," *Daily News* (July 6, 2009), http://www.nydailynews.com/sports/football/steve-mcnair-wife-unaware-affair-sahel-kazemi-husband-death-article-1.426240.

4. Seah Leahy, "Sahel Kazemi Called 911 on Norfleet After He Threw a Phone at Her," *USA Today* (July 8, 2009), http://content.usatoday.com/communities/thehuddle/post/2009/07/68493901/1#.Ui3-g4zn99B.

5. *Ibid.*

6. Wikipedia, the Free Encyclopedia, "Steve McNair," http://en.wikipedia.org/wiki/Sahel_Kazemi#Death (September 5, 2013).

7. Merrill, "The Woman Forever Tied to Steve McNair;" Flowers, *The Dynamics of Murder,* pp. 253-57.

8. Joe Edwards and Travis Loller, "Sahel Kazemi's Nephew Reveals She Expected Steve McNair to Divorce Wife," *Seattle Times* (July 7, 2009), http://seattletimes.com/html/seahawks/2009426210_nfl070.html.

9. Merrill, "The Woman Forever Tied to Steve McNair."

10. Sammy R. Saltzman, "Leah Ignagni, Steve McNair's Second Mistress, Was Busted for Drugs," *Crimesider* (October 23, 2009), http://www.cbsnews.com/8301-504083_162-5413540-504083.html.

11. "Steve McNair's Second Mistress Speaks," *WSMV-TV* (February 8, 2010), http://www.wsmv.com/story/14768356/steve-mcnairs-second-mistress-speaks.

12. *Ibid.*

13. Merrill, "The Woman Forever Tied to Steve McNair."

14. Crimesider Staff, "Adrian Gilliam, Man Who Sold Gun That Killed McNair, Wanted Affair with His Mistress Sahel Kazemi," *Crimesider* (December 18, 2009), http://www.cbsnews.com/8301-504083_162-5997302-504083.html.

15. Edwards and Loller, "Sahel Kazemi's Nephew Reveals She Expected."

16. Associated Press, "Feds Nab Murderer for Selling Gun that Killed ex-NFL Star Steve McNair," *Daily News* (February 17, 2009), http://www.nydailynews.com/news/world/feds-nab-murderer-selling-gun-killed-ex-nfl-star-steve-mcnair-article-1.385429.

17. Quoted in Kate Howard, Jaime Sarrio and Chris Echegaray, "Steve McNair and Sahel Kazemi Killed," *Tennessean* (July 4, 2009), http://www.tennessean.com/article/20090704/SPORTS01/90704013/Steve-McNair-Sahel-Kazemi-killed.

18. Michael O'Keefe and Jonathan Lemire, "Steve McNair, Sahel Kazemi Love Nest Became Blood-Soaked Crime Scene," *Daily News* (July 7, 2009), http://www.nydailynews.com/sports/football/steve-mcnair-sahel-kazemi-love-nest-blood-soaked-crime-scene-article-1.427036.

19. Howard, Sarrio, and Echegaray, "Steve McNair and Sahel Kazemi Killed."

20. *Ibid.*

21. Flowers, *The Dynamics of Murder*, pp. 253-57; Wayne Drash, "Police Call McNair Killing a Murder-Suicide," *CNN.com/Crime* (July 8, 2009), http://www.cnn.com/2009/CRIME/07/08/mcnair.shooting/index.html?_s=PM:CRIME.

22. Kate Howard, "Police: Jealous Kazemi Shot Steve McNair While He Slept," *The Tennessean* (July 8, 2009), http://www.tennessean.com/article/20090708/NEWS03/90708043?nclick_check=1.

23. Edecio Martinez, "McNair was Drunk Before Murdered," *Crimesider* (July 21, 2009), http://www.cbsnews.com/crimesider/?keyword=Steve+McNair.

24. "Cops say Kazemi Bought Gun," *ESPN.com* (July 10, 2009), http://sports.espn.go.com/nfl/news/story?id=4309196.

25. Ghianni and Lemire, "Steve McNair's Wife was Unaware of Affair."

26. "Adrian Gilliam, Man Who Sold Gun That Killed McNair."

27. Ghianni and Lemire, "Steve McNair's Wife was Unaware of Affair."

28. Colleen Starr, "Sahel Kazemi's Ex-Boyfriend Keith Norfleet, Questioned by Police," *Examiner.com* (July 6, 2009), http://www.examiner.com/article/sahel-kazemi-s-ex-boyfriend-keith-norfleet-questioned-by-police.

29. "Cops say Kazemi Bought Gun."

30. "Felon Arrested in Sale of Gun Used in McNair Murder," *WKRN-TV* (July 17, 2009), http://www.wkrn.com/story/10744385/felon-arrested-in-sale-of-gun-used-in-mcnair-murder.

31. "Adrian Gilliam, Man Who Sold Gun That Killed McNair."

32. Quoted in "Felon Arrested in Sale of Gun Used."

33. Sammy R. Saltzman, "Exclusive: Was Steve McNair Murder Investigation Flawed? Was Lover Really Suicidal?" *CBS News* (October 19, 2009), http://www.cbsnews.com/8301-504083_162-5390156-504083.html?tag=contentMain%3bcontentBody.

34. *Ibid*; Flowers, *The Dynamics of Murder*, pp. 253-57.

35. Quoted in CBS News Staff, *48 Hours*, http://www.cbsnews.com/2300-504083_162-5401821-19.html.

36. Sean Leahy, "Keith Norfleet's Grandmother: Sahel Kazemi was Dating Him and Steve McNair," *USA Today* (July 7, 2009), http://content.usatoday.com/communities/thehuddle/post/2009/07/68493789/1#.UiIYgozn99A.

37. *Ibid*.

38. Howard, Sarrio, and Echegaray, "Steve McNair and Sahel Kazemi Killed."

39. Quoted in Drash, "Police Call McNair Killing a Murder-Suicide."

40. *Ibid*.

41. Sammy R. Saltzman, "Sahel Kazemi and Steve McNair Final Texts Show Worries of Love and Money," *CBS News* (October 20, 2009), http://www.cbsnews.com/8301-504083_162-5400986-504083.html?tag=contentMain%3bcontentBody.

42. *Ibid*.

43. *Ibid*.; Flowers, *The Dynamics of Murder*, pp. 253-57.

44. Quoted in Drash, "Police Call McNair Killing a Murder-Suicide."

45. Flowers, *The Dynamics of Murder*, pp. 253-57.

46. *Ibid.*

47. *Ibid*; Drash, "Police Call McNair Killing a Murder-Suicide."

48. Merrill, "The Woman Forever Tied to Steve McNair."

49. Quoted in "Adrian Gilliam, Man Who Sold Gun That Killed McNair."

50. "Police Close McNair Case After nearly Six Mos.," *WKRN-TV* (December 18, 2009), http://www.wkrn.com/global/story.asp?s=11700859.

51. "Felon Sentenced to 2 1/2 Years in McNair Gun Case," *WKRN-TV* (December 18, 2009), http://www.wkrn.com/global/Story.asp?s=11699594.

52. "Man Who Sold Gun that Killed McNair Out of Jail," *WKRN-TV* (September 23, 2011), http://www.wkrn.com/story/15536044/man-who-sold-gun-that-killed-mcnair-out-of-jail.

53. Saltzman, "Exclusive: Was Steve McNair Murder Investigation Flawed?"

54. Merrill, "The Woman Forever Tied to Steve McNair;" Chris Echegaray, "One Year Later, Questions Linger About Steve McNair's Murder," *USA Today* (July 5, 2010), http://usatoday30.usatoday.com/sports/football/nfl/2010-07-04-steve-mcnair-anniversary_N.htm.

55. Echegaray, "One Year Later, Questions Linger;" Merrill, "The Woman Forever Tied to Steve McNair."

56. Quoted in "Adrian Gilliam, Man Who Sold Gun That Killed McNair."

57. Merrill, "The Woman Forever Tied to Steve McNair."

58. Quoted in Echegaray, "One Year Later, Questions Linger."

59. Merrill, "The Woman Forever Tied to Steve McNair;" *Associated Press*, http://sports.espn.go.com/nfl/news/story?id=4364855; Andy and Danielle Mayoras, The Probate Lawyer Blog, "Steve McNair's Widow Facing Estate Tax Nightmare," (April 12, 2010),

http://www.probatelawyerblog.com/2010/04/steve-mcnairs-widow-facing-estate-tax-nightmare.html.

60. "McNair Widow Asks Court to Give Cash to Heirs," *City Paper* (September 30, 2010), http://nashvillecitypaper.com/content/city-news/mcnair-widow-asks-court-give-cash-heirs.

61. "Judge Authorizes Sale of McNair's Restaurant," *WKRN-TV* (October 16, 2009), http://www.wkrn.com/Global/story.asp?S=11328893; "Gridiron 9 to Reopen Under New Ownership," *WKRN-TV* (August 30, 2010), http://www.wkrn.com/global/story.asp?s=13064996.

62. Marcus Washington, "Lawsuit Settled Against McNair Estate," *NewsChannel5.com* (February 11, 2010), http://www.newschannel5.com/global/story.asp?s=11973603.

63. Debbie Emory, "Murdered NFL Star Steve McNair's House Up For Sale: Take a Peek Inside!" *Radar Online* (May 30, 2012), http://radaronline.com/exclusives/2012/05/steve-mcnair-house-photos-sale/; Nevin Batiwalla, "Steve McNair's Green Hills home sells for $1.7M," *Nashville Business Journal* (February 22, 2013), http://www.bizjournals.com/nashville/news/2013/02/22/steve-mcnairs-green-hills-home-sells.html.

64. "McNair's Mom, Wife in Dispute on Death Anniversary," *WSMV-TV* (July 4, 2011), http://www.wsmv.com/story/15022632/wife-mother-dispute-over-money-two-years-after-steve-mcnairs-death.

65. Echegaray, "One Year Later, Questions Linger."

66. The Official Steve McNair Foundation, http://officialstevemcnair.com/events.html; "Future for McNair Foundation Uncertain," (July 30, 2009), http://sports.espn.go.com/nfl/news/story?id=4366805.

67. Brantley Hargrove, "McNair, Kazemi Estate Claims Resolved," *City Paper* (November 11, 2009),

http://nashvillecitypaper.com/content/city-news/mcnair-kazemi-estate-claims-resolved.

SERIAL KILLER COUPLES: Ian Brady & Myra Hindley

1. "I Wish I'd Been Hanged," *BBC News World Edition* (February 29, 2000), http://news.bbc.co.uk/2/hi/uk_news/661139.stm; Wikipedia, the Free Encyclopedia, "Moors Murders," http://en.wikipedia.org/wiki/Moors_murders#CITEREFStaff2007.

2. "Moors Murders."

3. Duncan Staff, *The Lost Boy* (New York: Bantam, 2007), pp. 49-50.

4. *Ibid.*, p. 50.

5. *Ibid.*, pp. 139-41.

6. R. Barri Flowers and H. Loraine Flowers, *Murders in the United States: Crimes, Killers and Victims of the Twentieth Century* (Jefferson, NC: McFarland, 2004), pp. 18-19, 170-71.

# # #

REFERENCES

"A Political Suicide." (January 24, 1955). *Time.*

Alphin, Elaine M. (2010) *An Unspeakable Crime: The Prosecution and Persecution of Leo Frank.* Minneapolis, MN: Carolrhoda Books.

American Female Executions 1900-2010. "Karla Faye Tucker, Justice Delayed?" http://www.capitalpunishmentuk.org/karla.html.

Amityville II: The Possession (1982). http://www.imdb.com/title/tt0083550/?ref_=fn_al_tt_1.

Anson, Jay. (1977) *The Amityville Horror.* Englewood Cliffs, NJ: Prentice-Hall.

Arnold Shapiro Productions. *Goodnight Sweet Wife: A Murder in Boston* (September 25, 1990). http://www.imdb.com/title/tt0099684/.

"Assert Hickman Said He Killed Toms." *New York Times* (March 18, 1928).

Associated Press. "Feds Nab Murderer for Selling Gun that Killed ex-NFL Star Steve McNair." *Daily News* (February 17, 2009). http://www.nydailynews.com/news/world/feds-nab-murderer-selling-gun-killed-ex-nfl-star-steve-mcnair-article-1.385429.

_____. "Hickman Attempts Twice to End Life Before Start South." *New York Times* (December 26, 1927).

_____. "Hickman Confused as Alibi of Cramer Proves He Is Lying." *New York Times* (December 24, 1927).

_____. "Mass. Man Convicted of Aiding In-Law Killing Dies." *Seattle Times* (September 4, 2011). http://seattletimes.nwsource.com/html/nationworld/20 16108848_apusstuartbrotherdeath.html.

Atlanta, Georgia. "Atlanta City Hall." http://www.nps.gov/nr/travel/atlanta/cit.htm.

Batiwalla, Nevin. "Steve McNair's Green Hills home sells for $1.7M." *Nashville Business Journal* (February 22, 2013). http://www.bizjournals.com/nashville/news/2013/02/2 2/steve-mcnairs-green-hills-home-sells.html.

BBC News. (January 30, 1988) "Special Report 1998: Karla Faye Tucker: "Portrait of a Repentant Killer." http://news.bbc.co.uk/2/hi/special_report/1998/karla_ faye_tucker/48816.stm.

"Begin Last Frank Appeal to Governor." (June 13, 1915) *New York Times*.

Bernstein, Matthew H. (2009) *Screening a Lynching: The Leo Frank Case on Film and Television*. Athens, GA: University of Georgia Press.

"Boston Mourns Pregnant Woman Killed by Robber." *United Press International* (October 29, 1989). http://articles.latimes.com/1989-10-29/news/mn-501_1_boston-police.

Brant, Marley. (2014) *The Outlaw Youngers: A Confederate Brotherhood*. Lanham, MD: Madison Books.

Brundage, W. Fitzhugh. (1993) *Lynching in the New South: Georgia and Virginia, 1880-1930*. Urbana, IL: University of Illinois Press.

Butterfield, Fox and Constance L. Hays. "Boston Tragedy: The Stuart Case – A Special Case; Motive Remains a Mystery In Deaths That Haunt a City." *New York Times*

(January 15, 1990).
http://www.nytimes.com/1990/01/15/us/boston-tragedy-stuart-case-special-case-motive-remains-mystery-deaths-that-haunt.html?pagewanted=all&src=pm.

CBS News Staff. *48 Hours*. http://www.cbsnews.com/2300-504083_162-5401821-19.html.

"Chemist Turns Detective." New York Times (June 10, 1927).

Clarridge, Christine. "A Plan to honor 130 Years of Fallen Seattle Officers." Seattle Times (September 14, 2014). http://seattletimes.com/html/localnews/2017162440_memorialsigns05m.html.

CNN Interactive. (February 1998) "Profile: Facing Death with Memories of Murder." http://www.cnn.com/SPECIALS/1998/tucker.execution/profile/.

"Cops say Kazemi Bought Gun." ESPN.com (July 10, 2009). http://sports.espn.go.com/nfl/news/story?id=4309196.

"Cramer Refutes Hickman. Police Reconstruct Crime with Kidnapper as Sole Killer." New·York Times (December 24, 1927).

Crimesider Staff. "Adrian Gilliam, Man Who Sold Gun That Killed McNair, Wanted Affair with His Mistress Sahel Kazemi." Crimesider (December 18, 2009). http://www.cbsnews.com/8301-504083_162-5997302-504083.html.

"D'Autremonts' Bail Put at $50,000 Each." New York Times (June 11, 1927).

Daly, Christopher B. "Young Stuart Pleads Guilty To Fraud; Alleged Wife Killer's Brother Gets 3 to 5." Washington Post (November 3, 1992). http://www.highbeam.com/doc/1P2-1033002.html.

"Death Witness Says Lynch Victim Innocent." (March 8, 1982) Bangor Daily News. http://news.google.com/newspapers?nid=2457&dat=19820308&id=EBE0AAAAIBAJ&sjid=YSMIAAAAIBAJ&pg=2860,2563887.

"Devoted Husband or Sick Psychopath." Dark Deeds
(February 11, 2012).
http://darkdeeds.susanfleet.com/blog_1.php?tag=carol+
dimaiti.

Drash, Wayne. "Police Call McNair Killing a Murder-
Suicide." CNN.com/Crime (July 8, 2009).
http://www.cnn.com/2009/CRIME/07/08/mcnair.sho
oting/index.html?_s=PM:CRIME.

"Earn $15,000 Reward. Solider and Cripple Get Shares for
D'Autremonts' Capture," New York Times (July 8, 1928).

Echegaray, Chris. "One Year Later, Questions Linger About
Steve McNair's Murder." USA Today (July 5, 2010).
http://usatoday30.usatoday.com/sports/football/nfl/20
10-07-04-steve-mcnair-anniversary_N.htm.

Edwards, Joe and Travis Loller. "Sahel Kazemi's Nephew
Reveals She Expected Steve McNair to Divorce Wife."
Seattle Times (July 7, 2009).
http://seattletimes.com/html/seahawks/2009426210_nfl
070.html.

Emory, Debbie. "Murdered NFL Star Steve McNair's House
Up For Sale: Take a Peek Inside!" Radar Online (May 30,
2012).
http://radaronline.com/exclusives/2012/05/steve-
mcnair-house-photos-sale/.

"Ex-Bank Messenger Positively Named Los Angeles Killer."
New York Times (December 21, 1927).

"Execution in Texas; Europeans Call Penalty Barbaric."
(February 4, 1998) New York Times.
http://www.nytimes.com/1998/02/04/us/execution-in-
texas-europeans-call-penalty-
barbaric.html?ref=karlafayetucker.

"Execution in Texas; Texas Governor Refuses to Intervene."
(February 4, 1998) New York Times.
http://www.nytimes.com/1998/02/04/us/execution-in-
texas-texas-governor-refuses-to-
intervene.html?ref=karlafayetucke.

"Execution Ordered for Pair Linked to Kentucky Slayings."
    Daily News (August 31, 1989).
    http://news.google.com/newspapers?id=8rQaAAAAIB
    AJ&sjid=HEgEAAAAIBAJ&pg=6842,6967599&dq=kill
    ers+cynthia+coffman+and+james+gregory+marlow&hl
    =en.

Famous Trials: The Leo Frank Trial 1913. "Testimony of
    Leo Frank."
    http://law2.umkc.edu/faculty/projects/ftrials/frank/test
    imonyleofrank.html.

Fattig, Paul. "D'Autremonts' Bungled Train Robbery in 1923
    Left 4 Dead." The Mall Tribune (October 11, 1998).
    http://www.angelfire.com/wa/andyhiggins/Greattrainro
    bbery.html.

_____."Great Train Robbery."
    http://tunnel13.com/history/robbery.html.

_____."Tunnel Smoke Blocks Access." Mail Tribune
    (November 19, 2003).
    http://www.mailtribune.com/apps/pbcs.dll/article?AID
    =/20031119/BIZ/311199998&cid=sitesearch.

Federal Bureau of Investigation. Famous Cases and
    Criminals. "Jack Gilbert Graham."
    http://www.fbi.gov/about-us/history/famous-
    cases/jack-gilbert-graham.

"Felon Arrested in Sale of Gun Used in McNair Murder."
    WKRN-TV (July 17, 2009).
    http://www.wkrn.com/story/10744385/felon-arrested-
    in-sale-of-gun-used-in-mcnair-murder.

"Felon Sentenced to 2 1/2 Years in McNair Gun Case."
    WKRN-TV (December 18, 2009).
    http://www.wkrn.com/global/Story.asp?s=11699594.

"Find Hickman Sane, Guilty of Murder." New York Times
    (February 10, 1928).

Flewelling, Stan. "The Dauntless Desperado: Harry Tracy."
    White River Journal (April 1998).
    http://www.wrvmuseum.org/journal/journal_0498.htm.

Flowers, R. Barri. (2013) The Dynamics of Murder: Kill or Be Killed. Boca Raton, FL: CRC Press.

_____. (2002) Murder, at the End of the Day and Night: A Study of Criminal Homicide Offenders, Victims, and Circumstances. Springfield, IL: Charles C Thomas.

_____, and H. Loraine Flowers. (2004) Murders in the United States: Crimes, Killers and Victims of the Twentieth Century. Jefferson, NC: McFarland.

"Frank James Dies at 72." New York Times (February 19, 1915).

Free Library. "DiMaiti Family Files Appeal." http://www.thefreelibrary.com/DiMaiti+family+files+appeal.-a018949219 (December 16, 1996).

Freeman, Mark. "Tunnel 13." Mail Tribune (November 18, 2003). http://www.mailtribune.com/apps/pbcs.dll/article?AID=/20031118/BIZ/311189998&cid=sitesearch.

"Fugitive Bandits Caught." New York Times (June 9, 1927).

Furio, Jennifer. (2001) Team Killers: A Comparative Study of Collaborative Criminals. New York: Algora.

"Future for McNair Foundation Uncertain." (July 30, 2009). http://sports.espn.go.com/nfl/news/story?id=4366805.

Gado, Mark. "Sabotage: The Downing of Flight 629." TruTV Crime Library. http://www.trutv.com/library/crime/notorious_murders/mass/jack_graham/index.html.

Gauss, Gordon. "Graham Spurns Appeal and is Sentenced to Die." Longmont-Times-Call (May 15, 1956).

Geringer, Joseph. "Karla Faye Tucker: Texas' Controversial Murderess." Crime Library: Criminal Minds and Methods. http://www.trutv.com/library/crime/notorious_murders/women/tucker/2.html.

Golden, Harry. (1965) A Little Girl Is Dead. Cleveland, OH: World.

Grave Spotlight. Marion Parker. http://www.cemeteryguide.com/gotw-parker.html.

Ghianni, Tim and Jonathan Lemire. "Steve McNair's Wife was Unaware of Affair with Sahel Kazemi Until Husband's Death." Daily News (July 6, 2009). http://www.nydailynews.com/sports/football/steve-mcnair-wife-unaware-affair-sahel-kazemi-husband-death-article-1.426240.

Gribben, Mark. "The Murder of Marion Parker." The Malefactor's Register: Crime, Punishment, Law, Writing. http://malefactorsregister.com/wp/?p=779.

"Gridiron 9 to Reopen Under New Ownership." WKRN-TV (August 30, 2010). http://www.wkrn.com/global/story.asp?s=13064996.

Grinberg, Emanuella. "Aunt Testifies Against Teen Niece Accused of Parents' Murder." CNN.com (February 21, 2005). http://www.cnn.com/2005/LAW/02/21/johnson/index.html?eref=sitesearch.

Grodd, Elizabeth R. and Jeffrey L. Diamond. "Primetime Crime: Teen Charged With Parents' Gruesome Murder." ABC Primetime (August 13, 2008). http://abcnews.go.com/TheLaw/story?id=3451371&page=1.

Guilfoil, John M. and Meghan Irons. "Stuart Found Dead in Shelter." Boston.com (September 4, 2011). http://www.boston.com/news/local/massachusetts/articles/2011/09/04/brother_of_charles_stuart_found_dead_at_cambridge_homeless_shelter/.

Gulick, Bill. (1999) Manhunt: the Pursuit of Harry Tracy. Caldwell, ID: Caxton Press.

"Hangman Captured, Admits Kidnapping." New York Times (December 23, 1927).

Hargrove, Brantley. "McNair, Kazemi Estate Claims Resolved." City Paper (November 11, 2009). http://nashvillecitypaper.com/content/city-news/mcnair-kazemi-estate-claims-resolved.

Handy, Delores. "The Murder That Forced A Divided Boston To Reflect." 90.9 WBUR (October 23, 2009).

http://www.wbur.org/2009/10/23/charles-stuart-anniversary.

"Hickman Admits Second Murder; Companion Jailed." New York Times (December 30, 1927).

"Hickman Confesses Murder and Robberies." New York Times (October 14, 1928).

"Hickman Convicted of Second Murder." New York Times (March 11, 1928).

"Hickman Conviction Upheld on Appeal." New York Times (July 6, 1928).

"Hickman Hanged as He Collapses." New York Times (October 20, 1928).

"Hickman Made Way as Far as Seattle." New York Times (December 23, 1927).

"Hickman Rejected by Juvenile Court." New York Times (January 12, 1928).

"Hickman to Invoke Leopold-Loeb Plea." New York Times (January 10, 1928).

"Hickman's Father Goes to His Aide." New York Times (February 1, 1928).

History and Archeology. "Leo Frank Case." (August 3, 2009) New Georgia Encyclopedia. http://www.georgiaencyclopedia.org/nge/Article.jsp?id=h-906&hl=y.

Holzer, Hans. (1977) Murder in Amityville. New York: Belmont Tower Books.

Howard, Kate. "Police: Jealous Kazemi Shot Steve McNair While He Slept." The Tennessean (July 8, 2009). http://www.tennessean.com/article/20090708/NEWS03/90708043?nclick_check=1.

_____, Jaime Sarrio and Chris Echegaray. "Steve McNair and Sahel Kazemi Killed." Tennessean (July 4, 2009). http://www.tennessean.com/article/20090704/SPORTS01/90704013/Steve-McNair-Sahel-Kazemi-killed.

"Hugh D'Autremont Convicted in Oregon." New York Times (June 22, 1927).

Idaho v. Johnson. Opinion 89 (2008).

IMDb. "Edward Hickman (1908-1928)."
http://www.imdb.com/name/nm1489218/.

_____. E! Entertainment Television. Too Young to Kill: 15 Shocking Crimes (January 10, 2010),
http://www.imdb.com/title/tt1686119/.

_____. Harry Tracy, Desperado (1082).
http://www.imdb.com/title/tt0084052/?ref_=nm_flmg _act_70.

_____. Leave it to Beaver (TV Series: 1957-63).
http://www.imdb.com/title/tt0050032/.

_____. Shattered Hopes: The True Story of the Amityville Murders—Part I: From Horror to Homicide (2011).
http://www.imdb.com/title/tt1786665/?ref_=fn_al_tt_ 3.

_____. Shattered Hopes: The True Story of the Amityville Murders—Part II: Mob, Mayhem, Murder (2012).
http://www.imdb.com/title/tt2150455/?ref_=fn_al_tt_ 2.

_____.Shattered Hopes: The True Story of the Amityville Murders—Part III: Fraud & Forensics (2014).
http://www.imdb.com/title/tt2295444/?ref_=fn_al_tt_ 1.

_____. The Amityville Horror (1977).
http://www.imdb.com/title/tt0078767/?ref_=nv_sr_2.

_____. The Amityville Horror (2005).
http://www.imdb.com/title/tt0384806/?ref_=nv_sr_1.

_____. The Crime of the D'Autremont Brothers (2012).
http://www.imdb.com/title/tt2357389/?ref_=fn_al_tt_ 1.

Investigation Discovery. Wicked Attraction. "The Folsom Wolf." (July 23, 2009).
http://www.imdb.com/title/tt1481516/.

"Jesse James Shot Down; Killed By One Of His Confederates Who Claims To Be A Detective." New York Times (April 4, 1882).

"Judge Authorizes Sale of McNair's Restaurant." WKRN-TV (October 16, 2009). http://www.wkrn.com/Global/story.asp?S=11328893.

Kaplan, Stephen, Ph.D. and Roxanne Salch Kaplan. (1995) The Amityville Horror Conspiracy. Laceyville, PA: Belfry Books.

Kean, Mary Phagan. (1989) The Murder of Little Mary Phagan. Far Hills, NJ: New Horizon Press.

Keeler, Bob. "DeFeo's New Story." Newsday (March 19, 1986).

"Last of Train Robbers Dies in Oregon at 84." Record-Journal (December 22, 1984).

Leahy, Sean. "Keith Norfleet's Grandmother: Sahel Kazemi was Dating Him and Steve McNair." USA Today (July 7, 2009). http://content.usatoday.com/communities/thehuddle/post/2009/07/68493789/1#.UiIYgozn99A.

_____. "Sahel Kazemi Called 911 on Norfleet After He Threw a Phone at Her." USA Today (July 8, 2009). http://content.usatoday.com/communities/thehuddle/post/2009/07/68493901/1#.Ui3-g4zn99B.

"Leo M. Frank: The 1913 Leo Frank Case and Trial Research Library." http://www.leofrank.org/alonzo-mann/.

Leshchinskaya, Nastacia."Is Convicted Parent Killer Sarah Johnson Innocent?" Crime Library: Criminals Minds & Methods (December 28, 2012). http://www.crimelibrary.com/blog/2012/12/28/is-convicted-parent-killer-sarah-johnson-innocent-lawyers-say-yes/index.htm.

"Let Murderer's Hang." Los Angeles Times (December 21, 1927).

Levy, Eugene. (2000) "Is the Jew a White Man?" In Maurianne Adams and John H. Bracey, eds. Strangers & Neighbors: Relations Between Blacks & Jews in the United States. Amherst, MA: University of Massachusetts Press.

Linder, Douglas O. (2008) "The Trial of Leo Frank: An Account."
http://law2.umkc.edu/faculty/projects/ftrials/frank/fra nkaccount.html.

"Los Angeles Killer Eludes All Pursuit." New York Times (December 22, 1927).

Lowry, Beverly. (2002) Crossed Over: A Murder, A Memoir. New York: Vintage.

Lynott, Douglas B. "The Real Life Amityville Horror." Crime Library: Criminal Minds & Methods.
http://www.crimelibrary.com/notorious_murders/famil y/amityville/2.html.

MacLean, Nancy. (December 1991) "The Leo Frank Case Reconsidered: Gender and Sexual Politics in the Making of Reactionary Populism." Journal of American History 78: 917-48.

"Man Who Sold Gun that Killed McNair Out of Jail." WKRN-TV (September 23, 2011).
http://www.wkrn.com/story/15536044/man-who-sold-gun-that-killed-mcnair-out-of-jail.

Martinez, Edecio. "McNair was Drunk Before Murdered." Crimesider (July 21, 2009).
http://www.cbsnews.com/crimesider/?keyword=Steve+McNair.

Mayoras, Andy and Danielle Mayoras. The Probate Lawyer Blog. "Steve McNair's Widow Facing Estate Tax Nightmare." (April 12, 2010).
http://www.probatelawyerblog.com/2010/04/steve-mcnairs-widow-facing-estate-tax-nightmare.html.

"McNair Widow Asks Court to Give Cash to Heirs." City Paper (September 30, 2010).
http://nashvillecitypaper.com/content/city-news/mcnair-widow-asks-court-give-cash-heirs.

"McNair's Mom, Wife in Dispute on Death Anniversary." WSMV-TV (July 4, 2011).
http://www.wsmv.com/story/15022632/wife-mother-dispute-over-money-two-years-after-steve-mcnairs-death.

Mehren, Elizabeth. "Civil Suit Is Filed in Boston Murder Case: Courts: Carol Stuart's Family Wants to Bar Her Husband's Heirs From Inheriting Any of Her Estate. They Claim 'Public Policy' Prevents Profiting From Her Death." Los Angeles Times (January 10, 1991). http://articles.latimes.com/1991-01-10/news/vw-11239_1_carol-stuart.

Merrill, Elizabeth. "The Woman Forever Tied to Steve McNair." ESPN.com (July 4, 2010). http://sports.espn.go.com/espn/otl/news/story?id=534 7315.

Montaldo, Charles. "Profile of Idaho Teen Killer Sarah Johnson." About News. http://crime.about.com/od/juvenile/a/sarah_johnson.htm.

Nakkula, Al. "44 Killed in Airliner Explosion." Rocky Mountain News (November 2, 1955).

"Nation in Brief: Massachusetts: Brother Charged in Stuart Slaying." Los Angeles Times (September 27, 1991). http://articles.latimes.com/1991-09-27/news/mn-2919_1_charles-stuart.

News Watch 12 Staff. "Oregon Trails: D'Autremont Train Robbery." KDRV.com (October 18, 2013). http://www.kdrv.com/oregon-trails-dautremont-train-robbery/.

Newton, Michael. (2002) The Encyclopedia of Robberies, Heists, and Capers. New York: Facts On File Inc.

O'Keefe, Michael and Jonathan Lemire. "Steve McNair, Sahel Kazemi Love Nest Became Blood-Soaked Crime Scene." Daily News (July 7, 2009). http://www.nydailynews.com/sports/football/steve-mcnair-sahel-kazemi-love-nest-blood-soaked-crime-scene-article-1.427036.

Oney, Steve. (2003) And the Dead Shall Rise: The Murder of Mary Phagan and the Lynching of Leo Frank. New York, NY: Pantheon Books.

Orion Pictures Corporation. (January 24, 1988) "The Murder of Mary Phagan." http://www.imdb.com/title/tt0095678/?ref_=fn_al_tt_1.

Osuna, Ric. (2002) The Night the DeFeos Died: Reinvestigating the Amityville Murders. Bloomington, IN: Xlibris.

Pinsky, Mark I. "Defendant Chose Love Life Over Victims' Lives. Courts: Woman Already Sentenced to Death for One Murder Describes Starting Strangulation of Huntington Beach Student at Ex-Convict's Request." Los Angeles Times (January 5, 1992). http://articles.latimes.com/1992-06-05/local/me-695_1_huntington-beach.

_____. "Guilt Conceded in Motel Murder: Trial: Attorney is Trying to Spare Convicted Killer James Gregory Marlow from the Death Penalty in a Huntington Beach Strangling." Los Angeles Times (March 5, 1992). http://articles.latimes.com/1992-03-05/local/me-4877_1_huntington-beach.

_____. "2nd Coffman Murder Trial Opens. Crime: Woman Already Under Death Sentence for Rampage With Lover Faces Similar Charges in College Student's Rape-Slaying in a Huntington Beach Hotel." Los Angeles Times (March 14, 1992). http://articles.latimes.com/1992-05-14/local/me-3208_1_death-sentence.

"Police Close McNair Case After nearly Six Mos." WKRN-TV (December 18, 2009). http://www.wkrn.com/global/story.asp?s=11700859.

Pou, Charles. "The Leo Frank Case." Georgia Info. http://georgiainfo.galileo.usg.edu/leofrank.htm.

Pressley, Sue A. (February 4, 1998) "Two Cases, Two States: Appeals Fail, Texas Executes Woman." Washington Post. http://articles.sun-sentinel.com/1998-02-04/news/9802040006_1_karla-faye-tucker-death-house-death-penalty.

Ravitz, Jessica. (November 2, 2009) "Murder Case, Leo Frank Lynching Lives On." CNN Justice. http://www.cnn.com/2009/CRIME/11/02/leo.frank/.

"Reopening Siskiyou Rail." Moving Ahead (September 28, 2012). http://www.odotmovingahead.com/2012/09/.

Reyes, David. "Coffman 'Instigated' Killing, Prosecutor Says: Trial: Deputy District Attorney Disputes Defense Contentions that She Acted Out of Fear, Saying in Closing Arguments that She Played a Major Role in the Crime." Los Angeles Times (June 23, 1992). http://articles.latimes.com/1992-06-23/local/me-970_1_closing-arguments.

"Ronald DeFeo Biography." Bio (September 17, 2014). http://www.biography.com/people/ronald-defeo-580972#synopsis.

Saltzman, Sammy R. "Exclusive: Was Steve McNair Murder Investigation Flawed? Was Lover Really Suicidal?" CBS News (October 19, 2009). http://www.cbsnews.com/8301-504083_162-5390156-504083.html?tag=contentMain%3bcontentBody.

_____. "Leah Ignagni, Steve McNair's Second Mistress, Was Busted for Drugs." Crimesider (October 23, 2009). http://www.cbsnews.com/8301-504083_162-5413540-504083.html.

_____. "Sahel Kazemi and Steve McNair Final Texts Show Worries of Love and Money." CBS News (October 20, 2009). http://www.cbsnews.com/8301-504083_162-5400986-504083.html?tag=contentMain%3bcontentBody.

Savive, Will. (2008) Mentally Ill in Amityville: Murder, Mystery, & Mayhem at 112 Ocean Ave. Bloomington, IN: iUniverse.

"Siskiyou Outrage." Slabtown Chronicle (May 5, 2006). http://portlandcrime.blogspot.com/2006/05/siskiyou-outrage.html.

Smith, Adam. "Remembering Carol Stuart DiMaiti 1959-1989." Daily Kos (October 24, 2008).

http://www.dailykos.com/story/2008/10/24/640950/-Remembering-Carol-Stuart-Dimaiti-1959-1989#.

Smith, Edward H. "Worldwide Man Hunt Started by a Chemist." New York Times (April 24, 1927).

Staff, Duncan. (2007) The Lost Boy. New York: Bantam.

Stark, Thomas J. People v DeFeo Memorandum Denying Motion to Vacate Conviction (January 6, 1993).

Starr, Colleen. "Sahel Kazemi's Ex-Boyfriend Keith Norfleet, Questioned by Police." Examiner.com (July 6, 2009). http://www.examiner.com/article/sahel-kazemi-s-ex-boyfriend-keith-norfleet-questioned-by-police.

Stein, Alan J. HistoryLink.org Essay 5375. Timeline Library (March 5, 2003). http://www.historylink.org/index.cfm?DisplayPage=output.cfm&file_id=5375.

"Steve McNair's Second Mistress Speaks." WSMV-TV (February 8, 2010). http://www.wsmv.com/story/14768356/steve-mcnairs-second-mistress-speaks.

Sutherland, Sydney. (1929) "The Mystery of the Pencil Factory." Ten Real Murder Mysteries—Never Solved. New Rochelle, NY: Knickerbocker Press.

Texas Department of Criminal Justice. (February 3, 1998) "Fact Sheet on Karla Faye Tucker." http://www.clarkprosecutor.org/html/death/US/tucker437.htm.

"Text of Hickman's Confession in Los Angeles Crime." New York Times (December 23, 1927).

The Official Steve McNair Foundation. http://officialstevemcnair.com/events.html.

"The People v. Leo Frank." (November 2009) PBS. http://www.pbs.org/programs/people-v-leo-frank/.

Tribal Theocrat. (April 2011) "The Leo Frank Murder: Semitism Birthing Anti-Semitism." http://tribaltheocrat.com/2011/04/the-leo-frank-murder-semitism-birthing-anti-semitism/.

Triplett, Frank. (2013) Jesse James: The Life, Times, and Treacherous Death of the Most Infamous Outlaw of All Time. New York: Skyhorse Publishing.

"Try to Prove Kin of Hickman Insane." New York Times (January 31, 1928).

Tumulty, Karen and David Treadwell. "Suicide of Man Whose Wife Was Slain Stuns Boston." Los Angeles Times (January 5, 1990).
http://articles.latimes.com/1990-01-05/news/mn-204_1_charles-stuart.

"Twin Bandits Held Under Heavy Guard." New York Times (June 10, 1927).

Verhovek, Sam H. (February 3, 1998) "Texas, in First Time in 135 Years, Is Set To Execute Woman." New York Times. http://www.nytimes.com/1998/02/03/us/texas-in-first-time-in-135-years-is-set-to-execute-woman.html?ref=karlafayetucker.

_____. (February 4, 1998) "Execution in Texas: The Overview Divisive Case of a Killer of Two Ends as Texas Executes Tucker." New York Times.
http://www.nytimes.com/1998/02/04/us/execution-texas-overview-divisive-case-killer-two-ends-texas-executes-tucker.html?ref=karlafayetucker.

_____. (February 5, 1998) "Karla Tucker Is Now Gone, But Several Debates Linger." New York Times.
http://www.nytimes.com/1998/02/05/us/karla-tucker-is-now-gone-but-several-debates-linger.html?ref=karlafayetucker.

_____. (February 8, 1998) "Near Death, Tucker Gave Suggestions to the Prison." New York Times.
http://www.nytimes.com/1998/02/08/us/near-death-tucker-gave-suggestions-to-the-prison.html?ref=karlafayetucker.

Walker, Adrian. "No Solace for Scapegoat." Boston.com (September 5, 2011).
http://www.boston.com/news/local/massachusetts/arti

cles/2011/09/05/stuart_death_brings_no_relief_to_ben
netts/.

Warner Brothers. (October 9, 1937) They Won't Forget.
http://www.imdb.com/title/tt0029658/?ref_=fn_al_tt_
1.

Warner Bros. Pictures. The FBI Story (1959).
http://www.imdb.com/title/tt0052792/.

Washington, Marcus. "Lawsuit Settled Against McNair
Estate." NewsChannel5.com (February 11, 2010).
http://www.newschannel5.com/global/story.asp?s=119
73603.

Wheeler, Sam. "Return of the Rails: Grant for Railroad
Repairs Likely to Bring Financial Benefits to Rogue
Valley." Ashland Daily Tidings (June 26, 2012).
http://www.dailytidings.com/apps/pbcs.dll/article?AID
=/20120626/NEWS02/206260305.

"Where Convict Tracy Made his Last Stand." Seattle Post-
Intelligencer (August 7, 1902).

Wikipedia, the Free Encyclopedia. "Anti-Defamation
League." http://en.wikipedia.org/wiki/Anti-
Defamation_League.

_____. "Charles Stuart (murderer)."
http://en.wikipedia.org/wiki/Charles_Stuart_(murderer)
(May 7, 1912).

_____. "Chipita Rodriguez."
http://en.wikipedia.org/wiki/Chipita_Rodriguez.

_____. "D'Autremont Brothers."
http://en.wikipedia.org/wiki/DeAutremont_Brothers.

_____. "Harry Tracy."
http://en.wikipedia.org/wiki/Harry_Tracy.

_____. "Industrial Workers of the World."
http://en.wikipedia.org/wiki/Industrial_Workers_of_the
_World.

_____. "Jack Gilbert Graham."
http://en.wikipedia.org/wiki/Jack_Gilbert_Graham.

_____. "The James–Younger Gang." http://en.wikipedia.org/wiki/James%E2%80%93Younger_Gang.

_____. "Leo Frank." http://en.wikipedia.org/wiki/Leo_Frank.

_____. "List of Individuals Executed in Texas, 1990–99." http://en.wikipedia.org/wiki/List_of_individuals_executed_in_Texas,_1990%E2%80%931999.

_____. "List of Individuals Executed in Texas, 2000–09." http://en.wikipedia.org/wiki/List_of_individuals_executed_in_Texas,_2000%E2%80%932009.

_____. "List of People Executed in Texas, 2010–." http://en.wikipedia.org/wiki/List_of_people_executed_in_Texas,_2010%E2%80%93.

_____. "Marion Parker." http://en.wikipedia.org/wiki/Marion_Parker.

_____. "Moors Murders." http://en.wikipedia.org/wiki/Moors_murders#CITEREFStaff2007.

_____. "Murder of Diane and Alan Scott Johnson." http://en.wikipedia.org/wiki/Sarah_Marie_Johnson (May 3, 2012).

_____. "Ronald DeFeo, Jr." http://en.wikipedia.org/wiki/Ronald_DeFeo%2C_Jr.

_____."Steve McNair." http://en.wikipedia.org/wiki/Sahel_Kazemi#Death (September 5, 2013).

Wilkes, Donald E., Jr. (May 5, 2004) "Wrongly Accused, Falsely Convicted, Wantonly Murdered." Flagpole Magazine. http://www.law.uga.edu/dwilkes_more/his38_wrongly.html.

Wong, Doris S. "Kakas Furs is Sued Over Gun in Stuart Slaying." Boston Globe (October 22, 1992). http://www.highbeam.com/doc/1P2-8764877.html.

Yeatman, Ted P. (2003) Frank and Jesse James: The Story Behind the Legend. Nashville, TN: Cumberland House, 2nd ed.

Woodward, Comer Vann. (1963) Tom Watson: Agrarian Rebel. New York: Oxford University Press.

Worthy, Larry. (Spring 2013) "Little Secrets: The Murder of Mary Phagan and the Death of Leo Frank." About North Georgia. http://www.aboutnorthgeorgia.com/ang/Little%20Secre ts.

Yarrow, Allison Gaudet. (May 13, 2009) "The People Revisit Leo Frank." Jewish Daily Forward. http://forward.com/articles/105936/the-people-revisit-leo-frank/.

# # #

ABOUT THE AUTHOR

R. Barri Flowers is an award winning criminologist and bestselling author of more than seventy books, including true crime, criminology, thriller fiction, and young adult mysteries. True crime titles include The Sex Slave Murders 1, 2, and 3, The Pickaxe Killers, Terror in East Lansing, Murder at the Pencil Factory, Killers of the Lonely Hearts, and Dead at the Saddleworth Moor.

Fiction titles include mysteries and thrillers such as, Before He Kills Again, Killer in The Woods, Dark Streets of Whitechapel, Fractured Trust, Murder in Maui, Murder in Honolulu, State's Evidence, and Justice Served.

Young adult fiction includes Count Dracula's Teenage Daughter, Danger in Time, Teen Ghost at Dead Lake, Ghost Girl in Shadow Bay, Out for Blood, and Summer at Paradise Ranch.

Follow R. Barri Flowers on Twitter, Facebook, Wikipedia, LinkedIn, Pinterest, YouTube, Flicker, Goodreads, and LibraryThing. Learn more about the author in Wikipedia and www.rbarriflowers.com.

# # #

CPSIA information can be obtained
at www.ICGtesting.com
Printed in the USA
LVHW081123161218
600596LV00033B/220/P